Wheels of Steel:
The Explosive Early Years
of the NWOBHM

Martin Popoff

WP
WYMER
PUBLISHING
Bedford, England

First published in Canada, 2015
Wymer Publishing
Bedford, England www.wymerpublishing.co.uk
Tel: 01234 326691
Wymer Publishing is a trading name of Wymer (UK) Ltd

ISBN: 978-1-912782-18-5

Printed and bound by
CMP, Dorset, England

A catalogue record for this book is available from the British Library.

Typesetting, layout and design by Eduardo Rodriguez.

Table Of Contents

Introduction

Well folks, good to be talking with you again. Here we are with another massive information dump of heavy metal madness, brought to you in the most dense manner I could conjure, the ol' detailed timeline with huge stacks of quotes from the archives.

Of course, this methodology started with the two *Deep Purple Royal Family* books, and then continued on into my Ozzy Osbourne book, the Iron Maiden book, and the forthcoming Yes book, not to mention *The Big Book of Hair Metal* and most recently, and probably best of this type of tome, 120,000 words of *Who Invented Heavy Metal?.*

I suppose you can also consider this a companion book, or follow-up, to *Smokin' Valves: A Headbanger's Guide to 900 NWOBHM Records*, because, of course, this book covers the happenings and the placement in time, mostly, more specifically, of all those albums and singles reviewed in that book. And with so much yummy talk from the participants itself, I was tempted to use the term "oral history" in the title, but, alas, it was getting unwieldy.

Now, hopefully you will be pleased to know that there is going to be a follow-up to this book as well, making it a true two-volume history of the New Wave of British Heavy Metal, with the second one called *This Means War: The Sunset Years of the NWOBHM.*

Okay, so it's time for a little explanation, or pre-answering of questions you might have as you read this book and celebrate all of this great music from a long time ago.

First a note on how the timeline works. The book is, of course, chronological, but when time of the year is not known, those entries are put at the beginning, before January of that year. When time of the month is not known, those entries are put at the beginning of the month, before January 1 or January 2. Things like spring, fall, early 1980, early June, those things are slotted into what is a logical, chronological, and hopefully consistent place.

Now, a point on quotes. I adhered quite strongly to the idea of not giving you quotes that could have conceivably shown up in some of my other books. Occasionally, the eagle eye amongst you might spot a few, but for all intents and purposes, all of the Iron Maiden quoting is new, i.e., not in my *2 Minutes to Midnight: An Iron Maiden Day-by-Day*. This should be pretty much all fresh material taken from other interviews.

As well, I was cognizant not to quote from the *Deep Purple Royal Family* books, nor should I, right? I mean, the debate is still out whether Gillan is a NWOBHM band, and so I split the difference, and included lots of Gillan entries, but not lots of Gillan quoting, adhering to a vague philosophy that borderline entries shouldn't take up a lot of real estate. Sticking with that family of bands, and speaking to a wider issue, there are indeed a smattering of Whitesnake and Deep Purple and Rainbow entries, but not a huge amount of detail, because we are talking about the story of the NWOBHM, and so when I include entries on bands not by any reasonable measure part of it, there's usually some justification of why this entry is here, why it relates to the story.

Which of course, brings up the contentious and quite vast amount of pre-1978 material. Let's remember one thing, what we are telling here is the story of the NWOBHM, rather than having every entry feed a question, such as it did in *Who Invented Heavy Metal?*. Having said that however, the astute reader can pretty much read the 1970 to 1978 portion of this book as "Who—or what—caused the NWOBHM?" because this baby steps part of the tale is all about the building blocks.

And of course—and this will become obvious once you start reading—there's very little in this book about the origins of heavy metal itself, because that was covered vastly and panoramically and pretty awesomely if I might say so myself, in *Who Invented Heavy Metal?*. And let's not forget, that book ended in 1971, and so everything past that date was fair game. But of course, it was only fair game if it adhered and contributed to the explaining of the predilections and likes of those who would go on to make NWOBHM music. So in essence, what you will see here is a celebration of the main records that someone like a John Gallagher from Raven would have in his angry headbanging young punter record collection.

So yeah, just to go back to this point, because I wanted to make it a little more strongly, had I not written *Steal Away the Night: An Ozzy Osbourne Day-by-Day*, well, you might've seen a little more real estate dedicated to the first two Ozzy Osbourne albums, that band being what we might call an honourary NWOBHM band. Because, as you will see throughout the book, we celebrate quite a few of these honourary bands—but again, the idea is to get in and get out. Celebrate them, remind readers that these bands, although they weren't from Britain, or were from Britain and had a bunch of old guys in the band, were peripherally part of the scene, or welcomed as part of the scene, but I'm not going to talk about every single they put out nor am I necessarily going to have them speak.

Fortunately, however, it's really only Maiden I've done a timeline and quotes book on that is true NWOBHM, and even *they* get kicked out by the purists who think that a band has to be poverty-stricken (or never tour America) to be included in the club. And since I had access to more quotes, well, this is indeed the book I wanted to write.

What else? Yes, just a note on the type of quotes you're going to read and hear. Again, because we aren't concerned with answering the question, "Who invented the NWOBHM?" but rather telling the story of the NWOBHM, I had no qualms about having these rockers talk about their albums and their songs, or stories about live gigs, touring, other specifics regarding their own little corner of the world. In other words, although there's lots of good conceptual, philosophical, general stuff about what the NWOBHM is and was, to my mind, the story of the genre is in the records, in the music itself, alongside the sociological stuff.

As well, I provide a "recap" section at the end of each significant period, mainly to highlight important milestones. One of the disadvantages of this format is the potential for the reader to be lost in a sea of factoids, without enough prioritizing of events. In the entry itself, I've tried to add contextual weight to red-flag importance, but the recaps help with this as well.

Actually, one other thing, I've decided to go with one image class for this book. You know me: I've proven this in something like a dozen books already that I love the advertisements. There was such a romance for me and my buddy Forrest Toop with going down to Spokane, Washington, and going into Magic Mushrooms or Strawberry Jams and buying *Sounds* and *Kerrang!* and seeing those ads for albums that were finally speaking to us in a direct voice. Now, the natural would be to include album covers and 45 sleeves, along with ads, which would open the door to live photography, ticket stubs and posters. But why I decided on the neatness of one image class is twofold: it provides a bit of conceptual focus, but also, the *Smokin' Valves* book, which most of you probably own already, is chock-full of nice, clear, sharp shots of all them rare album and 45 sleeves. Again, I'm endeavouring not to repeat myself across these 50+ books that I've done.

Finally, I must mention that as I write this appeal to you, *This Means War: The Sunset Years of the NWOBHM* is well in progress, and will be covering the years 1981, 1982, 1983 and 1984. We can all argue until we're blue in the face when the NWOBHM is over and done with, but I've always gone with 1984, backing that up with the records I've included in the *Smokin' Valves* reviews book. I suppose if you are actually from Britain, you would scale that back a bit, possibly even to 1982. It's an interesting parlour game—come visit my metal man cave (it's a dedicated condo office, so no distractions!) and we'll discuss. But bring beers; my fridge isn't always stocked.

All right, enough. These introductions are always the hardest things to do with these books, and writing them is one of the last things I do. Now it's back to editing, commenting, adding more quotes, hopefully winning a few more battles and unearthing specific dates, and getting this thing out the door to my designer Eduardo and then into print and having them boxes show up at pensioners' rock 'n' roll central here in Toronto. Thanks for listening. Up the Hammers and all that.

Martin Popoff
martinp@inforamp.net
martinpopoff.com

1970 ⁓ 1975 ⁓ "It's almost like the white man's blues, heavy metal."

Friday February 13, 1970. This date marks with utmost importance the UK release date for Black Sabbath's debut, *Black Sabbath*. The album contains seminal metal track "Black Sabbath," plus "The Wizard" and "N.I.B." The groundbreaking album reaches #8 on the UK album charts. Heavy metal needs to be invented for there to be, one day, a New Wave of British Heavy Metal. Arguably, *Black Sabbath* represents a first wave with so much focus and strength, that nothing all the way up until the collective NWOBHM, really, for all intents and purposes, counts as wholly "new" in-betwixt. Except, that is, for Deep Purple's *In Rock*.

Iron Maiden bassist Steve Harris:

Sabbath had the riffs and they had the dark element, the dark, dirgy, slow heavy kind of vibe, but also they had great melodies and great songs. I mean the bottom line of any band, lifespan of any band, I've always said, it's the songs. You can have a great technically-minded band, but if they're not playing good songs, then you're not really going to listen to them too much. So it's great songwriting abilities. And they were a lot more melodic than people would give them credit for. And us also, later, because I think a lot of people pass us off as being some metal band with not a lot of melody. Well that's obviously the people who didn't listen to it properly. But definitely, Sabbath had that kind of raw, earthy, very heavy and dark sound.

June 3, 1970. Deep Purple release *In Rock*. Recorded August '69 to May '70, *In Rock* can be considered, in some ways, the very first power metal album, and indeed more of a link to the NWOBHM than *Black Sabbath*. If *Black Sabbath* and *Paranoid* (and records by Uriah Heep, The Stooges, MC5 and Blue Cheer) can be considered earlier heavy metal albums, *In Rock* takes the prize for more of a modern twist on metal, being fast, keyboardy, and classical music-tinged. The album includes a true NWOBHM-styled metal gallop in "Hard Lovin' Man"—the blueprint for Iron Maiden is right here, and in turn, *In Rock* is ground zero for the invention of the NWOBHM, but not heavy metal in the wider sense, which still resides with *Black Sabbath*.

Deep Purple keyboardist Jon Lord:

For Ritchie, the speed of playing, when he was a young man, I think that was an end in itself for him. I think he just wanted to be the fastest guitarist on the planet. And when he was doing sessions for Joe Meek way back in the day, I think he was booked occasionally because, oh yeah, let's get Ritchie because he's the guy who can play really fast solos.

And some of these heroes from the American music scene in the late '50s and early '60s were guys who had real technique. I came out of a more improvisational school of music. Rhythm and blues kind of thing, after my classical training, and one of the things you're trained to be as a young classical pianist, is to be able to play that very difficult music, which is often very fast. So the technique was there— it seemed a shame to let it lie on the shelf. And of course you're young. You're full of spit and vinegar and you want to show off. I think part of the improvisational way of playing music is a preening, especially when you're younger. As you get older you put more in the service of the emotional content rather than the intellectual content, but I think it's all part of being young and proud enough to stand on stage and strut your stuff.

As for the riff, the guitar was becoming more and more important, much to the chagrin of people like me who were trying to elevate the importance of the Hammond organ. Still it's rock 'n' roll. The guitar is the symbol of rock 'n' roll, it's the sound of rock 'n' roll. Again, it's that animal ferocity that it's capable of. And it is exemplified by a great riff. The exception that proves the rule sometimes... if you listen to the riff of "Smoke on the Water" for example, which is often said to be one of the most famous guitar riffs, it actually achieves its strength by the confluence of the guitar and the organ being played in fourths. When the organ comes in on that riff, you know it's there. So I'm pleading my case a bit there. But generally, I think what exemplifies hard rock is a great guitar riff. It's a way of leading you in. It draws you instantly—a great riff and a killer chorus, and you've got it made.

With *In Rock*, we were responding to an inner compulsion, and the inner compulsion was driven by an exterior world, something around us that was driving us towards the way... I wanted the organ to get louder and fiercer and harder. I wanted the contrast. There was a feeling that barriers had to be pushed, had to be moved outwards. When we got to *In Rock*, everybody in the band knew exactly where we were going. We couldn't have named the place we were going to, but we knew what we were going to be doing when we got there.

Ritchie had this—it seemed to me—this sound in his mind that he was always after, and he came close. If you imagine a 30-foot cello being played at 1000 watts of volume, it might be what he had inside his mind somehow. That round and yet fierce sound that he got, as he got more towards his Rainbow days, I think, is where he finally found the sound he wanted. But it needed volume to make it happen and it needed control of feedback, which he became very expert at. And he was a great showman, of course, as well. Quiet as Bo Peep off stage, but on stage, capable of a kind of animal excitement. And I think he wanted more all the time. His famous phrase was, "Can we have everything louder than everything else?" And until you think about it, you go sure, and then you go, uh, what does that actually mean? He was a great believer in the power of volume.

Iron Maiden bassist Steve Harris: I think we were more influenced by Wishbone Ash-type stuff or Free and people like that more than Deep Purple. I like Deep Purple—we all did—but they weren't as much an influence. I think bands like Jethro Tull were actually more of an influence, believe it or not, than Deep Purple. I had *Made in Japan* and ended up buying a few Purple albums, whatever, but they weren't a major influence. Black Sabbath were probably more an influence and Led Zeppelin  as well. Some people thought that we were doing the twin guitar thing version of Purple at times, but that certainly wasn't intentional. Free were definitely a bigger influence. If you listen to Dave's guitar playing, he was definitely influenced by Paul Kossoff a lot and also Hendrix; Free were a massive influence.

Iron Maiden guitarist Adrian Smith on the topic of first heavy metal band:
It's gotta be Black Sabbath, hasn't it? I mean *Paranoid* was also quite a big hit in the UK, so you heard that on the radio. They were massively influential. But really, I never heard the expression heavy metal until the late '70s/early '80s. To me it was always hard rock or heavy rock, with Purple, Sabbath, even Free. And then the metal thing crept in at the end of the '70s/early '80s. But I suppose if you could call anything metal at the time, it was probably Sabbath.
It was just the whole atmosphere they created, I suppose. But again there's quite a lot of blues in the soloing side of it, you know.

But the sound of the guitar, some of the tunings, it was that very doomy kind of sound which you'd associate with metal rather than a happy poppy sound.

I suppose Zeppelin touched on it with "Whole Lotta Love" and some of the heavier stuff, but there was a lot more to Zeppelin, a lot of folk and loads of blues. They were before Sabbath, and maybe they touched on metal with "Communication Breakdown" and that sort of rock 'n' roll metal. It's almost like the white man's blues, heavy metal. Journalist Goetz Kunhemund:

Deep Purple was as classically influenced as Rainbow were. Rainbow took it a step further, but the classical influences, the medieval stuff, was heard in Deep Purple already, and yeah, Ritchie Blackmore told everybody who he took his influences from.

June 1970. Uriah Heep issue their quite heavy and modern *Very 'Eavy, Very 'Umble*, which was issued in the states as a self-titled. The UK edition's "Lucy Blues" was replaced by "Bird of Prey," arguably a proto-NWOBHM construct, if only through sheer modernity. Like *In Rock*, the album suggests keyboards for heavy metal, not out of the question for many NWOBHM bands, and touches down as well on many modern riff and rhythmic elements celebrated within the NWOBHM.

Metallica drummer Lars Ulrich:

There are a lot of bands that get left out when you talk metal, especially if you're talking to Americans. A band like Sweet, who were phenomenally big in Europe and had hit single after hit single and they made these great albums and had some really weighty, meaty, sort of Deep Purple-esque album tracks, and they're very talented musicians. And then you have a band like Slade who were incredible songwriters. Noddy Holder, incredible voice, massive in Europe. You have a band like Status Quo who were absolutely massive in Europe, one of the biggest bands ever in Germany, and you've got Nazareth also.

But the reason they don't figure much in these conversations is because they didn't really do much in America. Deep Purple's not in the Rock and Roll Hall of Fame because they didn't do much in America. Uriah Heep doesn't show up on the radar because they didn't do much in America. Zeppelin were the kings in America.

But when I was growing up in Denmark in the '70s it was all about Deep Purple and Black Sabbath and Uriah Heep; Led Zeppelin were not part of that conversation in Denmark so much. They were kind of bluesier and they had a different thing. I'm saying this not disrespectfully—I'm talking purely factually. When I was 12, Led Zeppelin was not a big thing on my radar or my friends' radar. It was much more Deep Purple, Uriah Heep, Black Sabbath.

It's difficult to have this conversation without... you don't want to dis anybody. I think a lot of people felt Uriah Heep were like a poor man's Deep Purple. That there was a pretty heavy presence on the Hammond organ. Ken Hensley was playing that so there was that element to their sound. But they didn't quite have the "Smoke on the Water"s or the "Highway Star"s. They had "Easy Livin'" and "Stealin'" and some of these songs, but it never became quite as well-known as Deep Purple. I mean for me, I saw Uriah Heep two or three times in Denmark. I saw Status Quo, I saw Sweet maybe four times, Slade numerous times.

At the end of the day there's got to be a song there, and Heep had some very good songs. Whether they're big or small, at the end of the day it starts and ends with songs. And they had some songs that were very, very good back then and that have stood the test of time. You take a song like "Easy Livin'," it sounds great 35 years later. It's just a great rock song. You take a song like "Stealin'," "Gypsy," "July Morning," they're just great songs. I would encourage anybody to go out and brush up on their Uriah Heep.

April 28, 1972. Wishbone Ash issue their third and most acclaimed album *Argus*. It has an ancient warrior on the cover, but most importantly, Wishbone Ash are considered one of the innovators of twin leads, a major NWOBHM element. Engineer on the album is Martin Birch, who would produce, in the early '80s, Whitesnake, Black Sabbath and Iron Maiden.

Iron Maiden basssist Steve Harris:
The *Argus* album was voted the best album of '72. Quite rightly so in my opinion. Absolute classic. I mean, I still listen to it now and it still sounds amazing to me. And incidentally Martin Birch was the engineer on the album, so that was a very influential album, I think. There were a lot of bands around playing Wishbone Ash covers at the time.

Everybody in the pubs and clubs at that time started off playing covers, same as we did, same as everybody did. The difference with us was we would always try and choose songs that weren't as well-known. So if we chose a Thin Lizzy song it would be something that was not one of the hits. And everyone was doing "All Right Now," so we might do that, but we'd also do something like "I'm a Mover," which wasn't as well-known.

Montrose's first album was very much a cult album, so we didn't really do much off that. We did something off the second album, *Paper Money*, which wasn't as well-known. We did "I Got the Fire," which we ended up recording, and that was one of the main songs of our set at one point. But everyone thought it was an original because they'd not heard that album.

So we consciously went out of our way to choose songs that weren't as well-known so that they would be refreshing. Because you could go every week to see a band playing "All Right Now" and "Stairway to Heaven," but not everybody was playing the sort of songs we were choosing. So even though we were doing some originals and some covers, the covers seemed like they were originals as well. And then as soon as we got more originals, we'd bin the covers anyway.

May 1972. Uriah Heep issue *Demons and Wizards*. The band enjoys its first US hit single with "Easy Livin'." With Heep, we see fantasy lyrics and mystical album covers, both recurring themes of NWOBHM bands. Heep return significantly to our story with the *Abominog* album, where the band make an appearance for an entirely different reason, namely as one of a handful of examples of bands essentially "bandwagoning" on the NWOBHM.

May 29, 1972. Following up on Mike Saunders' first accurate use of the term heavy metal to describe Sir Lord Baltimore in May of 1971, *Circular* calls Deep Purple's *Machine Head* "loud heavy metal rock," imbuing a clear NWOBHM influence with that identifier.

September 21, 1973. Thin Lizzy's third album, *Vagabonds of the Western World*, the last with guitarist Eric Bell. The album is the work of a band pointing in a heavier direction, and displays Phil Lynott's penchant for epic story-telling on "Vagabond of the Western World" and "The Hero and the Madman," but lacks celebrated Thin Lizzy signatures.

1974. Following upon use of the term "heavy metal" in a Black Sabbath record review in the *NME*, September '73, two more *NME* journos, Ian McDonald and Nick Kent, use the tern in 1974, as does Chris Charlesworth from *Melody Maker*. This widespread adoption of the term originates in Mike Saunders' now regular use of the term in the US, along with his illustrative pieces on what it means.

1974. Praying Mantis forms, although their first output wouldn't be until 1979, a *Soundhouse Tapes* EP, like Iron Maiden. Also like Iron Maiden, Praying Mantis are an example of a band quietly toiling away through the likes of glam and punk on their way to a new age for metal.

THE GREYHOUND
175 FULHAM PALACE RD., W.6

Thurs., Oct. 14	**PEACHES**
Fri., Oct. 15th.	**PEACHES**
Sat., Oct. 16th.	JUGGLER
Sun., Oct. 17th.	**HUNGRY HORSE**
Mon., Oct. 18th.	HEARTBREAKER
Tues., Oct. 19th	HANDBAG
Wed., Oct. 20th.	**BANDY LEGS**

★ ADMISSION FREE ★

1974. Birmingham's Quartz begins life as Bandy Legs. Like Saxon, they will transform through the years as their crowd signals to them that to do so would pay dividends.

1974. Raven forms in Newcastle, England.

Raven bassist and vocalist John Gallagher:

The music goes around in circles, and I think what had happened at the time was there was a lot of people, a lot of young kids like myself, who really liked the heavy bands and got inspired to play the music purely for playing the music, because the record companies in the business end wanted nothing to do with that whatsoever, which they usually don't.

We might as well have been in Goose Bay compared to where you are, you know? Middle of nowhere—Newcastle. Nobody cared about Newcastle, but we were very lucky in that there just happened to be this studio that had some success with some comedy records and recording demos for folk bands like Lindisfarne and stuff like that. They took a chance putting out a single by one local band called the Tygers of Pan Tang, and then after that, their manager came and saw us and said, "Wow, do you guys want to do a single?" We're like, "What? Yeah, yes please, we'll do that."

A similar thing happened with a few other places, but basically it was just a bunch of kids all over the country who loved the music and had their own take on it, and that's why what you would call the first tier bands, I guess, were very original. They all were playing basically the same thing but they all had their own take on it.

Tygers of Pan Tang vocalist and fellow Newcastle fixture Jess Cox on where the NWOBHM was located:
Around Yorkshire you had quite a few bands, but I mean there was no specific town. Saxon are from Barnsley, which is out of Yorkshire. You had Gaskin from Hull, which is sort of Humberside but it's still kind of east of main Yorkshire. There was nothing like London or Newcastle. I mean Newcastle, if you actually write them down, the amount of bands from Newcastle, you'd be shocked. Hellanbach, Raven, Satan, the Tygers, Venom, White Spirit, Saracen, Avenger, Tysondog, Warfare... you just go on and on.

February 16, 1974. *Melody Maker*'s Chris Charlesworth offers Blue Öyster Cult as part of "a new wave of heavy metal bands."

March 1, 1974. Rush issue their self-titled debut, on Moon Records. Canada's inventors of progressive metal are a regularly cited influence on NWOBHM bands. On July 1st of '74, the album gets reissued (and issued for the first time in the US) on Mercury. The album is Zeppelin-esque, but soon, the band emphatically is not.

July 1974. Nutz issue their self-titled debut. Dated blues rockers at this point, Nutz would change their name to Rage eventually and subsequently provide to the world a slightly less dated blues rock.

August 23 – 25, 1974. The third annual *Reading* festival. Heaviest bands on the bill are Trapeze, Hustler, Strider, Heavy Metal Kids and Nutz, who, as mentioned, would become middling NWOBHM participants Rage (after actually appearing on the first *Metal for Muthas* still as Nutz).

September 6, 1974. Judas Priest issue their debut album, *Rocka Rolla*. Priest is arguably the top most influential band on the creation of a NWOBHM portfolio of sounds, although not because of *Rocka Rolla*, which is more so a tentative and demure love letter to Black Sabbath.

November 1, 1974. Scorpions issue their second album, *Fly to the Rainbow*, which is creeping toward a modern sound, and certainly less "krautrock" than *Lonesome Crow*. Scorpions would be in that group of the top dozen or so bands igniting the imaginations of those who would man the bands of the NWOBHM.

1975. Witchfynde cook up some demos, documented on the *Lost Tapes of 1975*, through Vyper Records. Tracks are "Grimoire," "Madame Noname," "Halfway," "Pastiche," "Slow Down," "Valkyrian Ride" and "Tetelestai."

> Witchfynde guitarist Montalo:
> On a musical side in the '70s, we gigged everywhere. We were out playing constantly, at any little working men's club or bar or whatever. Before we got the deal, we had been doing it for a long, long time, before we ever did any recordings. We'd got quite a substantial following before we did any recordings. As you'd imagine, the type of bands that we were about were Sabbath and Deep Purple and Zeppelin, that sort of thing.

1975. Ian Gillan forms the Ian Gillan Band. Also in '75, Janick Gers, who will go on to play with Ian in Gillan, forms White Spirit, in Hartlepool, England.

1975. UK rock DJ Neal Kay establishes The Soundhouse, (or Bandwagon) in the back room of the Prince of Wales pub in Kingsbury. The Soundhouse was called "London's Only Heavy Rock Disco." The nights that he commandeered—one night a week and then the key Sunday night slot— began to take off. Then it was five nights a week and "denim-clad" patrons became the norm, while Neal spun records by Sabbath, Zeppelin, Purple, Thin Lizzy and Rush. It soon became known as Heavy Metal Soundhouse. Eventually the club started to book bands like Praying Mantis, Nutz, Iron Maiden, Angel Witch and Samson. In a few years' time, Iron Maiden's *The Soundhouse Tapes* gets produced, becoming Iron Maiden's legendary first release, an EP.

DJ Neal Kay:
    I was out of work and there was no exposure for any up-and-coming bands. There was hardly any exposure for the bands that everyone knew. Venues were not interested, no one was interested. The industry had suddenly decided that punk was the thing, and I was getting progressively more and more angry about the whole thing, and I was just an individual. I was a professional DJ, yeah?, but I was still very annoyed. And they took me to this pub one night. I was trucking, I was out of music, I just didn't want to work in it. And I was trucking for a living. And my driving buddy took me to a place one night after work on a Wednesday night near where we lived up in Kingsbury near Wembley. You know the football arena Wembley? It was near there and it was called the Prince of Wales, and they had a once-a-week rock thing happening there, DJs playing rock music, and he said to me, "You're going to like this. Come and have a beer."
    I went in there and I was so impressed. The sound system was fucking huge, man. It was really big. It wasn't a disco system, it was a fucking ginormous great band PA system. And I had a beer, and you know what? That night, they asked out over the PA if there were any DJs in the house that wanted to come up and work with them and present the rock show because they were not really sort of rock DJs. I went up there and got the job on the spot and that's how that happened. Remarkable.
    So the war was on. It was really vital to try and let the industry know that finally there was a place that would give exposure to rock, and the Bandwagon kind of picked up from that moment on. It was like the pop music of the day five nights a week, rock one night a week, and it was something else for the seventh. And there were a lot of underage kids getting into the commercial music nights, and the license of the place was threatened soon after I joined. I remember going to court to fight the license, and you know the most bizarre

twist of all? When it was discovered that there was no trouble on the heavy metal or hard rock night and people came in couples and they were older, the judge, the silly old fucker, he did, he swung around and said, "Well, I'll grant you your license on the condition that this form of music takes precedence at least five nights a week!" (laughs).

Yeah, oh wow! (laughs). So by appointment to her majesty. Un-fucking-believable. Fucking right (laughs). It was like I had a coat hanger in my mouth—I didn't stop grinning for a week. The old judge had just given me control of the old Soundhouse, as it became known. Where after that we worked hard, very, very hard indeed, contacting the various people, had all the seats thrown out, had new rules instilled. No one with a suit, shirt and a tie was allowed in. I threw all the stripes out and had my own doormen put in. I was a member of a bike club at the time and they became our door staff, actually.

And finally after an awful lot of work, Geoff Barton, the journalist from *Sounds* came down to see what we were doing and was absolutely amazed, and he wrote a double centre-page spread in *Sounds* magazine, which was the magazine of the day. And he subtitled it on the front page of *Sounds,* and would you believe it, A Survivor's Report From A Heavy Metal Discothèque!, exclamation mark, 'caxayed, as it's known now, classic rock. And by and by tapes started arriving, cassettes from all over the world, and it became apparent very quickly that record companies just weren't listening to anybody.

And bear in mind once again, the radio—or total lack of it—the DJ, the radio DJ, Tommy Vance, did a three-hour show once a week on Radio One called it *The Friday Night Rock Show*. And that was the only outlet that rock had. That was it on radio, and we had the Soundhouse, because *Sounds* had decided to get behind it and in turn other journalists came. Fuck me, I think the *London Times or the London Guardian* came to see what all the fuss was about on a Sunday night. We wiped them out; very funny actually.

I thought of other ways of raising the profile. I contacted CBS, Epic Records, and I got Ted Nugent and his band to come down and meet the kids on a personal appearance after a London Hammersmith Odeon show. He was the first. That had never happened before! But I had serious contacts up at the record companies by now, because I was playing all the rock and getting an awful lot of publicity for doing it, and I thought, well what better than that, if Ted Nugent—he was big in those days—if Gonzo came. Then others would follow and the press would follow too, and the profile of the club and the music would go sky high.

Look, the structure of the Soundhouse, musically, was very, very, very wide. I said I'd play Styx, Journey, all this sort of stuff. We played prog, we played everything that was good music. What we didn't play was shit. If you couldn't play, write or sing, then you weren't heard at the Soundhouse. That made the Soundhouse a very selective audience, actually, and it gave live bands a hell of a hard time. By then I had something like a 10K PA in there just for playing records on. It was so loud that we had to fly the discotheque console from the rafters on chains to avoid the rest of the low-frequency feedback, which we did, and it was sort of like a ship's compass if you know what I mean, kind of nimble-mounted. So if everyone jumped up and down and went bloody mad with their histrionics on the floor, the whole place shook. But if you're going to do it, that's how you do it. There's no point pussy-footing around.

February 17, 1975. AC/DC issue their debut album, *High Voltage*, only in Australia, with a different track list and cover art from the later worldwide issue. Brits-by-proxy AC/DC would become universally welcomed "honourary" NWOBHMers.

May 1975. Nutz issue their second album, *Nutz Too*.

July 1975. Rainbow issue their first album, *Ritchie Blackmore's Rainbow*. Rainbow forms when Ritchie gets annoyed that Deep Purple is getting too bluesy and funky. The album features vocalist Ronnie James Dio, poached from Elf (along with a couple other guys). The album sports a fantasy album cover and all sorts of "demons and wizards" lyrics. Classical-tinged metal classics include "Man on the Silver Mountain" and "Sixteenth Century Greensleeves." If the songs are all together too stodgy to be classed as proto-NWOBHM, the overall fanciful vibe of the record is not.

Journalist Goetz Kunhemund:
Rainbow were the inventors of classically-influenced hard rock. They were the first band to incorporate classical music in a way that everybody could grab. That everybody could understand. I mean others had done it before them, but with Rainbow the influence of Bach and Beethoven was so dominant and obvious that people picked up on that and realized there's a strong link between baroque classical music and hard rock music. In a way it's a similar music and it does fit together and it makes interesting listening. And people who love Rainbow... I mean Rainbow was huge all over Europe. Such an important band, and especially with Dio being the biggest singer in rock ever with this dramatic voice that could have been an opera singer and whatever in the middle ages.

Dio used a lot of fantasy stuff in his lyrics and he used a lot of drama, a lot of emotional stuff, which goes along well with the music. I mean Iron Maiden used to sing about everyday life. They used to sing about somebody running free, somebody trying to cope with everyday problems. Dio sang about stuff you would dream about or he would sing about the middle ages or dark times; that was pretty new at the time. I mean when the first Rainbow album came out I remember a few reviews that were mocking Dio's lyrics because they were so different—but they invented a genre.

July 20, 1975. An ill wind called Motörhead play their first gig, at the Roundhouse, supporting prog's forgotten band, Greenslade.

Iron Maiden vocalist Bruce Dickinson on the musical climate of the mid-'70s:

It was surprisingly quite a healthy scene, to be honest with you. I think, in retrospect, if you look now, the difficulties faced by bands, between not getting paid anymore for doing records and you know, people charging crazy amounts for getting insured just to go out and do the gigs and for noise regulations and "can't do this, can't do that" health and safety, all the bullshit, affects people just trying to do their gigs now... Back then it was a simpler time. You just turned up to the pubs—and there were quite a few pubs you could do gigs, as a metal band. In actual fact, it was that scene that kept the sort of underbelly of the metal scene going.

Because there was no Internet. There was no way of people getting together to talk to each other, except to go to gigs. People met at gigs. And they didn't meet pretty much anywhere else, unless you went to pubs, which played pop music. So that was sort of the metal scene in the period. You went to a pub and played metal stuff, or you went to a place where there were rock gigs. But at the same time, the punk thing was happening, and it was real; there was a degree of excitement about it, but it kind of coexisted with the whole metal thing. It didn't supplant it or replace it, because you could still go to all the major theaters and venues and see metal acts, and the place would be sold-out. Nobody was not going because they were going to see punk.

However, where it did supplant it was in the eyes of the media. And you know, you had kind of the art school media, which all wanted to be great artistes, and so music really just became an extension of their art school course. So in other words, music was not actually... music had no intrinsic value, as music. It was simply another form of performance art.

August 16, 1975. Motörhead's Lemmy, speaking with Geoff Barton from *Sounds*, is already wondering aloud to journalists whether "some" of the music he prefers is called "heavy rock and roll" or "heavy metal."

October 25, 1975. Nick Kent reviews for the *NME* a Blue Öyster Cult gig at the Hammersmith Odeon, panning the band, but saving his most stinging rebuke for opening act, Motörhead.

December 25, 1975. Iron Maiden forms, shortly after Steve Harris leaves his former band, Smiler.

Recap

Again, the birth of heavy metal itself is covered with insane detailed mania in *Who Invented Heavy Metal?*, and so what was an interesting exercise here was to point out the contours of a type of heavy metal that helps birth the New Wave of British Heavy Metal. In this light, you have to point out *Black Sabbath,* but in a sense, more importantly, Deep Purple's *In Rock,* and even Uriah Heep, with that band's gothic tones, high singing, and even keyboards, which were not particularly shunned by NWOBHM bands.

Within the framework of 1970 to 1975, you also start to see the first clear uses of the term "heavy metal." Why this is important to the present discussion is that the NWOBHM is characterized in a big way as the first heavy metal genre—and yes, we can debate whether it is a genre—in which heavy metal is something that can be experienced as a deliberate and identifiable thing, perhaps with all of the senses.

Within this timeframe, you also get the first records from bands like Thin Lizzy and Rush, both big NWOBHM influences, the former for their twin leads, the latter for their progressive nature, although both bands would blossom more so in the late '70s than early.

Importantly, we also get to see the birth of a handful of NWOBHM bands itself, proving the rostrum, "It's a long way to the top, if you wanna rock 'n' roll." Finally, we also see the birth of Neal Kay's heavy metal disco, the Soundhouse. Again, as articulated with great verve and intelligence by the man himself, Kay proves important in promoting and giving a home and a context to heavy metal music, both old and new. In fact, the DNA of the philosophy housed within Kay is similar to that of the guys starting bands at this time as well as the author of this book, in that it is the voracious consumption of old metal, to the point of satiation and even panic that there isn't any more, which gives rise to so much enthusiasm about new metal, when it suddenly starts appearing in clumps in 1980.

1976 — "We're like, we like heavy. Where's the heavy?"

1976. Rob Loonhouse shows up at the Soundhouse with a "hardboard" guitar and air guitar is born.

DJ Neal Kay:

Okay, this is all about the spirit of rock 'n' roll for me. I've seen it, I've been seeing it all my life. Joe Cocker, I will say, was the first, visually, ever to do this onstage at the Woodstock festival while they're playing the solo in "With a Little Help from My Friends;" Joe Cocker's standing there playing his imaginary guitar. The hero of heroes. I think that's the first visually recorded episode. I didn't invent it, it was already there. It's what people do when they are really taken with the spirit of the thing.

At the Bandwagon the Loonies went one further. Actually it went three further. The first thing that happened was Rob Loonhouse, one Rob Yeatman, a professional photographer by trade by day, and a glorious leader of the lunatics at the time, walked into the Soundhouse one day with a hardboard Flying V. No strings, but a whammy bar. And everyone said, "Rob, what are you going to do with that? There's no strings on it, man, you can't play it." "Don't need any." Ah, interesting.

Okay, get on with the show, play the show, lighting up, time, full lights, crack up the old sound system. The whole bar's shaking, fit to bust. Suddenly into the limelight steps one Loonhouse, picks up the Flying V, and whilst I'm playing the Judas Priest track, lo and behold Rob Loonhouse plays the solo! On the Flying V. And everyone saw him. And I thought that's novel. It's completely insane but it's novel. And afterwards I said to him, "Why did you do that?" And he said, "Well I felt like doing it, mate." All right. Sure. No problem, man.

Next week there was five of them. The week after, there was ten. Then there was 15. Then we started the triple-decker headbanging with them, and they'd stack up on each other's shoulders, three up. And there'd be a sea up there of air guitar players. At Christmas we ran Headbanger of the Year, or as it became known, Air Guitarist of the Year. The year after, it got so crazy, I finished up inviting an all-star guest panel to judge the final, amongst which were members from Rainbow, Priest, Maiden, all manner of high-falutin' stars were there. What is it? It's headbanging band of the year.

Rob Loonhouse by now had formed Willy Flasher and the Raincoats, and he had built himself a double neck Flying V and cardboard keyboards, and he had a cardboard drum kit for a drummer, and he had a whole stage set made of cardboard. And he had road crew. And in the middle of the set, they arranged for the drum set to explode all over the place; the road crew come running out onstage and start plugging in all these cables and rebuilding the kit. And it's just sensational. Absolutely sensational.

I would say this is a lot more to do with just the 'wagon rather than anything else, because you didn't see this so much elsewhere. It's partially my fault for driving them crazy, because I'd come from a show biz side, and I'm kind of a showman. I'm never satisfied with just playing records—any fool can do that. That's not it; you have to do more. And what I realized in the end was I'd grown a whole culture of rock 'n' roll loonies. I mean, we used to do the craziest things. In the middle of a set of fast-moving rock, I'd suddenly put in a tiny little bit of country and western, just about 30 bars, hoe-down music, real rapid, and then go straight back into the metal again. At Christmas show time, we'd do about 30 bars of "Snow White and the Seven Dwarfs" hi-ho, and the metalers would be on their knees going around the Soundhouse like the dwarfs. We inspired and encouraged total over-the-top behaviour.

Gillan bassist John McCoy:
It was a kind of club where you could go and meet people who were into rock and heavy metal and the bands we've been discussing. It was a pub in northwest London, really, just rooms in the back of a pub. And you knew if you went there you'd see somebody from some band and there would be a band playing and it was a crazy time. This is when all that air guitar stuff was going on—people used to do the air guitar. There were even competitions, who could play the best air guitar. I remember judging the competition and sitting next to Cozy Powell, and we sat there, and there's these guys having what can only be described as fits or Tourette syndrome in front of us, like very close, miming to whatever track they'd picked.

And Cozy and I just looked at each other and we just burst into laughter, and we laughed throughout the whole thing. It was a crazy time. There was a lot of freedom then. You didn't feel threatened in any way. There was something about that club—and it has to be said that Neal Kay made this happen—that just had an atmosphere. You know how certain places just feel right for whatever they're doing? I mean I'm sure you've got a favourite club that you go to. My all-time favourite was the old Marquee club. There was something special about that place. I suppose it was the heritage of all the people that played there over the years, but it was a great club with great sound and never any trouble and nice people.

And the Soundhouse was kind of the same thing. It just had an atmosphere where you could go and relax and enjoy good music on a great sound system. There was always one band on, and sometimes two or three, but Neal had access to the new releases and had a great sound system there. Back in those days you had to go travel quite a distance to find a place that had a good sound system that was loud and you could actually feel the bass. And Neal had all of that sorted out. Great sound. And he'd suddenly come out with, "I've got an Angel Witch demo here," or I've got something here by whoever it might be, that you hadn't heard before. And you felt kind of included in this phenomenon. At that time it wasn't named as anything. But I suppose there was a kind of movement to it that we were all part of without even thinking about it.

I think I played there in '76 with Bernie Torme in Scrap Yard. I think we played there, and it was just like a small rock gig, you know? That early period, it was very strange in the music business completely because that's when punk happened. Bernie and I were going around with this band Scrap Yard, we couldn't get arrested. We couldn't get a show for anything because punk had suddenly taken over, and punk bands were filling all the gigs, and that's what happened. You suddenly felt, oh, we're missing the point here somehow. But Neal was one of the few that sort of stuck it out and refused to bow. He was flying the flag for rock.

Journalist John Tucker on the birth of air guitar:

This is where you don't know whether a theory has been put together, or whether the evidence supports the theory. I've got no talent whatsoever. I've been playing imaginary guitar, as my friends called it, and we had a band with a guy looking like a little Muppet playing the drums. We'd divvy up who's playing the lead guitar, bass and vocals. There were five of us actually, who had an imaginary band. We knew nothing of… there was no TV… when the words air guitar became really big news, this was something we had been doing for donkey's years. We'd go to the local discos and try to get them to blast "Paranoid" or something like that, and have two-and-a-half minutes of fun. Headbanging was just something natural. I'm too old for it now, but it's something I did at the time. I'd go through an entire Iron Maiden set, pausing for breath. You'd go through a whole Scorpions tape in one go. But no one ever told us to do it. Not the group that sat in a provincial town in the middle of nowhere.

So where it became popular… I know the stories of Rob Loonhouse at the Soundhouse and things. He just turns up with a cardboard guitar one day, and takes it that one step further. So that when we read about it in *Sounds* then we made our own cardboard guitars. But before then it was completely imaginary. But no one told us to do it. I bought a bike jacket because that was part of the uniform back then and I had the money to afford it. But the denim jacket I bought was something that I thought was cool for a 17-year-old to be wearing. No one told me to wear it.

When I first went to university, which was my first time to meet people from all over the country in metal and to form a rock society in college and get bands and play music, I mentioned the word uniform to one guy and he shot me down. Uniform's not something you have to wear. This is something we wear out of choice. So it's bizarre. It's odd, yet I was being a bit old school. I was quite horrified when towards the mid-'80s people would turn up in surf jams and cutoffs. Because that, to me now, it wasn't the uniform. I'd been completely entrenched, and that's what I wore. I wore jeans, I wore denim jacket or a bike jacket. Black T-shirt, naturally, and that was it. There was no variation. But no one told me to do it; it just happened. And you went to a gig and saw loads of people doing the same thing and you'd think, it must be cool, it must be okay if everyone else is doing it.

1976. Jet Records signs Quartz, still known as Bandy Legs. The band tour, supporting AC/DC and hometown Birmingham chums Black Sabbath.

Quartz guitarist Mick Hopkins on the name change:
That would be just before we started recording. That was up until about 1975, '76, and then there was a chap who'd thought up Queen's name—I think he used to work for EMI. He's got a thing about the Q. And he says, "Quartz, that's a rock, it's big, you can use that as your name." We thought, yeah, all right.

1976. Bruce Dickinson bides his time in a band called Styx, followed by Speed, through '77 and '78. Meanwhile, Samson vocalist after Bruce Dickinson, Nicky Moore, finds himself roaring his way through two albums with his band Tiger, a self-titled and *Goin' Down Laughing*, both issued in '76.

Iron Maiden vocalist Bruce Dickinson on why punk had to happen around this time:
I think, to an extent, you had a generation of kids where some of them were into metal and the whole rock thing and the whole prog thing. But if you weren't into that, and you weren't into John Travolta and *Saturday Night Fever* and discotheques and youth clubs and all this, what were you supposed to be into?

At the end of the '70s, there was a great feeling that there were a lot of very smart people who didn't have a job that were pretty creative, and they didn't have anywhere to put their creativity. Rock was seen as a fairly traditional medium. It was already its own set of tribal gatherings and beliefs and things like that. If you didn't want to do that, you'd do something else. And so that, I think, is where punk came from, and the genius of the whole punk thing was Malcolm McLaren and Vivian Westwood. I mean, that was it—punk was started as an art school project.

1976. Ethel the Frog, named for a *Monty Python* sketch, form in Hull, while over in Wallasey, Spider open for business, anchored by two brothers.

1976. Saxon form in Barnsley, Yorkshire. The band's roots as Son of a Bitch can be traced back to 1975.

Saxon guitarist Graham Oliver:
We'd been through a period of punk in the '70s, and throughout all that period, we continued to play the style of the music that we played: heavy rock. And I'm talking about the late '70s, really. The original lineup of the band came together about '76. Me and Steve Dawson started the band, and did a few gigs with a couple of people, and it wasn't working, and then we heard about the singer, Biff Byford, and he used to play bass, and he was available, and we heard a demo of him singing, and so we auditioned him.

If a wasn't for me and Steve, there never would've been a Saxon. Because when we came together in '76, we did all the gigs like The Music Machine in London, all these early gigs that were punk strongholds, and played our style of music which was really unfashionable at the time. You had Deep Purple and Sabbath 'round about '70, coming out, and Zeppelin were on the peak from '68 to '72, and then punk started.

So rock became unpopular, although we were like really heavy rock. We had the aggression of the punk people, but we didn't like the music, although we were the same age. And we ended up doing gigs like Manchester with The Clash. We even played with the Sex Pistols one time, when they were coming up. So we had all the energy and aggression. I don't know if aggression is the right word, but the fire of the punk feeling, but we wanted to play music without the long drawn-out, self-indulgence of the bands of the early '70s.

That we didn't really like, to be honest. When bands like Yes came out with those long and drawn-out songs, we just didn't connect with it. We connected with the punk feeling, but not the poor music. I think the good stuff like The Clash came through, but it was really difficult for us. We were playing gigs in London, like £20, and it cost us £50 to get there and back. But we just believed in the music that we all grew up with collectively. And that belief and dedication in the music probably comes through in the early Saxon stuff. It got into the grooves of the vinyl. It's hard to categorize something that you've done yourself, because obviously people who were not involved in it will perceive it in a different light. We're that close to it. But I believe the passion that we felt at the time does come out of the tracks, and probably that's why we wrote songs like "Dallas 1 PM," with lyrics about subjects rather than just booze and girls or whatever.

Saxon guitarist Paul Quinn:

We were based around Yorkshire but we got around a lot. We went to the Northeast of England, forayed into Wales and London. Basically, whatever we saw in the newspaper that was advertising rock music, we'd call up or send them demos. The gigs were either pubs which were "working men's clubs," drinking clubs basically. Workers with cheap booze (laughs). A lot of them wouldn't accept bands that were playing new material so we didn't tell them (laughs.) We kind of went in and built up a following that used to ask us whose song we were playing and we'd say, "Well, ours in this case."

It got so that when the punk explosion happened, people were telling us to shove off because we were old hacks now. That didn't faze us. We upped the aggression levels and became more like musical competitors for them, but still as aggressive if not more so. You kind of have to compete when that happens.

Saxon vocalist Biff Byford on the musical climate of 1976 and 1977:

Actually it was a bit rough because the punk thing was really heavy then. It was right in that London thing, and what you could call punk. And we found it quite pitiful, actually, being a long-haired band playing more rock-based stuff rather than frantic energy fashion music. Although we've had the influences quite a lot in our songwriting later on. I mean we quite liked a lot of the stuff like Sex Pistols and Clash because it was a bit rebellious. But they didn't really like us, if you know what I mean. They were all like short hair, green, blue hair with spikes and nose rings. It was definitely a bit of an against society-type movement, punk.

And we were, as well, actually. In those respects we were definitely antiestablishment as well. But in them days, '76, '77, we weren't really writing songs like that. We started writing songs like that a bit later on, 1979, '80, "Backs Against the Wall" and "Never Surrender" and all that type of sentiment. But yeah, it was quite difficult for us to get gigs, but we had strongholds of followers. Like, Wales was a great area for us—South Wales, there was a great stronghold of heavy rock. And the northeast of England, what we called Geordie-land, Newcastle area—that was a big stronghold where we could play. And obviously Yorkshire, where we were from, was good. So we had this area where we used to tour around the clubs playing our own songs, really, and we created a following.

Saxon bassist Steve Dawson on Son of a Bitch:
Very basic, and very much like an extension of punk music. A lot of the songs that we played were very fast, very up-tempo, and we wanted to get as much energy across as possible. Like when you listen to a lot of the early metal stuff, it is just an extension of punk music, but played to a higher degree of musicianship and singing. And that's basically what we sounded like. Because when you're just starting out with anything, you're not very good at it. You get better the more you do it. The first Saxon album, the first Iron Maiden album, don't really sound anything like the later ones because we were just naïve, really, on how to make a record and on how to write a song.

February 1976. Motörhead, having recently replaced Lucas Fox with Phil Taylor, now hires Fast Eddie Clarke. The band's other guitarist, Larry Wallis promptly quits.

Motörhead guitarist Fast Eddie on joining Motörhead:
I was still chomping at the bit at that time. In my early 20s, I had kind of stopped playing. I used to jam with people and that was about it. I had some trouble with the law and that is when people told me that I needed to get serious about music and change things around. I auditioned for Curtis Knight's band and I got the job. Up until then, I was not that serious about music. Once I got in that band, I started to take things more serious. When I got out of Curtis Knight, I did

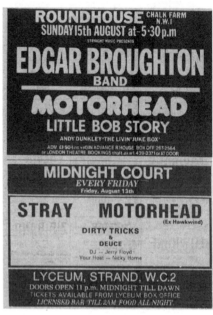

a thing that was on Anchor Records but I never finished it, as I fell out with the guys. I then did a solo thing and at the same time I was working on a houseboat; I was building it. I met Phil Taylor because he came and applied for a job on the houseboat. I gave him a job and then we got talking that he was a drummer and we had a jam and we had a bit of fun.

Phil went off and I didn't hear from him for a while. The next time I did hear from him, Phil said, "Hey, I'm in this band called Motörhead and we need another guitar player. I thought you might like to do it." I went down to rehearsal and I was going to be a rhythm guitarist behind Larry Wallis. Larry didn't really want to do Motörhead anymore and he left the band right there. He got me in the band so he could exit the band.

I set up a rehearsal for my audition—that's the way it was with Motörhead. Phil had taken me over to meet Larry a couple of weeks before so I thought it would be fine. Lemmy, Phil and I started jamming about 3:00pm but Larry had not showed up. Lemmy called every half hour and Larry kept saying he was on his way.

The three of us were having a really good time playing together but at 6:30 the room was booked out to someone else. Fortunately, there was another rehearsal place upstairs, so we moved up there and Larry promised he was on his way. Around 7:30pm Larry showed up. He had a roadie who set up his Fender Twin amp. I only had an AC30 so I couldn't hear shit. He said hardly anything to anyone, plugged in and started playing a tune off their album, which I fortunately had learned.

The vibe in the room was awful and it got worse but, no lie, we must have played the same song for 30 minutes. Lemmy was getting pissed. Lemmy suggested we do something else and the same thing happened. I am thinking, "I haven't got this job." Lemmy then took Larry outside and they were gone awhile. I packed up my stuff. Phil was totally bemused by all this so we talked about other things. When Larry and Lem returned, I said my farewells, paid for the rehearsal room on my way out and that was that. I am thinking, "That didn't go very well."

I heard nothing over the next few days. Phil and Lemmy didn't have phones, so I figured no gig. Three days later, on a Saturday, there's this banging on my door. I drag myself out of bed in my underpants, open the door and Lemmy is standing there with a bullet belt in one hand and a leather jacket in the other. He handed them to me with the words, "You've got the gig" and then he turned around and off he went. I didn't know what to think but I was over the moon. It's always nice to be wanted.

March 23, 1976. Judas Priest present their second album, *Sad Wings of Destiny*, a huge NWOBHM (and power metal) influence and inspiration, given its variously dark, religious and serious lyrical themes, high, operatic vocals from Rob Halford and expert riffing and epic structures—as well as its epic cover art.

Judas Priest vocalist Rob Halford on the record's seminal second wave metal classic "Victim of Changes:"

I think the great special feeling about "Victim of Changes" from *Sad Wings*, it's become almost the archetypal metal song. It seems to have so many ingredients of what great metal music is about. You've got the incredible dual harmony lead break that brings the song in. Then you've got the crushing riff. And it's a very unusual rhythm in time sequence if you break the song down. It's kind of sparse as well. It doesn't have a lot going on musically if you really break it down, again, but it's got all those great elements of metal. It's very primitive to some extent just from my point of view, and from a singing aspect, again you are doing everything. You know, you're doing the vocal gymnastics; you are doing the nice kind of break down slow passages.

So it's like a metal combo of all the things that we love in that one track. It has to be in the repertoire. It's a great title isn't it? "Victim of Changes?" It's got that whiskey woman and all of this business, and it's about the breakup and all the classic type of attitudes of relationships put into a metal song. It still does the business all those years later—it still connects.

"Victim of Changes" definitely put me into a different way of singing. I've never really approached a vocal in that way before. So to get to all of those extreme places, all the high stuff was a first for me on that particular track. You know, you don't really think that much about... is it time to show off? Is it time to like, hey guys, check what I can do. It's not about that; it's all about doing the best that you can do for that song. As a singer I was still learning my craft. I was still a new singer to a great extent. I was learning as much as any new band is when you are making those first releases. You constantly are exploring. What is the potential? What can you do? Okay this is a different song, this is a different level of intensity, let's see how far we can push it. That's where I was going as a singer particularly on "Victim of Changes."

Led Zeppelin expert Dave Lewis on the idea of Priest being metal for a new generation:

Judas Priest—and I'm only talking an English perspective, where over there it may have been very different—probably was, because you had things like Kiss, which attracted huge numbers, and for what it was, was very entertaining. You got Rush, who cultivated the album-buying public and the big stage show. And in between that you got things like Queen going on, which was quite flashy. Not NWOBHM in any sense, but they'd been around. But there was a cultural shift towards youngsters wanting to listen to music played by people their age group much more than listening to people who were ten, 15 years older than them.

Because Zeppelin didn't play in the UK for four years. And when they're away people still want to see live music and still want to do other things. I think by the fact of their absence, that created careers for some bands without a doubt. Judas Priest might be in there; I'd have to look at the timeline of where Zeppelin's out from '75 to '79.

But you did get the emergence of things like Rainbow. And if they were visible and playing, I think they'd be more of an attraction to go and see them. In the end, 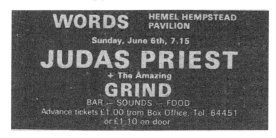 what Zeppelin traded on, in a way, was their reputation, when it came to Knebworth and also their legacy. A lot of kids who went to Knebworth, it was definitely the only time they saw Zeppelin, and a lot of people went to stand there and say these are the gods of rock, as it were. The fact that they gave a good performance anyway, in my view, was great and there was still a future for them, and there were places to go, and *In Through the Out Door* had enough ideas for them to take it further.

But Deep Purple is either breaking up or they're on drugs or gone playing Australia and Japan. And later Sabbath had fragmented, and if you're using those as the three iconic bands of that genre, then yeah, there was that to it.

Journalist John Tucker on *Sad Wings of Destiny*:

It's my personal favourite Judas Priest album. There was something new about it. It didn't have the... pretention is perhaps the wrong word, but some of the Led Zeppelin stuff was getting a bit ethereal for your standard broad stroke metal fan. We were still rock fans at the time; I don't think we were metal fans back then. And you get an album that comes out, okay, production-wise now it sounds a bit weak in places, but what an album. What songs. "Tyrant." "Genocide"—great stuff. Songs that stretch things a bit in a way that Priest collapsed on later on and went back to three-and-a-half minute formulaic stuff, when here they were stretching the confines of what they could do quite radically.

There's no bad tracks on the album at all; there's nothing wrong with that album at all. Everyone says that punk blew metal away, but it was already getting rather quiet. And if you're not a great fan of extremely long Yes albums, which I'm not, by the middle '70s there wasn't a lot going on.

Diamond Head guitarist Brian Tatler:

Punk rock got all the attention for that period, '77, '78, but yeah, I liked *Sad Wings of Destiny*; I bought it, and it was almost like going on separate to punk rock. Punk rock was over here, but also, you have all of a sudden Judas Priest, AC/DC, and I would be listening to all this as well, and it all just helped influence me. Possibly the energy of punk, but I didn't really want to be a punk rock band, but I did like the energy, the do it yourself, the get up and go, but there I was, leaning more towards becoming more like a classic rock band. At the end of the day, songs are important. So if there aren't enough good songwriters, and the songs don't last the test of time, people will probably go off it fairly quickly, to the press determining the next thing. So there are a few great songwriters that came out of punk, but not many.

And punk seemed a little bit more disposable, a little political, and if you're interested... there seemed to be a lot of records about bringing down the government and anti-police and things like that, and I didn't really think along those lines. I was more interested in maybe the fantasy lyrics and things like that. I didn't do lyrics, but that's probably what drew me towards certain bands. Certainly the long epic-type songs I always seemed to like. I don't think we had any political agendas, really. It was more about making an audience react, getting an excitement out of an audience, and just putting energy over on stage and on record.

March 26, 1976. Thin Lizzy issue *Jailbreak*. The hit album by the band is a favourite amongst budding NWOBHM players.

Iron Maiden guitarist Adrian Smith:

Well obviously the twin guitar thing, the guitar harmonies. I think the Allman Brothers were doing it probably a little bit before in America. I think maybe that's where Lizzy might have got the idea from, but it certainly wasn't a typical thing. But it was always attracting me. I've always played in bands with another guitarist. I think the first bands, we used to do a couple of Wishbone Ash songs, we used to do the harmonies and thought it sounded really cool. Which it does; it's very melodic. So you have that melodic almost folky influence. Some of Wishbone's stuff was almost folky, and like I said some of Maiden's stuff is like that. So they were definitely an influence.

And Lizzy, of course, were just super cool. You know, Phil Lynott, really tight songs, great guitar, great sound. They just had the whole package, really. With the guitar harmonies, probably you have to be a little more disciplined in your playing. If you listen to Purple live, while it's tight and very musical, there's a lot more space in it for the guitar to weave in and out. But I think with two or three guitars, as we've got now, you've got to be a lot more disciplined in your playing.

Journalist John Tucker on the lack of good hard rock in the mid-'70s:

I think there was. And the reason I agree with that is a sort of generational thing: what happens when this current generation of bands grows old? What happens next? Because there was nothing coming through. Later on when you had Raven and Iron Maiden and things like that coming through, then it was an interesting time. But there were a few bands. There was UFO kicking around, Thin Lizzy, Judas Priest, and then you start drumming your fingernails on the table and asking who the hell else is doing something interesting? And that's about it. It got very quiet.

The big bands were still doing very good business, but my own favourite, Purple, sort of called it a day in '76 and that was the end of them. In the UK, the singles and the album charts are very different. By '75 the singles charts were almost exclusively soul. A lot of that time had gone through the glam era, and there's a lot of soul bands dominating the singles charts. Singles is what gives an awful lot of young people exposure to music. Bowie went his way with American soul, Elton John following suit. There was still a teeny boom. I'm not too sure where you'd put the likes of David Cassidy in there, but a lot of pretty boy image stuff was always doing good business. But to get a metal single on the chart by then I would have thought would be almost impossible.

But Led Zeppelin had lost the way a bit. They'd had their own personal problems by then. Deep Purple are sort of beginning to unravel in places with *Stormbringer*. Uriah Heep, the change of vocalist didn't go down particularly well and they were always playing second fiddle to Purple in a certain way. If you look at the album charts, sure those bands were still doing good business. Sabbath still made some good albums. And like I said, there's still the likes of Thin Lizzy starting to make waves for themselves—*Jailbreak* was '76, and things really started to happen for them. I'm sure they had cult status at that time, and I'm sure if you were in the know and you didn't live in a scraggy, provincial town in the middle of nowhere, there were bands you could go see. But there wasn't a lot going on. There was Motörhead, of course. They were starting to make waves, and roughly at the same time that punk was starting to do its thing. But it was a bit of a quiet period; you could put it in those terms: a very quiet time.

But the other thing from our point of view, a certain time in the States, as soon as a band gets big here, the next thing they do is crack America. So you're losing your profile in the UK but hopefully you're going to get really, really big money on the other side of the Atlantic. But again, you nick some of your home base. Purple were doing 30-day tours, maybe four or five different dates in London alone, then come back in '76 and we get five dates and that's all you get for your UK tour. And that does opinionate your fans after a while. Zeppelin was spending a lot of time in America too. That's where the money was but that's not much good to me.

So I think there was a void to be filled; there were things that needed to be done. And the likes of AC/DC who came along and started playing tiny bloody clubs... there was a space for them. People were hungry for something new and Priest were new. Their image took a lot to catch on, but once they'd cracked that as well you had a force to be reckoned with.

March 31, 1976. Led Zeppelin issue *Presence*. Increasingly knowledgeable fans of hard rock both sides of the pond are not impressed with the band's insolence, lack of care, lack of energy and fall from grace after the immense *Physical Graffiti*. What's more, they aren't fooled by "Achilles Last Stand," the band's rickety, bumbling attempt at heavy metal.

April 1, 1976. Rush release their fourth album, *2112*. Conceptual, sci-fi, spacey, heavy and dark, the surprise hit record—a surprise as much to the band as to the industry—is lyrically and thematically an influence on future metal-makers from England.

May 1976. Key NWOBHM predecessor band UFO are now three records into their fine Michael Schenker era, issuing *No Heavy Petting*. UFO is a celebrated pastiche of hard rock melody, European-accented guitar leads and lyrical Britishness, plus the guys can always be found down at the bar.

May 1, 1976. According to Steve Harris' diary, this qualifies as Iron Maiden's first gig, although there is some   show that expert Garry Bushell considers the first show).

Iron Maiden bassist Steve Harris:

It was actually '75 when we formed, and then it took us four-and-a-half years to get a record deal, and I think it was purely what was happening—or not happening, in our case—back in those days, in the music biz at the time. I think it was just the whole reaction... I mean, we were around for the punk thing; the punk thing happens around '77, so it was difficult at first to work, and then the whole sort of backlash with that was really tough.

I think it was a good thing in a way. In retrospect I suppose it's easy to say that, but at the time it was being really annoyed at not getting attention and not getting gigs. But it was a good thing in a way, because it was four-and-a-half years before we got the deal, and everything happened after that. Making the album, going on tour, consequently tour after tour, the whole thing happened really quickly, from playing sort of pubs to playing big places. And we wouldn't have been prepared for that if we had got signed after a year or something. Going out and playing all those gigs, just kind being together as a band for that amount of time, it stood us in good stead for later.

May 17, 1976. Rainbow issue their second album *Rising*, a definitive "second wave" metal classic, given two eight-minute epics in "Light in the Black" and "Stargazer," and lots of ancient/mythic themes throughout. As well, there's Ritchie and his classical-based guitar work and the presence of a keyboardist/synthesizer player in Tony Carey. Finally, in a nod to the concept of being proud to be heavy metal in that all six songs on the record are heavy metal songs—a first not to be repeated until *Motörhead* and AC/DC's *Let There Be Rock*.

Rainbow keyboardist Tony Cary on Ronnie James Dio's lyrics:

You gotta remember Ronnie was making music. He was a lot older than anybody else. Well not Ritchie, but a lot older than I was or than Jimmy was, and he basically spent 50 or 55 years doing exactly what he wanted to do. He didn't do anything he didn't want to do, Ronnie. So by the time Rainbow started he was already 35 and he was a mature musician and he had his own voice; let me put it that way. He didn't need to write somebody else's idea of what a song was or fill this cliché or fill that spot.

Which is the problem I had with a lot of... we're the warriors of 666... I won't say the number of the beast, but you seem to be aiming at a target audience. Ronnie's audience, he made his—he built his audience. He was really the first to combine this tarot card sorcery, *Lord of the Rings*-type thing, the wizard flying over and then a fist coming out of the ocean grabbing a rainbow, this whole fantasy thing, with hard rock. That in itself, I'd never heard anybody doing that until that point.

Venom drummer Abaddon on the double bass influence of Cozy Powell: It was mainly because he was somebody that I'd gone to see quite a lot with bands like Rainbow and others, and he was just... he just sounded like thunder. I liked what Phil Taylor was doing, but Cozy just sounded like he invented it. I loved Ian Paice, I love what Ian Paice was doing, but Ian Paice was only playing one bass drum, although he was playing double top notes with one bass drum. But it still didn't sound like Cozy who had that really driving kind of thing. And it was something I wanted to do as soon as I could play, as soon as I could pick up sticks and have a go.

Saxon vocalist Biff Byford:
Rainbow *Rising*... vocally, melodically it was a step forward with Dio singing. There were some great songs, huge passages of fantastically mixed melodies and riffs, really. I don't see that as a starting point for the '80s, though. We did tour with Rainbow a bit, but my favourite Rainbow was with Dio, without a doubt, which was more rockier than commercial. It's like UFO. They were around. I think UFO, and Priest and bands like that... they were like the connection

between the more long, drawn-out solos that used to happen in the '70s. I think UFO and Judas Priest were more song-orientated, as were Rainbow, actually. I don't think it influenced us a lot, though, because we were more into playing the song as powerful as we could. And for us, playing a song fast had to fit the lyric.

Journalist Carl Begai:
Dio was telling stories; it's fantasy, it's escapism, and an inspiration for all these bands nowadays. If Dio did it, it's okay if we do it, basically. You're going to get your detractors, but you can't really fault them for that because look where it came from. As a journalist and a critic, occasionally you roll your eyes and go, "Oh, more *Dungeons & Dragons.*"

Rainbow bassist Jimmy Bain:
I thought that from the first rehearsals we had, Ritchie was definitely into getting a more raw sound than he had before. Purple had become a bit more commercial, so he wanted to get back to that sort of rough edge. I made the bad move of putting on *Stormbringer* in the limo one time, and he took it out and chucked it out of the window. He wasn't too taken with that record. I really liked *Stormbringer.* I thought it was a great record, but he didn't care for that period of Purple at all.

When I was with Rainbow it was like being in the Marines. The physical energy you had to put out to play these songs at the intensity Ritchie wanted them was pretty heavy, and you had to be in pretty good shape. I remember Cozy and I would look at each other onstage and go, "Is this song ever going to end?" It was such a fast tempo and it was so really heavy at the same time. You couldn't slow down or stop playing; you just had to go at it until the end, and it was sometimes pretty intense, physically.

So it was a very demanding gig, but we all loved it. He just took it to the next level, I thought. He seemed to be really happy at the time, and I think that helped. He was in a great studio, great place, he loved Germany, so everything was exactly the way he wanted it, and I think that's where you get the best from people, if you give them the atmosphere and the area they like to be in, so he loved it.

We only had six songs, six tracks on the *Rising* record. It seemed like not too many songs, but judging by the popularity of the thing it seems to still have stood the test of time. It was exactly what people were looking for at the time. We just kind of hit it right on the head as far as timing went, as far as the style went, the music, and the whole vibe of the band. And we had Ronnie's voice, as well, which was not too shabby.

But they were really hardcore songs, and when they were written they seemed to have that edge, and when we recorded them they had that nastiness that really good metal should have. I think it has that edge to it that everybody's playing flat-out. You got that in the recording, and of course when the band played live, as well. "Stargazer" and "A Light in the Black" were just heavier than anything that I'd heard up until that point. I'm not sure if it was a conscious thing or whether it just happened that way, but we did get it in the performance. If there was any lightness to the songs, they lost the lightness when we went into the studio and recorded them. It went bye-bye.

And Ronnie, I'd never seen anybody perform like that at any time in the studio before that. It was just phenomenal. He took it to another level, or two or three levels higher than anybody else. And with the heaviness of the bass, drums and guitar and keyboards, his voice just slid right on top. It couldn't get any heavier. It was like okay, we got it. He had the pipes to just sit right on top of that heaviness, and it didn't matter how heavy you got with the rhythm section or guitar or whatever.

Journalist John Tucker on *Rising*:
You can draw directly a niche between that and the Purple predecessors. You can see where Blackmore is getting frustrated and why he came out with an album that is what it is. But I think again, in certain quarters you'd get lynched by suggesting that it was a metal album. And I think because its progenitors definitely lie in what the likes of a Blackmore, Dio, and Cozy Powell were doing beforehand, in a very rock arena, despite the fact that it's all metal to me at the end of the day. If you're going to draw a line and say what goes in the rock box and what goes in the metal box, I think Rainbow *Rising*, great album though it is, is definitely a rock album. I don't think it would actually consciously be anything different, though I do like the point about *Sad Wings of Destiny* as stretching something new.

June 1976. Uriah Heep issue *High and Mighty*, their last album with David Byron on vocals. A once high and mighty NWOBHM favourite from the old days enters a period of irrelevance, not emerging from hibernation until it barges its way into near NWOBHM status itself, with 1982's *Abominog*.

June 9, 1976. Iron Maiden play the Cart & Horse, Stratford, UK, a show that many consider their first official gig. The next night, Steve goes and sees Genesis, writing in his diary, "Bloody brilliant!"

July 1976. Ian Gillan Band issues their debut album, *Child in Time*, recorded at Musicland in Munich and produced by Roger Glover. The band's sound is jazzy, funky, progressive rock, quite unfashionable in the middle of the punk explosion, with Ian still trying to rebel against the proto-NWOBHM roots of his time in Deep Purple Mk 2.

Raven bassist and vocalist John Gallagher on the shortcomings of the '70s:

When we were going through that... first and foremost we are fans. We saw every band that came through Newcastle and soaked it up like a sponge. That was all education and picking up music. We didn't get the DVD from whoever, Joe Satriani. It was like go and see Pat Travers, engrain it into your brain and see that this other band sucks because they're not into it. This band is great because you can tell they really care, and it really hit home.

Like I say, everyone you can pretty much mention came by. But there's a tendency to the tail end of the '70s where a lot of bands wanted to do this funky kind of thing, which got a little bit annoying. But by and large there was good music and then there was the media and the *Top of the Pops* culture trying to force this punk rock on you or the New Romantics or whatever. And nobody was interested in that. We're like, we like heavy. Where's the heavy? And it turned out that all those people that were into the heavy, a lot of them started their own bands.

August 1976. Future Iron Maiden guitarist Adrian Smith's band Evil Ways become Urchin and land a deal with DJM Records.

Iron Maiden guitarist Adrian Smith on the blues:

There's a definite connection there. Dave's the same. He listened to Hendrix a lot. He was greatly influenced by blues. I think probably all of us are influenced a bit by Hendrix, but blues is a big influence on metal and if you take AC/DC, I mean, what Angus plays is very blues; it's amped up, but a lot of it comes from blues.

The first thing I listened to was a band called Free. *Free Live!* — classic album, with "All Right Now" and all those great songs. Just electrifying, and the guitar was really kind of raunchy and raw and loud. And I just had to, you know, get a guitar and plug it into a big amp and away you go. Of course it's not that simple, but you know what I mean.

So it was the guy from Free, Paul Kossoff, all the Lizzy guitarists, Gary Moore, Scott Gorham... Pat Travers I already liked, and Johnny Winter. So it was more kind of blues guys. I think I'd already been playing five or six years before Van Halen came out, so when he came out he probably didn't have the influence on me that he did on the kids that started playing just after that. Then we're coming out with the finger-tapping and all that.

I was kind of entrenched in my own style before that, although Van Halen was incredible. He was like the late '70s/early '80s version of Hendrix. He took it up even further. But my early influences were more the second generation rock blues guitarists. And I still play like that. People say Maiden are metal, and I suppose it is, but there's a lot of other influences. There's almost a folky influence in what Maiden does. In a convoluted way, there's a bit of blues in there, in the soloing, the scale patterns; you know, Maiden's pretty unique. It's kind of a mish-mash. And there's a progressive influence—Steve loves all the progressive bands.

October 22, 1976. Led Zeppelin issue a disappointing live album in *The Song Remains the Same*. The album is full of bloated, meandering, tired renditions of songs fans were tired of hearing all over radio. It had been seven months since the also disappointing *Presence* album, and it would be three more years until the band would release the also somewhat disappointing *In Through the Out Door*. But *The Song Remains the Same* is significant in that it represented graphically in the grooves, this idea of the old guard bands boring the pants off of us with long jams of pointlessness. What's more, even if the punks didn't like the material from these hard rock bands and maybe hard rock fans still could champion it, many from both camps could agree that 26:30 of "Dazed and Confused" and 14:25 of "Whole Lotta Love" was a bit rich.

Led Zeppelin expert Dave Lewis on Zeppelin's compromised standing in rock consciousness in the late '70s and early '80s:

From my point of view, it's a fact that after they disbanded, Led Zeppelin became quite unfashionable. When you think about that now, it's a crazy thing. But in the 1980s up until *Live Aid*, they had five years out in the wilderness, really, because they were almost forgotten, and because so many other things were happening, nurtured by the NWOBHM and bands like Scorpions. I think it became much more what I would say treadmill, because you didn't have the titanic acts, really. They were all bundled in there. You couldn't pick three out, really.

The Ritchie Blackmore thing came out of Purple and he discovered Dio and certainly took it to a very good audience that were ready for it. And you got David Coverdale with Whitesnake. Again, the other thing really, is from Zeppelin's point of view, they weren't very productive because many things were happening and they weren't on the road for two years. So two years in the '70s was like ten years from any other time. And while that's going to happen, other acts are going to emerge. The people want to buy and listen to hard rock and there isn't a Led Zeppelin album in 1977, so you're going to buy a Rainbow *Rising* or whatever else had come out that year because they were conditioned.

I know a lot of bona fide rock fans that bought *Sounds* music weekly here every week, would only want to listen to that type of music. So that's where Rainbow got an audience; certainly Judas Priest did, and again, moving into something like in '80 where you get the beginnings of Maiden, Saxon and Def Leppard and all that came with that. Which almost made Zeppelin redundant because people have very short memories and were just getting caught up in all the bands that were coming out here. It took rock to grow up a bit after *Live Aid* and I would also say when the remasters came out in 1990; that project suddenly catapulted Zeppelin back into the consciousnesses of people, and they realized what a good band it had been, and since then it's just grown and grown and grown.

But the big bands, the honeymoon period for those bands was way over, and if you say '70 or '73 that's when it was, from then on, for a lot of the bands mentioned, it became harder work for various reasons, including musical differences and people leaving. But again, I think if you talk to rock buyers at that time who were only interested in that genre, then yeah, if they weren't getting their rocks off from those bands, then they're going to go somewhere else, and I think that probably happened.

Song Remains the Same probably wasn't received that well. *Presence* didn't sell anything like Zeppelin *IV*; *In Through the Out Door*, at the time sold a lot of records, but wasn't well received by the press. That's a sure fact. So yeah, I think maybe there was a bit of a void, and bona fide rock kids in their early 20s, late teens, they wanted their fix, and be it Peter Frampton or Whitesnake or whatever, they'd go elsewhere.

And there's also a lot to be said for self-creativity—you can only make so many *Paranoid*s and you can only make so many Zep *IV*s, and the musicians at the time have to please themselves. Plus you've got to look at the hedonistic things that were happening in terms of drugs and drinking and what have you with the big bands. Creativity was being slowed for those reasons. Again, it just got too big. It doesn't happen now because it's a very different era and we live in a different world in terms of health and all these things, but at the time it didn't matter.

November 1976. San Francisco's Yesterday and Today (later known as Y&T) issue their self-titled debut; they will become a beloved honourary NWOBHM act, beginning most pronounced with their third record, *Earthshaker*, in 1981.

> Journalist John Tucker:
> Y&T, the first two albums, Yesterday and Today albums, were just bargain bucket jobs like Starcastle and various others. Those you could buy for next to nothing. It wasn't really until *Earthshaker* came out... that was the sort of thing you'd go and buy with the first Raven album. I did buy the two on the same day. So whereas they were very influential albums in their own right, they didn't do a lot an awful lot for the NWOBHM because it was already happening by then. Lots of bands got rediscovered. Not re-invented themselves, but were reinvented by the likes of us—the things that might have been a little bit dodgy, then you'd welcome them with open arms. Could be quite heavy but you wouldn't touch it with a barge pole. All of a sudden now, yeah, that's cool, we'll have some of that.

December 1976. Birmingham's Jameson Raid takes shape, from roots back to 1973 and a number of band names, including Notre Dame.

December 4, 1976. Deep Purple's Tommy Bolin dies of a heroin overdose, nail to the coffin, so to speak, for one of old guard hard rock's biggest acts, even if UK fans had already loudly demonstrated their displeasure at the bluesy, funky guise of Purple without The Man in Black.

Recap

The big story of 1976 is the emergence of a second generation of heavy metal bands, after the first big British bands, and before the NWOBHM bands, who I'd argue are essentially a third generation.

Sure, we see UFO, Rush and Thin Lizzy making fine records by this point, but more crucially, Judas Priest bestows upon the landscape *Sad Wings of Destiny*, and Rainbow gifts us *Rising*, two crazy-good, very modern heavy metal albums, and two records that are very much blueprint records for the British bands of 1979 and 1980. An added amusing point about the Rainbow record is that, arguably, this is the first suite of songs that we hear that is heavy metal from start to finish, belying an elevated if not overtly voiced sense of pride in this type of music.

Also, we get three of the genre's biggest bands forming, or already formed and getting more active, namely, Motörhead, Iron Maiden and Saxon.

Another trend, in tandem with the rise of these second-generation bands, is the toppling of the larger-than-life first-generation bands, with both Uriah Heep and Led Zeppelin turning in inferior music, and Deep Purple imploding upon the death of Tommy Bolin.

It is also interesting to note that what is happening in America barely matters to this story, first, because it's physically happening in America, with the big four—namely Ted Nugent, Kiss, Aerosmith and Blue Öyster Cult—spending most of their time there, and second, because American hard rock music didn't possess quite as much NWOBHM DNA as did the second generation British bands.

1977 — "That's why Maiden's crowd was almost like a football crowd."

1977. All-female NWOBHM act Rock Goddess forms in Wandsworth, South London. Guitarist and vocalist Jody Turner is 13 and her sister, Julie, is nine.

1977. Possibly the first NWOBHM band—now settled on the name Samson—is born.

> Samson bassist John McCoy:
> It was a hectic period, but I was already sort of involved in that before I did the Japanese album with Gillan. I was fully aware of the new wave, if you like, and what was going on there. Because if I can just take you way back in '76, I had a band with Bernie Torme called Scrap Yard, which was like a basic heavy, three-piece band. We didn't do too well, but we worked. And we enjoyed playing together.
> Bernie went off from that to form his own Bernie Torme Band. We got a replacement in called Paul Samson, and Paul was a great player, great singer, nice guy. We got him immediately and we started writing material. And then it was such a strange time that we actually called the band two names. One week we'd be McCoy, and the next week we'd be Samson, so that we could play the few gigs that were available to us; we could turn up under a different name and get paid again. We were pretty desperate in those days. So there was like a McCoy-come-Samson band around that time. And it slowly became not McCoy—it slowly became Samson because I was, as I said at that time, heavily into doing sessions and productions and I wasn't always available.

> Journalist John Tucker:
> Samson were a really big deal. There were those singles they did, which by now sound nothing like what you associate Samson as being, but they are old and collectible—very, very old.

1977. Spider, otherwise known as the baby Status Quo, issue their debut single "Back to the Wall"/"Down & Out," which finds the band straddling their future boogie metal style to a curious punk ethic.

Wheels of Steel | 45

February 1977. David Coverdale, a year out of Deep Purple, issues his first solo album, *White Snake*. A bluesy, funky record, it is recorded at Kingsway Recorders in London, the studio which would also give birth to the Gillan band.

February 1977. Nutz issue their third album, *Hard Nutz*. A new member is keyboardist Kenny Newton who would play with Nightwing. The band are a graphic example of a third-string old guard hard rock act adrift.

February 10, 1977. Diamond Head play their first show, at the High Park school hall.

Diamond Head guitarist Brian Tatler on the degree of punk influence on his band:

I liked punk. I thought it was very important for the music scene. I think it really got rid of a lot of the deadwood. It seemed like prog bands were getting out of control. Bands like Yes, they were making double albums and triple albums and it was just becoming a bit leaden. And Emerson, Lake & Palmer, and you could only see these bands if you went to see them at Wembley or something like that. And so certainly punk rock happened and it was back to little tiny clubs and you could feel the energy.

And it sort of said to me, instead of spending 15 years learning to play the guitar to a very, very high standard, you could get going now and you could form a band. Of course, all I wanted to do was be in a band, but instead of having this incredible benchmark of say Deep Purple to look up to, certainly I could play the guitar like Steve Jones in the Sex Pistols. Or you could see these bands appear on *Top of the Pops* or the John Peel show; I used to listen to John Peel quite a bit. And of course he played a lot of punk rock, and I would record it, and I just thought it had so much energy and do-it-yourself attitude— make your own record and get out and do your own gig—and I think some of that rubbed off on me and my band.

The Zeppelins and Sabbaths and Purples of the world, they were untouchable; they were like gods from another planet or something. You didn't breathe the same air as Led Zeppelin, but suddenly you could go watch a punk band in a club. Yeah, the excitement, the energy, and I think it gave thousands of kids the idea that you can go make your own music, get a guitar, write your own songs, just get crackin'—don't wait to become a virtuoso. The big bands were kind of on the wane by then. It was time for something new and exciting.

Punk was something new, shocking. You'd get a front cover with someone with a safety pin in their nose. It's more exciting than a big review of the new Led Zeppelin album or something. You're going to do that anyway, but it's just fresh, isn't it? It's fun.

February 18, 1977. The Damned issue their debut, *Damned Damned Damned*, which is considered by many to be the first UK punk album.

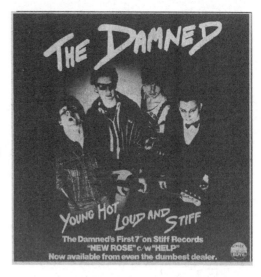

The Damned drummer Rat Scabies on the punk tribe versus the metal tribe:

There wasn't a lot of mixing going on with that. It was kind of a bit strange, because I don't think the punk crowd really cared who turned up. Lemmy used to be around a lot; he crossed that bridge quite a lot, between the metal scene and the punk scene. He made it kind of okay. Because Motörhead really picked up the energy thing, and I don't think a lot of the hard rock bands were really doing that. It was all kind of very slow and laboured. Motörhead and The Damned... it was kind of both gangs turned up, and I think it moved everybody into the frame of actually, it's okay, even though we're not in the same gang. I think it had to do with the rebellious nature of both types of music, in that both are considered unacceptable by the mainstream. So there's an affinity that is naturally there and so I think the two crossed over.

I think there was a lot of resentment from rock bands because they were sort of the darlings of the media in '76, and then by '77, a lot of them were washed-up. People had that, "Oh fucking hell, if it wasn't for that lot, I would still be on the circuit" sort of thing. So we were darlings of the media; once punk arrived, all that fluffy hairstyle fell to the wayside. Because don't forget, heavy metal and rock at that time was considered a joke by the mainstream. It wasn't regarded as real music; it was kind of too cartoon, I guess. So as far as the media was concerned, it was quite easy to ignore them, still. They would only kind of print the big band stories.

Motörhead drummer Phil Taylor on bridging the gap between punk and metal:

Well I think it was because I didn't really want to be a long-haired hippie, because I was still quite violent, and I'd been a skinhead, and I had kind of a Rod Stewart/Ron Wood kind of hairstyle, and I had a leather jacket, but it was like a biker jacket. It was like a punk rocker jacket. And then if it was a punk looking at record sleeves, and they saw maybe me, with these other two guys, they would think, "Oh, that's strange—he looks like a punk," and then maybe the punk would buy that. And then maybe some long-hair would look, "Hey, two long-haired guys playing with this punk; that might be interesting." But I think the punks latched onto us because we were playing fast, and that's what most punk rock bands were. That's all they were about really, "1,2,3,4, dah-dah-dah, the end." In a way Motörhead was like that, but a bit longer. And the punks just got off on the energy, and the fact that from a fan's point of view, it was kind of weird to like a band that had two sort of hippies in it and one punk on the drums.

But it was Motörhead music, really. I guess it was unlike anything that had been heard before. But again, we only realized that years and years later—with hindsight. We just realized that we played a lot faster than most bands that were around. But we didn't do any of that stuff consciously. I mean, at the time, when we lived in London, and we all lived along at Chelsea, which was sort of the bit that where you're Malcolm McLarens and the Pistols were from; that was Chelsea—rich area. You got a better class of pauper. A better class of squat, which was us, and a lot of punks.

It was not just the music, I mean, for us, either. We came up with Billy Idol and The Damned, because they're buddies that go to the same boozers, in Chelsea. So it was a social thing as well as a music thing. We didn't discriminate between metal or punk or rock or big band or jazz or whatever, or black or white, or anything. It's just like, "Oh, where's the party; where's the action going on?" As you are, wherever it was happening, that's where you went. And so we mixed and rubbed shoulders with all kinds of people, as one does.

Journalist John Tucker on punk fans versus the headbangers:
As fans, I'd say pure hatred. I think the bands probably recognized
that they were both doing something different and there was room for
everyone and they could co-exist. In terms of fans, it was completely
bloody tribal warfare as far as I was concerned. So much so that the
first Metallica gig I went to at the end of '84, that was the first time I'd
been in the company of so many punks—and skinheads come to think
of it—and I was terrified as I went to the venue because these were
people I'd routinely been bottled by, spat at by, and being a mild-
mannered person, I'd been hassled to no end. So in terms of fandom,
we had nothing in common whatsoever. The bands... because you're
living around the same circuit, you're going to run into each other
occasionally. So I think bands had mutual respect for each other.

Tygers Of Pan Tang guitarist Robb Weir on punk versus metal:
I wouldn't say we were enemies, but from the hard rock, heavy
metal, NWOBHM point of view, we kind of felt that punk was a
cop-out because a lot of the punk players—and I don't mean to be
disparaging—but a lot of the punk players weren't particularly good.
It was plug in and everybody jumped up and down and spat and did
what they did at sort of 85 mph, where hard rock and heavy metal
music was, for me, a lot more well constructed and thought put into
it, and the players were top notch.

Early 1977. Angel Witch forms in London, under the name Lucifer. There's
an Iron Maiden connection in that early member Steve Jones went on to
form Speed, with Bruce Dickinson. Also significantly, Satanic themes are
being revived, which, despite the light rock of Coven and Black Widow, more
logically align with heavy metal as a natural musical soundtrack.

Angel Witch guitarist Kevin Heybourne on the name Lucifer:
We played one gig under that name and then promptly changed it.
My main influence was always Black Sabbath. The thing that they had
which was different to all the others like Deep Purple, Black Sabbath
had a darker sound and I was really into that. And their guitar sound
was so muddy and heavy, it just filled the whole thing out. And that
was the angle I was trying to take. I listened to loads of stuff, Black
Sabbath, UFO, Schenker as a guitarist, even Ted Nugent (laughs),
whatever you could get your hands on at the time; Thin Lizzy also
with the dual leads, which of course Priest had as well.

March 21, 1977. AC/DC issue *Let There Be Rock*, one of the first five albums of all time with no ballads or "mellow" songs, pointing the way to a pride in heavy metal ownership, the idea that an album can be, unapologetically, nothing but hard rock.

AC/DC guitarist Malcolm Young: That's right! Well, that was the idea, you know. We thought with *Let There Be Rock*, we needed some new stage material; that's how we looked at it. We wanted to get the kids up more with it, get tougher. Well that was us with everything back then— no ballads (laughs). Every band had ballads. Foreigner, bands like that at the time, they needed the ballads. Even though they had a couple of good up-tempo tunes, it was always the ballad that made them sell more. So you get that thing, get the ballad, get a slow song for radio, middle of the road radio. And we were like, "Screw that, you know? Every time we play, we play to more kids. We're happy doing it this way. We don't mind building this outfit." So we took our time and that. And it's difficult, because you get a lot of pressure. But we were just like, "Screw youse."

April 23, 1977. Judas Priest's first album for CBS, *Sin After Sin* is issued, and it's a highly technical affair, with super-fast speed metal and double bass in "Let Us Prey"/"Call for the Priest," space-themed songs like "Starbreaker," and a general complicated heavy metal vibe that paves the way for a "new wave" of heavy metal that is as far from the other new wave—punk—as rock could possibly be.

Judas Priest vocalist Rob Halford on the changing times: If you were in a metal band in the '70s, what a great time that was because it was still finding its place. This metal experience was still finding its places as we were moving through the mid-'70s to the '80s, and the brink of the New Wave of British Heavy Metal. We were looking around and checking out what everyone else was doing. There wasn't that great amount of influence and inspiration within metal because there were only a handful of metal bands. I was certainly listening to Zeppelin and Purple obviously, The Who—some of The Who stuff is very intense, you know—Crazy World of Arthur Brown, John Mayall's Bluesbreakers, Taste with Rory Gallagher, Medicine Head.

With all of these bands it was really exciting then because we also had this great level of musicianship that we were able to look at. We've always said in Priest that the people we were listening to were really craftsmen, great singers, great guitar players, drummers, bass players. So that's where we were at in a metal sense of things. It was a great time of very, very slow growth but you could sense something was building, that on the horizon would be some good things.

April 15, 1977. The Ian Gillan Band issues their second album, *Clear Air Turbulence*. Unfortunately, punks liked fusion about as much as they liked prog. Same with Ian Gillan's old fans—most of them would rather listen to prog than their old hero squawking along to jazz rock.

May 13, 1977. Urchin issue their "Black Leather Fantasy"/"Rock and Roll Woman" single. Guitarist in the band is future Iron Maiden axeman Adrian Smith. For a brief time, future Maiden player Dave Murray is also in the band.

Iron Maiden bassist Steve Harris:

Adrian... it was difficult because we tried to get him and Dave to join before the first album and he was still doing his thing with Urchin, his band Urchin, and he'd been with them for years and he was fronting it and singing lead vocals for that, so he sort of had to see that through, really. And it's not like we were hoping and praying it wouldn't work for him, because we didn't think like that, really. We just went on ahead, got someone else and carried on with it. But when it didn't work out with him we just got straight back on it and said, look, you're joining this time, no argument, that's it. You're in. He was like, okay then. That was it, really.

But they played together in sort of an early band before, young band writing together when they very first started learning. So they had a good affinity anyway. And because they're such different styles of playing they really complimented each other. Wishbone Ash, Thin Lizzy... there were elements of that playing going in their playing, but the fact that we were a much more aggressive, heavier band lent itself to the fact they were able to play more aggressively, but melodically over the top also.

May 21, 1977. *Sounds'* Phil Sutcliffe reviews a Judas Priest gig at City Hall, Newcastle, calling their fans "heavy metal kids," a suggestion that a crowd at a hard rock show might be a homogenous entity, essentially the type of jean-jacket heavy metal army that would attend future NWOBHM shows.

June 1977. Holocaust forms, in Edinburgh, Scotland, first adopting the name Buzzard, and later Apollo and Preying Mantis.

June 1977. Motörhead issue their first single, "Motörhead"/"City Kids," the b-side being a throwback to guitarist Larry Wallis' Pink Fairies days. Also available on 12" and later reissued in 1979. Motörhead quickly become the bridge band between the punks and the metalheads, who are confused in equal measure about the band's motivations.

Motörhead bassist and vocalist Lemmy on punk:

It made me realized that coming around in the morning was all right. I went down to the Roxy in London when they first started it, and I went to see what all the fuss was about. They viewed me with entire suspicion, the flares and long hair, and all these kids with orange crew cuts and safety pins through the mouth, and they're looking at me weird, and this voice behind me said, "I loved Hawkwind. I used to sell acid at your gigs." And it was Johnny Rotten. And I remembered him. He used to have long red hair and an army coat and sell acid out of his pockets. I remembered him. Kings Cross Cinemas, all nighters on Sunday. So I was cool then, see.

Punk was fast and loud and raucous and pissed-off. I liked the fuck you-ness of it. We came out the same time. We were only a year before them, and I always liked The Damned the best. I thought they were the epitome of a punk band. They still are. We just did a tour with them in England, and they're still... Captain Sensible, what a great name. And Rat Scabies—isn't that a great name for a drummer?

Rock was quickly vanishing up its own asshole. There was very contemplative stuff going on. People staring at their shoes while they played in checked shirts and it was all getting very tedious. The punk thing was really good. I remember seeing Johnny Thunders down at the Roxy with the original Heartbreakers, and last time I saw him was with the New York Dolls and they were fucking rotten. They were terrible, the New York Dolls, and then he shows up with the Heartbreakers and he was fucking marvelous. Great band. And of course heroin killed two of them, Jerry and John.

We sounded like punk and we looked like metal. Actually I had long hair way before heavy metal was even conjured as a name. Funny enough, the name heavy metal for music only came up about two years before punk hit, so it's a joke anyway. Categories are fucking unimportant anyway. They're for the papers to write about. Categories in music don't exist. Any band should be friendly with any other band because we're all in the same army. We're all fighting the same shit and we're all doing the things we have to do to make it, and there shouldn't be any enmity between bands. We should be brothers. And I've always said that and I've always practiced that and it's always worked.

Journalist John Tucker:
Motörhead predate everything. Motörhead, as far as I'm concerned, were doing everything far too early. I did discuss this with Lemmy at the time, that they were far too early. They were an influence but not so much. They were more an inspiration than an influence. Because they did what they did; they stuck to their guns. They did an album they recorded that was canned and wasn't released until they were popular. There was also a single that didn't come out, but they stuck with it and they didn't change the formula, and eventually someone realized that actually, they were completely missing the point and here you had something that was quite novel—the punk band hybrid.

Iron Maiden vocalist Bruce Dickinson, offering another perspective on the mixing of the tribes:
Well, I'll give you an example. I mean, I was a history student in college in the East End, and I roadied for two or three years, I was the social secretary at the college, and so, let's look at the bands that I brought as a social set. I booked the Ian Gillan Band, because I was a fan. I booked Hawkwind—I roadied for them. We had two BBC shows, which would be like the *Old Grey Whistle Test*-type stuff, like the *Sight and Sound* in concert; one was Supertramp, one was Manfred Mann's Earth Band, and then I brought The Pirates and Bethnal, who were a punk band. And I think The Lurkers might've

done a show there as well. So we were booking punk bands. Bethnal were interesting, because they were a punk band with an electric violinist, and they did a great version of "Baba O'Reilly." We had The Jam, played there. So The Jam were kind of local; they were East End.

And one of the guys who was a geography student, he was a guy called Steve Dagger, and Steve and I used to stand around the jukebox and he's going, "Rock 'n' roll is over, mate. It's all going to be punk from now on." And shove another Deep Purple track on, "Rubbish," and then he would put something else on. Anyway, he went off and managed Spandau Ballet, and so yeah, we kept bumping into each other. And I sort of go, "Well, I've done alright for a washed-up old rocker, haven't I, considering…" "Well, yeah, all right." But if you look at Spandau Ballet, they were a band that adopted the fashion of punk, but actually were a complete pop band. I mean, punk was ambushed very quickly by pop music, because it didn't have the musicianship—or the desire—to be anything else other than a transitory thing.

You know, when you look at those punk bands who got together, who could barely play their instruments, they jumped around and had a laugh—that's as far as it was ever going to go for those guys. If you look to what McLaren did with the Sex Pistols, he took a bunch of metal guys, who were really good musicians, and said, "Right guys, you just go and do what you do. I don't care what it is, don't care about that; we'll dress you up and all this." But the main thing is we're going to have this sneering guy pissing everybody off, dressed in Vivian Westwood's favourite, you know, pajama trousers and safety pins. You know, annoying grannies up and down the nation.

And he was very, very clever, and so to that extent, yes, there was some take-up of things. I mean, I could see how punk was entertaining. I could see a band like The Stranglers, for example, who were actually really good at what they did. And they would attract a mixed audience of rock guys and sort of like punk chic-type people. You had Motörhead, who were adopted by punk guys, who just because it was such a blinding wall of noise that nobody would comprehend, oh, it was punk in the first place.

And you had other strange things, this band The Pirates, which were from Johnny Kidd and the Pirates, which goes right the way back to the '60s. But they were just an amazing R&B band, R&B in the proper sense of the word. Another band—Dr. Feelgood. Dr. Feelgood came from Canvey Island, and if you look back at the musical genesis of punk, they were a rhythm and blues band with harmonica and just really, really harsh, chopping rhythms. And if you look at their style and what they did, they morphed into bands like Madness. So all those bands, they sort of… very quickly, from being punk... how long did punk last? Well, let's look at the Boomtown Rats. You know, Boomtown Rats, punk band, they were a pop band! They were produced by Mutt Lange. And Mutt Lange is a pop producer! He doesn't even like heavy metal! I mean, he really doesn't. And so "I Don't Like Mondays" had all the Mutt Lange devices; very clever guy, great producer, but it was a pure pop record, dressed up as something else.

Raven bassist and vocalist John Gallagher on metal versus punk:
Punk was still floating around. When we were rehearsing before we did the first single—there's actually photos out there—I got my arm broken because a bunch of punks came in and tried to steal one of my basses. I ended up wrestling it off them and hitting them, and then 15 came around the corner. That didn't go down too well. But at the time, to be honest, where we were in Newcastle, most of the bands wanted to be The Eagles, so they really hated us. We didn't go over well at all with that. We had our own little cult following there and it just built from that.

But there was a divide. It was what you'd call the punks and the hairies, and they would get into pitched battles occasionally. And we'd play gigs around the northeast at some pubs and working man clubs, and you'd get both. I remember one famous show we played in Sunderland, which is a town about ten miles south of Newcastle; again, being England, you might as well be 400 miles away. And a punk band called The Angelic Upstarts, who were flavour of the month at the time, they used to kick a pig's head around onstage. They canceled, so all the punks came to our show, and before long they were kicking one of our lighting guys around on the floor, flying through the air in front of us. But they got into the energy when we played. We played with a band called The Motors who were popular at the time; we opened for the Stranglers, who were a great band. They were a full-out punk audience and they got into it because we were nuts.

I mean it was kind of in the back of our heads, without really being spoken, that there was a DIY kind of culture in punk, and if they can do it we can do it. But I mean a lot of it was really funny. There was bands like The Toy Dolls who played really fast and had hilarious lyrics and stuff like that. But a lot of it, we were just like ah, it's rubbish. You can't play properly. But the energy factor was obviously a breath of fresh air, rather than having people standing there wearing very ornate trousers and standing on the $15,000 carpets contemplating their navels.

June 2, 1977. The classic jagged Iron Maiden logo starts to appear in gig ads.

July 1977. Judas Priest make their first assault on the US; in June of '78, Jon Young from *Trouser Press* talks about witnessing "headbanging" at a Chicago show.

July 11, 1977. After only two studio albums, Rainbow issue a double live album called *On Stage*. The record's long jammy tracks underscore the idea that old guard bands are a bore and a chore live.

Stratovarius guitarist Timo Tolki:
      The first record I ever bought was Rainbow – *On Stage*. It was this double vinyl and I'd heard "Smoke on the Water" on the radio. Up until that I had been listening to Beatles and Abba and Shadows. Nothing to do with metal or heavy rock. And then I hear this riff and it was a live version of "Smoke on the Water" from *Made in Japan*, and I was like, what is this?! I still remember that day how it was resonating in me, that riff. And I really wanted to be like Ritchie. Blackmore became so big an influence to me. He gave me my identity when I was a kid, like 14, a teenager.
      Rainbow was always, to me, very melodic, and Ritchie's sense of humour is widely known. Very similar to John Lennon, which I really love as well. The humour aspect, you know. But first of all, there was a guitar hero. I was a 13-, 14-year-old teenager with a very low self-esteem, and I found something that gave me an identity—a guitar player. And Blackmore's that idol for me; he gave me the role model, so to speak. And because of that, I just admired him so much and I really loved the songs and the melodic aspect. His solos were incredible at that time. Now when you compare his solos to the guitar players of today, of course everything has evolved but you still recognize the guy when he starts playing.

September 1977. Quartz issues their self-titled debut, on Jet Records; it is produced by Tony Iommi. Not much of a NWOBHM blueprint, the album nonetheless includes convincing metal. Two singles from the album are also issued in late '77, the a-sides being "Sugar Rain" and

"Street Fighting Lady." Still, despite the variety, there's a sense of validity to the argument that maybe this is the first NWOBHM album. Interesting that the record emerges the same month as the first Motörhead album.

Quartz drummer Malcolm Cope:
We teamed up with Albert Chapman as our manager, and Albert Chapman is a close friend of Tony's. We just all built on that. We used to rehearse every week, changing our style of music, and the type of music we wanted to write. Tony was coming to our rehearsals and spending hours and hours with us, and giving his input into where he thought some of the song should be, and one thing or another, and we went and recorded the first album.

I thought it was a bit too clinical, to be honest with you. I think we were all a little bit nervous in what we were doing. And Tony was very precise in what he was doing. A lot of the songs on there, we'd rehearsed and played them many times, but when we'd come to record them, we changed them as we were recording them. And it's not quite the same, as opposed to when you're really familiar with what you're doing.

September 24, 1977. Motörhead issue, on Chiswick, their self-titled debut album, an uncompromisingly dirty rocking affair, unapologetically heavy but not so much characteristic of NWOBHM conceits, other than the cover art, which suggests mascot as well as a biker image. It rises to #43 on the UK charts.

Motörhead guitarist Fast Eddie Clarke:
The band was close to quitting and we had one more show at the Marquee in London on a Friday night in April 1977. We asked Ted to record the gig, as it might be our last and he said he couldn't pay the type of money the Marquee wanted for recording there. Ted suggested we make a single and he would pay. Speedy Keen, from Thunderclap Newman, organized a studio in Kent and drove us down there after the gig. We got there about 2:00am and set up the equipment and started jamming.

I had done an album with Curtis Knight in 24 hours. I told the guys this, and as we had been playing the tunes over and over, it made sense. So we started recording about 4:00am on Saturday and finished everything at about 6:00am Sunday morning. We crashed out and left Speedy and John, the engineer, to do the mixing and they had anything that was left to keep them awake. Ted came at about 6:00pm Sunday evening and we proudly announced we had an album and not a single. He was bowled over by this and we did some remixing at Olympic Studios. We had our first album. Once we had an album, the whole landscape changed. We had hope again and there was interest from promoters thanks to Ted and our part-time managers Doug Smith and Frank Kennington. They had something to work with so it was game on.

October 1977. Nutz issues *Live Cutz*, their last album before a name change to Rage following their appearance on *Metal for Muthas*.

October 7, 1977. Ian Gillan Band issue their third and last album, *Scarabus*. Its quick death helps give rise to the NWOBHM, through Ian's formation of the harder-rocking, more frantic Gillan.

October 27, 1977. Punk reaches its apex with the Sex Pistols at last issuing their one and only album, *Never Mind the Bollocks*. As wry irony to all the "rockers" who can't get work because of punk, it's somewhat of a heavy metal album, with multi-tracked guitars, muscular grooves, epic riffs everywhere, and overall solid production values.

Tank guitarist Mick Tucker on the NWOBHM's ties to punk:
There was the punk thing, so I think it's a natural progression from that, really. Loud guitars, a bit of attitude, and I think it progressed from that, really. You look at the Pistols, bands like that. They're all good bands. The Damned, UK Subs. The Stranglers are pretty good, quite a lot of hit singles. There's quite a few bands. I was into all the classic rock stuff at the time, but I could appreciate what was going on with punk as well.
Algy, he was in the thick of it with The Damned. I mean all the bands he likes are Deep Purple, Free, Mountain, and he's playing for a punk band. So he's actually a rock 'n' roller, really. I think it was just a case of like 16-year-olds, they could get up there and do some gigs and get some money as well. I think that had a lot to do with it. In The Damned, Captain Sensible, he's quite a good jazz guitar player,

believe it or not. You look at Scabies, he ended up playing with Jimmy Page, didn't he? I think everyone's got to learn from somewhere and I think they learned from the rock side.

Iron Maiden bassist Steve Harris on punk:
It was a reaction against the big bands, really, I suppose bands like Zeppelin and things like that didn't play very often or anymore, and when they did, they played these massive venues, and the whole sort of business was geared towards that kind of stuff. It was a reaction against that, really. But I grew up listening to that stuff, the early '70s stuff, rock, progressive rock, classic rock. And that's the stuff I grew up on and really loved. So that's the stuff we wanted to emulate. Even when we did covers, it was those types of bands, and we sort of learned our trade like that. And once the punks came along, they couldn't really play very well. It's not like the punks now—they can play. But the ones at the time couldn't really play their instruments very well, so it didn't go down too well with bands like us.

Journalist Garry Bushell on why the NWOBHM had to happen:
It was parallel to punk and some of the reasons it happened were the same reasons punk happened. People had just got fed up with superstar bands, stadium bands being completely out of touch or living a playboy lifestyle and not relating to the sort of things the kids who were coming to see them were into. Someone like Iron Maiden came along and they were exactly the same as the kids in the audience. They were young, they were all working class, their music was wild, it was heavy, it was direct. They connected immediately with the crowd and there was that instant rapport, and that's why Maiden's crowd was almost like a football crowd, they were almost like a terrorist crowd in the fact that they were boisterous, they were loud, they were just as blue collar as you can be. The atmosphere of those early Maiden gigs was very much like the working class that was at punk gigs.

Journalist John Tucker on the struggle of being rock in 1977:
No one would book them because they weren't doing punk, and Biff Byford in his book is quite open about the fact that when they found out they were a metal band it was very hard to get bookings, because the rising thing at the time was to be a punk band. It was to cut your hair, limit your chords and thrash it out. And if you fly against the

face of fashion, it's really hard to get bookings. There's some good hard bands. Northeast, obviously. South Wales is always a good metal place, and the Midlands. But otherwise, metal bands wouldn't get booked—it was all punk bands because that was flavour of the month.

November 1977. After a particularly bad gig at the Bridgehouse, Steve Harris re-thinks Iron Maiden and fires the entire band. Don't worry, he still hates punk.

Iron Maiden bassist Steve Harris:

Anything to do with punk, we didn't want to have anything to do with it—at all. I remember going down to a gig somewhere in west London, and a band called Chelsea were playing, punk band, and we went in there, it was just people diving about all over the place, spitting over the band and all this, and we just said, well, there's no way we could play. Because if our audience came down here, and they start spitting on us, it's just all going to go off anyway. It'll kick off. So we didn't bother to play there.

It was just, I hated everything about it, absolutely everything. There was no respect with the punks. There was a brotherhood and respect going on with the rock community, because I think everybody was feeling a bit hard-done-by, because they weren't getting the gigs anymore. The punk bands were getting the gigs. Anything that was more mainstream rock wasn't even looked at anymore. And so it was really tough for bands at the time. I mean there were a lot of pubs and clubs around, there was just nowhere to play, because it was all locked out with all these Herberts diving about all over the place and spitting (laughs).

Journalist John Tucker on whether there was the stirrings of a NWOBHM as early as '77:

Yes, there were things happening, but the big problem is they weren't getting reported because no one was interested. But all those bands were slugging away somewhere. I'd hate to think how many gigs Saxon played before they actually got signed but that's how you honed it. You just keep going. You play for people like a dog, but you play your guts out and you learn the good bits and the bad bits.

So yeah, very much. These bands weren't manufactured; they didn't come from nowhere. They were already doing what they thought they were doing best. Being true to yourself, I suppose. Playing the music that… assuming this is what you were brought up on, this is what you listened to, maybe your older brother had it, whatever. But this is what you heard and this is what you want to do.

Speaking personally, I never ever got punk. I never bought a punk single. I got the vibe behind it, I couldn't stand the vocals, I didn't see the point of it. So speaking personally, I just kept buying what I wanted to buy, what I wanted to listen to, and I presumed that these people who were brought up on the same things as I listened to just wanted to be true to themselves and just play what they wanted to do, even before they knew it was never, ever going to be fashionable again. I mean how long do you plug away is a whole question in itself. How long would Steve Harris have kept Iron Maiden going if by '82, '83, it was still completely unfashionable. You gotta pay the bills after all, somehow. But be true to yourself. That's one of the things we can do. We can be true to ourselves.

Recap

In 1977, unsurprisingly, we see the formation of yet more bands that will soon be key NWOBHM characters, namely Diamond Head, Samson, Spider (actually, with their first single), Angel Witch and Holocaust. What's more, both Motörhead and Quartz make debut albums. Now Quartz is more of a personal favourite, but there's quite a bit of importance in the Motörhead story, given the waves they immediately make with their shockingly nasty sound, but also the fact that here's another record with no ballads, no mellow songs on it, loud and cantankerous start to finish.

Also in that camp is AC/DC, with their third record, *Let There Be Rock*, again, no mellow tracks, although, amusingly, us as kids considered "Problem Child" so poppy, that it counted as an up-tempo ballad!

And who else is in this camp? Well, surprise, The Sex Pistols! Yes, 1977 is the key year for punk rock mania, and that band's *Never Mind the Bollocks* is essentially a wall-to-wall hard rock record, although philosophically speaking, the punk rock ethos put into practice by this band is annoying every long-haired hard rocker who takes pride in his playing, most notably Steve Harris. Of note as well, punk introduced a culture of independent singles and albums that the NWOBHM would both survive and thrive upon. Previous to punk, both in the UK and stateside, the large majority of music was recorded in establishment studios and disseminated on major labels.

Other than that, 1977 really playing out much like 1976, offering a few more pretty decent and pretty important hard rock and heavy metal records (of note, *Sin After Sin*), but also like 1976, dominated and subjugated in the press by the firestorm that was punk rock.

1978 ─ "All the original frontrunners had gone asleep."

1978. Belfast's Cobra issues "Lookin' for a Lady," on Rip Off, suggesting that metal existed on the emerald isle as well, as would the presence of Sweet Savage and the collectible *Green Metal* compilation of 1985.

1978. Dedringer form in Leeds, while Black Rose forms in Saltburn by the Sea, initially as ICE, changing their name in 1980. Meanwhile, in Mansfield, immense NWOBHM talents Savage open for business proper, after a false start two years earlier.

1978. Midlands-based boogie rockers Eazie Ryder issue "Motorbikin'," on Graduate. Vocalist Geoff Bate would resurface for Quartz's brooding *Against All Odds* album from 1983.

1978. Ethel the Frog issue their first single, "Eleanor Rigby"/"Whatever Happened to Love."

1978. Sweden's Heavy Load issue their debut *Full Speed at High Level*. It is one of the heaviest albums of the '70s, and in the modern NWOBHM style, that is to say, proto-power metal. However, few take notice of the obscure, barely distributed album.

1978. The Next Band issue "Four by Three," on Gannet. Frank Noon would be the drummer on Def Leppard's inaugural EP and then move on to a number of slots with luminaries gone solo. Rocky Newton would do time with Lionheart and MSG, with John Lockton ending up with Wild Horses.

1978. No Sweat issue "Start All Over Again," on Rip Off while Overlord issue "Lucy," on Airbeat.

1978. Son of a Bitch, now called Saxon, record a three song demo tape.

1978. Tygers of Pan Tang form in Whitley Bay, England.

> Tygers of Pan Tang guitarist Robb Weir:
> I think the NWOBHM happened because the music scene was searching for something new and fresh. We had the '60s kind of movement, the flower power and love and all that. Bands like Black Sabbath and Zeppelin just kind of stepped their tune up a little bit heavier, more progressive. There was glam like Mott The Hoople, and then punk, and what it got from that was the spontaneity and the attitude live; let's go and do this, plug and play, and get everybody excited, that kind of feel.

February 10, 1978. Judas Priest's fourth album, *Stained Class*, hits the shops. Like *Sin After Sin*, it is a major leading edge metal milestone front to back. "Exciter" is both proto-power and proto-thrash. "Stained Class" is framed upon a classic NWOBHM/power metal gallop. Rob Halford continues to present an operatic vocal style that we will hear imitated often within the new and younger wave of metal bands. And, again, as they do on the two previous records, when Priest write mellow music (here it's "Beyond the Realms of Death"), it's not a love ballad per sé but a funereal dirge, a throwback to Sabbath and a throw forward to the dark and doomy balladry of many a NWOBHM band who felt compelled to stick a quiet moment or two on their records.

Journalist John Tucker, on the likes of soft songs from Nazareth, UFO, Slade and Thin Lizzy being essentially, boy/girl material: Yes, you're right. I mean all those bands you name, again, all of those, you'd get lynched for calling them metal bands. All those bands, yeah, they were love songs and there's nothing wrong with that. There's a place for everything. But when you look at things like "Last Rose of Summer" or "Epitaph," things like that, yeah, they always seem to be about the bleaker side of things, the end of something. It's not an area that Purple explored. So you are looking at some of those early, very good Sabbath songs. Again you've got this divide; Sabbath would have to go in the metal bucket whether they like it or not. But there is a bit of a line there, compared to "Heart's Grown Cold" by Nazareth or something—you've got a very strong divide there.

Judas Priest vocalist Rob Halford on the band's evolving and increasingly focused use of twin leads:
You have to go back to Wishbone Ash 'cause KK was a huge fan of Wishbone Ash. As you know, for the longest time Priest was guitar, bass, vocals, drums. So when my decision was made to have two guitar players, everything changed—everything changed. I think again to some extent it set a new template for bands to go, you know, when you have two guitar players and the one plays lead, that rhythm is

still roaring—it's not like this hole that suddenly appears sometimes. And also if you've got two distinctive lead stylistic players thinking and playing totally different to one another, this is great because look again at the potential. It's always great to be able to share the load in what you do no matter what it is in life.

So if you've got two guitar players that are looking at each other and playing, not against each other but with each other, and checking each other out—I've got this great riff and if you play it this way—you know, it's all that wonderful sense of potential and growth, and that optimism of the way you can go by having two guitars instead of one. There are a load of great players; I mean look at what Dimebag did. God! Look at what Eddie Van Halen did. Tony Iommi. But that was very important for us. Suddenly Priest... to the best of my knowledge, surely we were the first heavy metal band with two guitar players. That's very important in the make-up of the music we made in Priest.

Judas Priest guitarist Glenn Tipton on how two guitars made Priest heavier:

In many ways. First of all there is a writing level. We're both writers, and we write well together, particularly as a trio, with Rob. So that was the first thing that really gelled, and suddenly we ignited in that area. But you've got a lot of power, because you've got two rhythm guitars playing in stereo, if you like. If Ken takes the lead, I can play rhythm, so you don't get something falling out. If I play lead, Ken can play rhythm, exactly the same, then we can do harmonies, and we can do fast harmonies together, which is heavy metal harmony, guitar playing, as opposed to the Wishbone Ash sort of thing.

But you've also got quieter passages, and we very often pooled our ideas, with quiet ideas, and we've got a sixth sense with each other now, where Ken can play one thing and I will enhance it and vice versa. And so it just opened everything up, and it was exciting for all of us, really, because suddenly with two guitar players, you can do a lot more than just with one guitar player. And that's not to say anything about the band, as well, because the band's got five members, we've all got great character, and it will all gel together.

With me and Ken there are no rules. We just did what we wanted to do. When we have writing sessions, a lovely melodic song like "Last Rose of Summer" will go just as well with something like "Painkiller." There are no rules. We love heavy metal, but we also love melody, and we always believed that you can do whatever you want to do. You shouldn't be restricted by the so-called code of heavy metal. You can do what you want, and I think that gave the band a lot of inner strength, really. The other good thing is, if you play rhythm guitar, and you stop playing rhythm guitar to play lead guitar, there is a drop. There isn't the risk... now the riff continues over the lead break. And the trade-off is very exciting, and the fast, like "Freewheel Burning" or whatever, there are fast trade-offs and it all adds excitement to the metal moment.

Judas Priest guitarist K.K. Downing on the benefits of two guitars in a live setting:
Personally, I think it's very exciting when I see guys with two guitar players in the band, and when the guys are just pounding at a riff, or just headbanging together, or just like trading off solos, as we did. It's an exciting thing to look at. I think there's a lot more energy when you look at bands with two guitar players, thrashing at it.

Journalist Carl Begai:
Who was doing that back then with the exception of Maiden? As Halford was developing his voice and his style, you had the twin guitars. Priest just took things five steps further than anybody else, with the whole twin guitars especially. You know, this is what you can do with this and they weren't shy about it at all. And Rob, he sounded better live than recorded, which was insane. You had your Helloween stuff that happened later on, but early Priest, they were doing things that you had to stop and listen, check your head and see, what is he doing? And there were bands that were listening to that and going crap, this works. You know, I can build on this, I can copy this.

SPV Records executive Olly Hahn:
Judas Priest is very important for every kind of metal because they put all the bands like Zeppelin, Deep Purple and Black Sabbath together and created their own thing. I think the song which stands out and was the first power metal, heavy metal or whatever, song is "Exciter" on the *Stained Class* album. Because you never heard double bass in this intensity, with this voice and the screaming. So I think this was the start of everything. Also with the guitars, normally you had a lead guitar player and a rhythm guitar player, but now you had two lead guitar players, and this was very rare.

Venom guitarist Mantas:
    For myself, when I put Venom together, I was always into guitar-based things. The first band that I really got into was Slade. The two-guitar type thing, it was rock music. It was loud rock 'n' roll, really. Looking back on it, it was a bit of a quest for me. Looking for something heavier all the time, and I discovered this band from

America called Kiss, and this was still sort of mid- to late-'70s, really. And then you find out about Motörhead and people like that.

But the band that changed everything for me was Judas Priest. I saw them on the *Stained Class* tour at Newcastle City Hall. And seeing them on stage, that was the epitome of heavy metal for me. I don't think it's any great secret that I've cited K.K. Downing as my biggest influence for wanting to be in a band and wanting to be a guitarist. I was dabbling in guitar at the time. I've got a signed ticket from K.K. and Rob Halford as well. But that was it for me. That completely changed my destiny, let's put it that way.

March 1978. Liverpool's Marseille issue their debut single, "The French Way"/"Cold Steel," followed the next month by debut album *Red, White and Slightly Blue*, both on Mountain. At a stretch, Marseille are to Def Leppard what Y&T are to Van Halen.

March 10, 1978. David Coverdale issues his second solo album, *Northwinds*, on Purple Records. Like the debut, it is produced by Roger Glover. Later in the year, half of the album (four of eight tracks) would be combined with the *Snakebite* EP to become the debut Whitesnake album. Whitesnake, Gillan and Rainbow, as well as Ozzy Osbourne, would represent old guard rockers rebranded and benefitting from the enthusiasm for all things heavy within the UK rock scene of the early '80s.

Spring 1978. Girlschool form, when Kim McAuliffe and End Williams dissolve their formative band Painted Lady.

Girlschool bassist and vocalist Enid Williams:
Kim and I had our first band in 1975. But the band went through different phases, and Kim and I grew up together. I mean literally, we can remember looking at each other when we were sitting in our prams. So some good memories. And we went to the same primary school, at least. And her mother still lives ten doors away from me. And we had this band, and we went through various lineup changes, and it was very unusual, because we started playing, and this was just before we knew The Runaways. We hadn't heard of Fanny at that point, and we were just like aliens from outer space. Everyone just laughed at us. There were no other female musicians around, and everything had changed.

With punk there was that can-do attitude, and all of a sudden there were loads and loads of girls picking up instruments. Most of them were shit, but still, most of the guys were shit too. So it was like having a go, sort of attitude. And we had a lineup change, and we got in this guitarist called Kathy Valentine. She was a rhythm guitarist. And we had a few rehearsals and she was really nice, and then she got really ill and she couldn't do our first gig.

So the drummer said, "Oh, I know a guitarist." And it was Kelly, and Kelly stepped in. And for various reasons, obviously Kelly worked really well. Kathy was primarily a rhythm guitarist. She was pretty wild in those days and we were pretty innocent. And we were sort of like whoa, this woman is kind of like… little realizing that Girlschool was going to be just as wild in its own way a few years later. And then she went back to the states, and shortly afterwards, she heard about an audition, she learned bass in three days, and she joined The Go-Go's (laughs).

Girlschool guitarist Kim McAuliffe:
In the early days, we were quite influenced by punk. I think the Sex Pistols' *Never Mind the Bollocks* is still one of the greatest rock records ever made. It still sounds good today and we were quite influenced by it back then, as well as being big fans of heavy rock. Plus when we were growing up, glam rock over here was massive. You had The Sweet and bands like that, Alice Cooper, and we grew up listening to a lot of that, as well as the heavy rock around at the time. We actually all were quite influenced by the glam rock scene, which was just great fun. But as soon as we started to write our own stuff we didn't try to sound like anything. It's just literally the way it came out as we were writing it.

Funny enough, Motörhead were just becoming well-known then as well, and we didn't really know that much about them. They were quite new then, as I said, so the first time we actually heard anything of them was somebody gave us one of their records, the original single, "Motörhead," and we put it on and went, "What the hell is this?!" (laughs). There was nothing around like that, so it just so happened that we were doing the same stuff around the same time. Because, as I said, we didn't actually make any effort to sound any particular way. When we would write the songs and rehearse them, that is just how we ended up sounding.

April 1978. Adrian Smith joins Maiden for a second time, leaving Urchin, who issue their second single, "She's a Roller"/"Long Time no Woman" this year. Also this month, future MCA signing Fist open for business, first as Axe, before their name change the following year.

April 13, 1978. Rainbow issue their third studio album *Long Live Rock 'n' Roll*, which includes the Egypto-mystical power metal staple "Gates of Babylon" along with speed metal rocker "Kill the King." Speed metal would soon become a journalistic term to describe the faster songs by NWOBHM bands, and then, when applied to American and Canadian bands from 1983, 1984, it would signify a brief transition genre tag toward thrash.

Rainbow bassist Jimmy Bain, on flying the flag for hard rock as a "second wave" metal band:
Absolutely, yeah. And kept it going, too, I think to a certain extent, because it was veering away from that. Several layers, kind of thing, or more experimental. It was good because—and we didn't realize at the time—but we were doing just that, and it was kind of good for us, in a way, too, because it kept us kind of on top for a while.

May 25, 1978. AC/DC issue their beloved fifth album, *Powerage*. The Australian band with roots in Glasgow spends a lot of time in the UK exciting and inspiring many a teenage metalhead.

Saxon vocalist Biff Byford on AC/DC's huge influence on the band:

That came from me, because I really got into that *Dirty Deeds Done Dirt Cheap* period. And I actually took the band to a little pub in Sheffield to see AC/DC with Bon Scott in '70-something. And all that playing the same riff with the chorus appealed to me. It had a certain power, you know what I mean? Obviously, without AC/DC there wouldn't have been a "Wheels of Steel." Much the same as if there wasn't a Motörhead there wouldn't have been a "Heavy Metal Thunder."

You can't pin down your influences on one thing. It just all fucking goes in there through your ear and bounces around your brain for a few years and then it comes out in different ways. That's the thing. So it's never a rip-off. It's a slight influence or a slightly different... or it's the same sort of arrangements but different approach. I don't think they had an influence on the guitar riffs, because they were really into other things. But after I took them to see them, that changed us a little bit.

June 1978. Marseille issues, on Mountain, non-LPer "Kiss Like Rock 'n' Roll," backed with "Can-Can."

June 2, 1978. Thin Lizzy issue *Live and Dangerous*, considered one of the great live albums of all time. Lizzy is an influence, no doubt, on the NWOBHMers, but it becomes enhanced through the band's accessibility for a pint in the pubs about London town.

June 2, 1978. "David Coverdale's Whitesnake" issue their first material, the *Snakebite* EP, consisting of "Come On," "Bloody Mary," "Ain't No Love in the Heat of the City" and "Steal Away." The four tracks from this EP would be combined with four tracks from *Northwinds* to become the debut album, also called *Snakebite*. The additional four tracks are "Keep on Giving Me Love," "Queen of Hearts," "Only My Soul" and "Breakdown."

July – August 1978. Gillan work on the tracks that will become a self-titled debut album, also known as the *Japanese Album*, given its release and profile in Japan.

August 1978. Scorpions issue a double live album called *Tokyo Tapes*.

> Journalist John Tucker:
> To be fair, they didn't really do much over here until *Tokyo Tapes*. That was my introduction to the Scorpions, and *Tokyo Tapes* knocks the spots off the studio albums. And from there on in they got slots at Reading '79 where I think Thin Lizzy pulled out and they were drafted in, and from there they could do no wrong. *Lovedrive* comes out and they are big. But before that time, before *Tokyo Tapes*, in my mind, up to that point they weren't doing much in the UK at all. I'd be surprised if any of their albums charted at all. After that, those albums on the Harvest label over here were really big business.

August 19, 1978. Geoff Barton visits Neal Kay at his new "heavy metal disco" and writes a piece in *Sounds* about it entitled Wednesday Night Fever.

August 27, 1978. Gillan play their first show, at the *Reading* festival. It is a significant NWOBHM moment. The band is billed as Ian Gillan Band but it is in fact the real heavy metal deal. Other than Gillan, practically no one else heavy was on the bill, save for Status Quo, headliners on the Saturday.

September 1978. After his hard rock/jazz-fusion Ian Gillan Band fizzles after three albums, Ian is now set up with Gillan, very much a NWOBHM band. The self-titled debut was issued in September '78, but only in Japan, Australia and New Zealand. It is a candidate for first NWOBHM album ever, as is Gillan's second album, *Mr. Universe* (if one doesn't buy the argument vis-à-vis the debut), which is heavier and more convincing with respect to musical match with the young hard rock bands exploding onto the scene at the time.

> Gillan bassist John McCoy on whether *Gillan* was the first NWOBHM album:
> That's a hard question. I don't think so. I don't think you'd class that as a heavy metal album. That was kind of the crossover album from Ian Gillan Band to becoming Gillan. The songs were great songs but they

were still not really heavy. There was a couple of tracks that were heavy, but it was the crossover period. I think that the Samson *Survivors* album has to be up there as maybe the first NWOBHM full album.

September 1978. Guillotine change their name to Venom; at this point the five-piece act's only classic Venom lineup member is guitarist Mantas. Meanwhile, Cronos is busy in his own two-years-running band called Album Graecum, soon to become Dwarfstar.

September 7, 1978. The Who loses Keith Moon, felled by an abundance of self-medication. New rock stars are needed.

September 28, 1978. Black Sabbath issue what would be the last album of the original Ozzy Osbourne era. *Never Say Die* would represent yet another old guard heavy metal band tired and running on fumes.

September 30, 1978. Motörhead issue their laid-back cover of "Louie Louie," with b-side "Tear Ya Down" turning up the intensity significantly.

Motörhead guitarist Fast Eddie Clarke on first meeting Lemmy:

I was surprised how friendly he was and keen to have the rehearsal for my audition. I have to say I liked him from the start and was looking forward to a jam together. Having been with Hawkwind, he had toured the States and had all that experience to pass on to Phil and myself. I think I always thought of him as a big brother.

As for the booze and drugs, we were all like that in those days. It's kind of what made the world go 'round back then. I was not

Martin Popoff

particularly into speed but I soon got the hang of it. I wasn't a big drinker, but after six months with Motörhead it seemed a natural progression. Of course when we started we did not have a pot to piss in. That always keeps you pretty healthy.

But for me, they were great years and we made some great music. It was a good time to be in a band. I think we were really lucky. Right place, right time. We really had nothing to lose and a lot of our fans could identify with that as they were in the same boat. We never sold out and we rubbed a lot of people up the wrong way, but were honest about it. I miss those times; things were much simpler. I think life is more fun when it is a bit of a struggle.

October 1978. Bernie Torme, soon to be Gillan's guitarist, issues, as the Bernie Torme Band, a single called "I'm Not Ready"/"Free."

October 1978. Whitesnake issue their first album proper, their first record of material all recorded at once for one project, first under the shortened name Whitesnake. The album is called *Trouble* and is produced by Martin Birch. It reaches #50 on the UK charts.

October 1978. Samson issue their first single, "Telephone Man," produced by future Gillan bassist John McCoy. Of the four tracks split between the band's first two singles however, only the b-side on the second one, from 1979, "Drivin' Man," puts its back into planting NWOBHM seeds.

Producer John McCoy:
Before the album, we'd done a couple singles, both with Clive Burr on drums. One single was called "Telephone" and one was called "Mr. Rock 'n' Roll." And "Telephone," in particular, was sort of highlighted as one of the first NWOBHM singles. It was kind of a cheesy pop song, really, but it was heavy, and that's what mattered.

October 9, 1978. Judas Priest issue *Killing Machine*. The album contains "Take on the World" which the band mimes on *Top of the Pops*, looking metal and singing the praises of metal. It's a watershed moment for the NWOBHM in that a band that's not exactly new, but not exactly ancient either—father figures as it were but still relevant—overtly fly the flag of metal musically, lyrically and visually.

THE BAND IS JUDAS PRIEST.
THE ALBUM IS
'KILLING MACHINE.'
THE SINGLE IS
'BEFORE THE DAWN.'
THE NATIONWIDE TOUR
IS UNDER WAY.

The rest is up to you

KILLING MACHINE

Judas Priest vocalist Rob Halford:
Heavy metal music is full of anthems. It's full of these great resounding songs that really capture what is the heavy metal spirit. Again, you gotta bring the fans

into the picture. Put yourself in our hands and together we'll take on all the world. That's not just the band saying it, that's everybody saying it. It's just a statement of confidence. Like we're not going anywhere, this is who we are and we believe in what we do. And so that "Take on the World" track is a shout, it's a real demand for attention. And to get on a show like the British *Top of the Pops*, some of the fans didn't like that. They didn't like that at all. It was like you were selling out onto the commercial TV show. We said no, no, no, we're spreading the metal. We're spreading the gospel of metal, and the best way you can do that is through something like *Top of the Pops*, which without a doubt really helped the band grow.

Again, the great tradition and heritage, and the history of metal from a lyrical point of view, it goes everywhere. It touches every subject, every idea. But I think for Priest especially we were always aware and we are always grateful of those early days. Even now, the only way you can progress is with the people that support you. The people that buy a ticket to your show, buy a record, buy a t-shirt. That all goes in the pot that keeps the whole machine moving. So you recognize that. You look around and you see these fans and you go, God bless these fans because we can't do this without the fans. We are without a doubt united in that heavy metal spirit.

So you think about how you can make that connection. When the band is singing those words, the fans are singing those words, we are all singing about the same thing, the same idea. This heavy metal community, this spirit of the whole thing that we are doing together, it just makes that bond stronger. It's like yeah, we recognize each other; this is really important to us. And again from those early days and even now today you get the detractors that look at it and go, what is that? Well we don't care what you think. This is who we are, this is what we love, and this is how we're combining our forces to support each other.

Judas Priest guitarist Glenn Tipton on the band's anthems to metal:
It's never us and the audience when we're on stage, it's the whole thing. The audience sing along with our choruses, verses, and even lead breaks now. So tracks like "Take on the World" and "United," are fantastic for the audience to sing and join in with, and that's something we love. When we do a concert, it's not all about Judas Priest, it's about Judas Priest and our fans in the audience and the atmosphere that creates. I suppose we consciously do compose some music with that in mind. They can join in, and we can all sing together.

Journalist John Tucker:
When *Killing Machine* came out—or *Hell Bent for Leather* for you guys—that's when they codified their image. And the first thing I can remember about Judas Priest as something a bit different was when they performed "Take on the World" on *Top of the Pops*, with the leather. All of a sudden they had an image, and if you wanted to do a picture that screamed this is heavy metal, a clip from that footage—

which was released on one of their DVDs a while ago, the BBC footage—that was it. I'd not seen anything quite like that. I saw that and thought bloody 'ell. I'd seen pictures of a caftan-wearing Rob Halford, I'd seen the likes of Sabbath do their thing, but I'd never seen anything quite that metal.

Saxon vocalist Biff Byford on singing the praises of heavy metal:
We do it and we did it, obviously, with songs like "Heavy Metal Thunder," and obviously Judas Priest did. And to a certain extent, so did Queen. So to sing about your audience and to sing about the music that you love, I think some bands can do it and have done it, and I think as the audience grew, then we can sing more about it.

About the link between the audience and the band, it's denim and leather—that's what that's about. We're basically singing about the audience, we're basically praising the audience. We're saying you're a fantastic bunch of people. And Judas Priest did do that, obviously. But that sort of passion from an audience affects me. And if it affects me in a profound way, then it will end up as a song. Some people would say that was a bit cheesy and would say love songs are what it's all about, but I'm not one of those people. I like to say it how it is, and from the streets, basically. That's what we felt like. We felt like we were one big fucking tribe of people all together.

Tyger of Pan Tang vocalist Jess Cox:
When you think of metal, I guess Judas Priest has got to be the one, really, that was the first like complete metal band, because I mean Sabbath were a bit doomy, Zeppelin were kind of like a heavy version of the Beatles half the time. Deep Purple were there and a bit metal, but with keyboards in there, it softened it up a bit. When you say this was the beginning of metal, you start talking about the Yardbirds and things like that from the '60s. I mean, "You Really Got Me" by the Kinks, for instance, that's one hell of a metal riff, but you wouldn't exactly call the Kinks metal. So heavier sounds started in the '60s, but if you want to talk about a metal band, I suppose Priest must be the first to say "I am metal."

Raven bassist and vocalist John Gallagher on the importance of the "Take on the World" video:
That just made them more popular, giving them the opportunity to be on TV in England. They were like eh, it's all right, it's fun, what the hell. You knew why they were doing it, but it wasn't so much a selling-out type thing. It was appealing to the football hooligan in everybody, kind of sing-along things, which are very popular back in the old UK. It was the soccer thing. It was take on the world together, united, all that kind of thing. United, united—that's obviously a direct correlation to soccer. They basically sealed that uniform of the leather jacket and the bullet belts and the studs and all that stuff, which is pretty funny considering where Rob got it all from. They brought that out; they really did. It was *Killing Machine* in England and *Hell Bent for Leather* in the US—that's when it got solidified.

Diamond Head guitarist Brian Tatler on the invention of the "metal anthem:"
That might be a way of connecting with the audience, have a good time. You could say, write an anthem, as something that will connect with the people in the audience. You're still on your way up, anyway. Like Saxon, you haven't reached the plateau. You're still trying to connect with as many people as possible, so to write the songs that would embrace this music—great idea. When Diamond Head started, there was no New Wave of British Heavy Metal; we just wanted to be a rock band, just a heavy rock band, not even heavy metal, because even heavy metal didn't really come along until Judas Priest and maybe *British Steel*, where it started getting called heavy metal. So we didn't ever say right, we're a heavy metal band. As I say, we wanted to be like your Zeppelins and Purples and Sabbaths.

Judas Priest engineer and producer Chris Tsangarides on Priest's identification with heavy metal:
I think they took it quite seriously, about the metal community; it's about the brotherhood. It still is. You can go anywhere in the world and you see someone with long hair and a T-shirt, you can go speak to them and it will be fine. You've got something in common. They were so into it. The type of people they are as well. They are very family, they are very caring about each other and whatnot, and so the way they were brought up, from the areas they lived in, in the Midlands, it really, I think, contributes to it all. And I'm glad, because it's kind of a unique thing to them. That's their uniqueness, the way they write their stuff, the way they sound, and even through it all, they've gone from songs like "United" and "Breaking the Law" to "Painkiller," for goodness sakes. But it all fits. It all still fits.

Late 1978. Angel Witch begins recording some of their early classics. Angel Witch and the Iron Maiden of the debut album (and maybe, at a stretch, the Witchfynde of *Give 'Em Hell*) will come to represent the dark, brooding, depressive, hopelessly heavy metal heart of the NWOBHM.

Angel Witch guitarist Kevin Heybourne on the band's first song ever, "Angel Witch:"
The basic premise of the rhythm is something like the one from a band called Pink Fairies. I can't remember the name of the track, it's so long ago. It was something like, "She took me to a room and hit me with a broom;" it kind has the same rhythm and the same chord progression.

November 1978. Stiff Records include in a box set what was to be Motörhead's first single, intended for release in December '76. Comprising "Leaving Here" and "White Line Fever," the a-side is an old school cover but the b-side rocks quite hard and modern, for all intents and purposes, an example of pure metal and emphatically not punk.

November 25, 26, 1978. Def Leppard record *The Def Leppard E.P.*, later known as the *Getcha Rocks Off* EP, at a cost of £150.00.

Def Leppard vocalist Joe Elliott on the NWOBHM:

We didn't want anything to do with that, so we were absolutely the enemy. We spent every given opportunity in the press telling everybody how crap they all were. Not that you have anything personal against anybody, apart from maybe Saxon. But like, we've known Maiden for over 21 years and they're decent guys. You can sit at the bar with these guys or go for a curry with them and have a really good time, because they're all nice guys; known them since they were this big.

But we don't have anything in common with them musically. In fact, we've got a lot more in common with Oasis than we have with Iron Maiden. And that blows people's minds. And I say, think about it! We don't do the obligatory guitar solos because we're a rock band. It's not that we have Phil and Vivian going, "Oh, I've got to have my 20 seconds," because it's not important. The thing is, you listen to all the songs that have won Grammys, the songs that are going to be in the book of all-time great songs in the world, from "Love Me Do" to "Jumping Jack Flash," they don't necessarily have guitar solos in them. So what's the important thing? It's the shell for the solo, the delivery of the thing from start to finish.

I mean, we've worn leathers, but we've worn leathers the same way Lou Reed has worn leathers. It's not because of the, "We swear allegiance to rock" bullshit. I mean, you take a look at Lou Reed on the front of *Metal Machine Music* and you could argue that he could have been the lead singer for Judas Priest. You shouldn't be tainted by it, but unfortunately you are. You've got to be very careful if you wear a leather jacket nowadays. George Michael can wear one and nobody thinks he's in a heavy metal band. We wear one and all of a sudden we're metal. And we've been trying so long to just get out of any movement and be our own thing. We don't want to be part of any movement.

Def Leppard guitarist Phil Collen on leather:

I was talking to a guy the other day from Austria, and he says, "Things have changed; you don't wear the leathers anymore." And I said we never did! Even when I was in Girl, I mean look at that— that's not very metal. I said, we were always more Duran Duran than we were Judas Priest. In fact it embarrassed us to be put in that kind of thing. And even the people who bought the records, it wasn't the rock fans per sé. I mean it was, but it crossed over. I mean, I remember when we were on the front of *Seventeen* magazine.

December 1978 – January 1979. Motörhead record what will become *Overkill*, a suite of songs that is a huge step up from the ragged debut.

Motörhead bassist and vocalist Lemmy on making angry music:

The British are generally angry because of our climate, and the lack of things to do after 9:30 at night because the police close them all down as soon as we start liking it. It's bloody impossible in England. It's so fucking miserable. The weather there is just going to depress the hell out of you before you get out of bed. Just as soon as you look out the window, "Oh fuck, I gotta go out in that again?" It rains all the time. You have no idea.

And rain is worse than freezing to death. Freezing to death, at least it's quick. But constant rain really beats you down and it ruins your hair, if you've got long hair. Life is a bitch, right? And so are you. You can't get around life being a bastard because it is, and it's not anybody cursing you, it's not the devil getting on your case, it's random shit. And it can happen to you. A piano can fall on you as you walk down the street on a sunny day. And if you're lucky it will.

Motörhead drummer Phil Taylor on playing fast:

I guess Motörhead were the first, as far as I can remember, to play really fast. At the time, we just thought of ourselves as a rock band, and then the term heavy rock came in and then we figured well, we're a heavy rock band. But we happen to have played that little bit faster than anybody else. But as they say, again, it wasn't intentional at all. But I can see why I would be the influence of a lot of thrash metal kids, because all the bands that came after us, a lot of them, they intentionally wanted to play that fast, whereas for myself, I never intended to play intensely that fast; that's just how it ended up. So, it's very nice and it's a great complement to be cited as sort of an influence; I'm very flattered by that.

As Motörhead got faster and faster and faster I was always wishing that it would slow down, so that what we were playing could maybe be actually heard by people. Because there's an old adage that goes, volume can cover up many mistakes, just sheer volume and speed— and it can. And it would have been nice to have been recognized by other musicians at the time, as being good musicians. But I don't think we were thought of like that. I mean, it's great to be admired by the fans, but at the same time, you kind of want to be acknowledged as a good musician by your contemporaries as well, and I don't think we ever got that, because we just played so fast and so loud.

December 30, 31, 1978. Iron Maiden records "Prowler," "Invasion," "Strange World" and "Iron Maiden," at the Soundhouse, later to be issued as *The Soundhouse Tapes*, onthe band's own Rock Hard Records. As the year comes to a close, suddenly quite a bit of very heavy metal is being tracked at studios about the UK, by newer, younger punters—and Lemmy.

Iron Maiden bassist Steve Harris:

We tried to do something different, really. I suppose it was the aggression in music and playing faster maybe, but also incorporating things like twin guitars, melody, prog-type stuff as well, time changes. But it was just a more aggressive attitude, and I think that's where a lot of people tried to liken us with the punk thing. I mean, we still play "Iron Maiden" in the set now, and the song tends to get a lot of liking to the punky side of thing because it's fast. But it's got harmony guitars in it, so I don't think it's punk myself. But I think a lot of people lumped it in with that, because that's what was happening at the time.

But we didn't want to be associated with it at all. It's not like we wanted to ride on the crest of the wave with punk—we didn't. We didn't want anything to do with it. We hated it; we absolutely hated it. We really didn't want to be part of any of it. To you living overseas maybe you look at it a different way, but in England at the time, it was absolutely punk on one side… it was a bit like Mods and Rockers—it was like punk and rock, classic rock, whatever, and they didn't like each other at all.

Iron Maiden guitarist Dennis Stratton on what caused the NWOBHM:

That's a big question. Basically, I think that the original frontrunners like Deep Purple, Black Sabbath and Led Zeppelin had been around for quite a long time in the late '60s and '70s. You've got to remember that we're England—it was a very small country so the music influences, the music scene, it changes very quickly. It's nothing like America where you have loads of radio stations.

I think that what happened was bands were playing in and around England—I come from East London, so I can only talk for London— but most of the bands were from London or around the outer areas of London. Everyone was playing their own kind of music but nothing was happening because there wasn't many bands touring at the time. UFO, they went to America. But you had all the bands like Maiden, Saxon and Def Leppard and the Tygers of Pan Tang all rehearsing and trying to write songs to make it bigger.

I remember about 1976-'77, the band I was playing with, RDB, which was Remus Down Boulevard, we were signed to Quarry Management who managed Status Quo. And the next minute, we were on tour with Status Quo, and we're going back in '76, '77, and we had to go abroad. It was Europe, Scandinavia, Germany, France, all over. No concerts in England because I think, at the time, the music scene in England regarding heavy metal or heavy rock just seemed to disappear, so these bands had to go abroad to get audiences. I think when Maiden came along, they had been doing all the gigs for many, many years but not doing big concerts, like just clubs. I think, at the end of the day, after the punk scene happened, with Neal Kay and Maiden and Saxon, there was a new wave of heavy metal that had to happen because all the original frontrunners had gone asleep. or they were in Japan or America.

Recap

In 1978, much to Steve Harris' satisfaction, punk is considered dead. It's not so much that a vacuum is created, because really, what happens is that all of those punk bands become post-punk, and new post-punk bands emerge. It's easy to put the blinders on and forget all these other forms of music, but it's an almost joyously creative period in England outside of heavy metal as well.

But back to our happy story, more NWOBHM bands sprung into action in 1978, including Marseille, Tygers of Pan Tang, Ethel the Frog, Venom, and Def Leppard. As well, Samson issues their first single, arguably the first piece of definable NWOBHM product.

In the world of dinosaur rockers in decline, Ozzy Osbourne makes his last record with Black Sabbath, the trashy and casual *Never Say Die*, before the band rises from the ashes two years later with Ronnie James Dio at the helm. And speaking of Ronnie, he's making his last album with Rainbow, *Long Live Rock 'n' Roll*, even if that band recovers fairly quickly with the creditable *Down to Earth* the following year.

In the world of big bands thriving, well, this would necessarily fall upon the second-generation bands as opposed to the first. AC/DC is flying high with the charming *Powerage* record, while both Thin Lizzy and Scorpions issue landmark double live LPs. Most impressive of the lot, however, is Judas Priest, who strike out with *Stained Class* early in 1978 and *Killing Machine* by the end of the year. Essentially, by this point, Judas Priest has emerged as pretty much the #1 inspiring force calling for a heavy metal renaissance, Halford, Tipton and Downing promising to "Take on the World" on behalf of the blue army.

But also calling for that renaissance is the ever-present Neal Kay and his nuclear powered PA, which influential journalist and soon-to-be heavy metal champion of baby bands Geoff Barton, experiences firsthand this year. Kay further finds himself at the flashpoint of NWOBHM history when at the very end of the year, his buddies Iron Maiden record the scary tracks for what will be their legendary *The Soundhouse Tapes* EP, perhaps the most important early suite of songs baying at the moon for the invention of a NWOBHM.

1979 —"This kind of music is absolute."

1979. The first wave of indie NWOBHM singles arrive throughout the year. Some of these minor releases for which exact dates within 1979 are not known are as follows: Angel Street - "Midnight Man:" Dave "Bucket" Colwell ends up with Samson and Adrian Smith's ASaP before landing the late period Bad Company gig; A.R.C. Rock Band - "Home Made Wine;" Blazer Blazer - "Cecil B. Devine," on Logo. Blazer Blazer is pre-Maiden in a slight way, having barely contained Nicko McBrain and in a later incarnation as Broadway Brats, Adrian Smith; Clientelle - "Can't Forget;" Everyone Else – "Schooldays;" Full Moon - "Stand Up;" Jodey - "The Rocker:" this band is pre-Chinatown, leaning toward both prog and pop; Alec Johnson Band - "Busman's Holiday," produced by Strife's Gordon Rowley, who snatched personnel from the band to form Nightwing; Juno's Claw – "Barbara;" Kick - "Rough 'n' Smooth," a surprise early NWOBHM play for EMI, earlier even than the *Metal for Muthas* comps; The Law - "Be My Girl;" Pheetus – "Nomads;" Rough Justice - "Black Knight," from the Outer Hebrides; Snatch-Back - "Eastern Lady;" Toad the Wet Sprocket - "Pete's Punk Song" and Triarchy - "Save the Khan."

1979. In a metal and punk crossover moment, Thin Lizzy's Phil Lynott teams up with Steve Jones and Paul Cook in the Greedy Bastards (changed to the Greedies), recording a novelty Christmas single, "A Merry Jingle," and playing just one live gig. Sociable Phil is rightly regarded as one of the few from traditional rock to give punks the time of day.

Raven bassist and vocalist John Gallagher on staying away from the punks:

We kept away. One of the few times we ran into them I ended up getting my wrist broken, so it wasn't a lot of fun with them at all. And it was very delineated. There was a punk culture, and there was what they called the hairies, which was basically the rock fan. Long hair and leather jackets. We prided ourselves on musicianship. Very much so. That's what pissed us off. I mean well-noted when the whole stagediving thing started getting popular, which we ran into in '83, I think, when we played California for the first time. I think they'd started out there. Did a little stagediving and going crazy, and we'd stop because it's like, yeah, I've spent the better part of seven or eight years of my life working on my trade, so when I'm up here I own it. Get the fuck off. What are you doing on my stage? You want to get onstage? Learn to play.

And we had this whole thing, we played crap, horrible gigs, and when we'd be introduced as the boys from Newcastle in the next town, who hated Newcastle, and people would come up with their little coasters and they'd usually give you requests to play, and when you were down there most of them just said fuck off. You'd look at them and go, oh, that's nice (laughs). So we felt like we earned our stripes. We went through an apprenticeship. We learned to play, we learned how to deal with cords going wrong, strings breaking, microphones going off, entertain the audience because when you play to those places, the working men's clubs, they just want to be entertained, and they would let you know very quickly if they liked you or didn't like you. We figured it out, and there's been a long, slippery slope ever since then where people can just kind of learn in the bedroom and the next thing you know they're playing onstage in front of 20,000 people.

1979. Grim Reaper forms in Droitwich, England, while Satan opens for business in Newcastle. Over in Cardiff, a new band called Persian Risk includes Jon Deverill, soon to defect to Tygers of Pan Tang, and Phil Campbell, later of Motörhead.

1979. Mythra issue, on Guardian, *Death and Destiny*, one of the higher quality, well-regarded indies within the genre. It would be reissued in 1980 on Street Beat with a picture sleeve and one less track, in both 7" and 12" formats.

DJ Neal Kay on the birth of the NWOBHM:

There's not a single point that you can actually look at. It was a sort of progression. Basically behind the closed doors of Bandwagon, the first thing I know we needed to do was get a name for the club. I saw an opportunity and felt strongly that here, if only I could get the media's attention—this was before punk by two years—I felt that we had an opportunity

Bandwagon Heavymetal Soundhouse
Kingsbury Circle NW9
(Nearest Tube Kingsbury on the Jubilee Line)

Presents Special Evening
Sunday 7th October
Personal appearance of

MOTORHEAD

Doors open 8pm. Admission 50p
(strictly 18 + only)

to present our case for some much-needed publicity. If only we could get the weight of the media behind us, then maybe the record companies would jump up and pay some attention. It wasn't just us. There were bands out there, new bands, young bands, sent me demo tapes, once Geoff Barton's exposé of what I then called the Bandwagon Heavy Metal Soundhouse—I hate the word discotheque and did then—that's why I called it a Soundhouse, to get away from the term of discotheque.

And also I had this massive sound system there. It wasn't a discotheque club system. It was a band PA, and it could blow windows out, and it was the only place in the country that had one at discotheque level. In 1977 they used my picture onstage at the 'wagon as the front page advert in *Melody Maker* for *Sounds Expo* at Earl's Court that year. We had the biggest club sound system in the country, and you couldn't blow it up. Not with records. It was impossible.

It was a really broad spectrum for a start, because I personally have a love for all things rock, not just heavy metal. We hadn't heard that phrase. Let's get this sorted. We hadn't heard the phrase heavy metal until it came from the States. We didn't know what that was. It was something new. Everybody had a different definition for it, and I think they still do today depending on their angle. Musician, DJ, promoter, record company, no one knows exactly how to describe it. When I first heard the phrase whilst I was looking for a new name for the Soundhouse, I took it to mean high-energy rock. Which doesn't necessarily have to be as heavy as heavy metal. It doesn't have to be Black Sabbath moving at the speed of light. It doesn't have to be Motörhead thundering along at the speed of light. There were other bands out there that had high energy, but may not have necessarily been a heavy metal band.

But the point is, I guess the key thing is that, a) you believed in rock, and b) you didn't believe in punk, and you wanted to play music that was musical for young people. That was rock. I already had an audience there. I mean I had a lot of help from the years I spent as a club DJ in London. The '60s taught me how to be a professional disc jockey. How not to speak over records. How not to lose a floor. How to have a lot of respect for musicians, how to have a lot of respect for great music. I had all that behind me and a lot of years. I'd also worked outside the UK, so when I went to the Bandwagon I brought all that with me, and of course my own family's stage legend with me, too, and that mattered.

As for sending these heavy metal charts to *Sounds*? Right, well that's easy enough, really. It's like this. For two years from 1975 to 1977 I worked at building the 'wagon up. I had it five nights a week, including Friday and Saturday and Sunday nights. I had the best nights. Hell, I could do what I wanted, and because of that I could broaden everything. We tell this story of Floyd in Quadraphonic. The company that supported me just rolled in another couple of PA towers, and we'd do the Floyd story, we'd do the Thin Lizzy, the Free/Bad Company story, we'd do all these things.

And at the same time I was cracking away at the media every day that I could. I kept phoning up *Sounds*, which was the big metal rock paper at the time. In the end Geoff Barton took notice. I said to him, if you come up you will not be disappointed. I will show you something you have never seen before, I promise you. And in the end he came. And we deafened him. He was Deaf Barton after that. He couldn't believe it. And neither could I, because when we saw the results it was astonishing. He put a center page, double spread about us in *Sounds*, and he'd explained about the whacking great PA system we had. He became famous in the end, he really did.

We kept punk outside—it never existed. Nor was anybody even interested in listening to it. No one wanted to know. The cross section of the audience came from all different walks of life. They were not just working class heroes. The odd thing was that they crossed into hierarchy as well. Hell, we had a rocket scientist. We had a geologist from the oil rigs used to come and see us. We had a total cross section of humanity that expressed a love and desire, a spirit, a total lifestyle given over to rock.

It was his little piece of Heaven. That's what Geoff said. It was his little piece of Heaven. He couldn't believe it. He wrote on the front page of *Sounds*, a survivor's report from—would you believe—a heavy metal disco. That was on the front page. His exposé took in everything. I mean as time went by, within a few months the popularity of the Soundhouse was unbelievable. They came from everywhere. From across the Irish Sea, from Scotland, from Wales, lunatics from Norway, maniacs from Europe. We were totally inundated with this unbelievable surge of young rock humanity.

But it didn't stop there. In Geoff Barton I'd found a kind of a brother—a kindred spirit—and he was as passionate about it as I was. And I knew that he was going to be the man that was going to help me do what I must do. And Geoff came to me one day and said, "Look, we've had a yak down here at *Sounds*. Would you be interested in doing a chart, a heavy metal chart, for the paper every week?" And I said, "Well actually I'm thinking about doing a Soundhouse one; we collect the punter's requests each night and I'll take them home at the end of the week and shuffle them into a kind of a Top 20 or something, and when I've sorted it you can have it for print if you want." And he said, "Yeah, that's a cool idea." And it happened.

But at the same time, I was getting hundreds of cassettes from bands all over Europe. Mainly of course from the UK, but they didn't stop there. There was no outlet for young bands. Record companies weren't interested. It was punk or nothing at the time, and these rock bands, these youngsters, some were only kids. They had nowhere to go, no one to listen to, no one to support them, no one to move the product higher, no one to press it, print it, release it and get it there. And it began to get me really annoyed, because I thought this is crazy. There's something happening here, but no one's listening again.

Concerning this phrase New Wave of British Heavy Metal, I mean that's a difficult one to actually define. Al Lewis, the editor of *Sounds* at the time, is the man who invented the term, the New Wave of British Heavy Metal. He came up with it. We had so many tapes coming in from all over the place, that by then I'd also started putting on bands, too, actually. I think a young band called Heroes possibly was the first to ever play the Soundhouse. I think Pete Townsend's cousin or nephew or someone like that was in the band. We did actually establish in the end a NWOBHM circuit of these bands, right? But it was early days because we weren't really equipped to put live bands on. And the other problem for them was that my PA was five times bigger than theirs.

And it had another effect. Because we had such a superb system, my audience was used to listening to vinyl, then, because there wasn't anything else, and cassettes through an unbelievable PA. Plus I was playing a broad spectrum of music. It could be anything from Motörhead to Styx and back again through prog rock to AC/DC. The earlier stuff we included, as well, as a kind of a feed and follow on, but didn't major in, was your first generation bands, Sabbath, Purple, this sort of legacy from the legend at the end of the '60s, obviously Led Zeppelin because I mean all these major bands had their first albums out by '69. Hendrix, of course, who went very heavy. It was completely across the board.

Once they'd done the article on the Soundhouse and started printing our chart, something else happened that we weren't actually expecting. All these kids in these bands suddenly saw an outlet for their tapes. And where upon they're all fed up sending them to big corporate record companies, the only thing... the most useful thing that punk actually gave was the independent track. It said that, well you know, stuff the labels, who cares? You can do your own thing. Maybe this is an alternative route. I would listen. I did a lot of interviews back then with *Sounds*, and Geoff would phone up and say what's happening this week? And I'd say look, put it in print, ask the guys to send all their tapes in. I'll listen to them. And if I can I'll pass them on, because at the same time I was real busy trying to get the attention of the record companies. Because I realized without them no one's going anywhere.

Led Zeppelin expert Dave Lewis on his ties to the NWOBHM infrastructure:

I did a piece in *Sounds* in '78, with Geoff Barton. We did a full week, ten years of Zeppelin thing, which I was involved in, and I went up to the *Sounds* office a few times and there was this... Neal Kay was the DJ, and it was the first time I ever saw pictures of people on a dance floor playing air guitar, which would be viewed, at the time, suspiciously, but suddenly became quite acceptable. And I think there was a switch to heavy metal not being this kids' thing. It was looked down upon very much so by the likes of the enemy. If you look at the journalistic marketplace here, you had the *Melody Maker*, which were the musos, and at the time the rock music press here were very influential—hugely influential. You would read a review in the *NME* and if it was good, you would go and get it. I think *Kerrang!* had that later, in the '80s with their five K's and all that.

But you had the enemy, which had to be hip and trendy, and Zeppelin had a good relationship with them and just about held in there, but *Sounds* were definitely hooked on the metal and that's where you got this guy Neal Kay playing at this place in London, and then that spread up north and you've got rock clubs in Newcastle.

Also what you've got to consider here is rock radio, because then you've got things like Tommy Vance doing his *Friday Night Rock Show*. You gotta remember, there was only one rock show a week and that was it. So that became... if you think now, you can go on and have however many stations you want. We had two hours a week in England in the late '70s, and that definitely made people really want to be in this club. It became less of a joke, if you like. I think metal for a while had been a bit like that, and again, I think because Zeppelin had been around, they weren't really in that. They were seen as a bigger thing. It wasn't the first name that people would put a patch on their jacket. Zeppelin might go on there, but it would go on after Maiden or countless others.

So I can remember going in the office and Geoff Barton telling me... I think they did an early feature around that period, '78, '79. Definitely when Knebworth was announced he was doing it later, because on Friday nights I think they had some sort of competition to win tickets with them or whatever. It was beginning, then, to get some profile, and that transcended a bit to other areas. Certainly Birmingham, Manchester, Liverpool... again, rock up north was always a very big thing. It had a bigger following in Newcastle area and places like that. That's where some of the NWOBHM bands began. Like Saxon was from Yorkshire—it wasn't all London.

But you'd get people going to clubs and forming their own bands, and that's where you get the likes of Diamond Head. If you spoke with Geoff Barton, he's credited with that. And it was the beginnings of going to see Def Leppard in Sheffield. I've got an advert for Zeppelin at Knebworth, and on the left-hand side you've got a half-page advert for the first Def Leppard single, which was "Rocks Off," I think. It was the one they did off their own back, and suddenly you've got this new band that have got a similar type of name, they've got the permed hair, and this is where it was going to go. And these kids were only 17 or whatever. And they were always going to attract a similar audience age group.

When Led Zeppelin did Knebworth it was a fantastic thing and a lot of people came, but we're never going to know what would happen to Zeppelin in the '80s. Whether they would have held that audience or not. And they may have had a bit of trouble because of the change in musical landscape. I think maybe their audience would have grown up with them, but whether they'd attract new kids, I don't know. I think the kids would rather go see Def Leppard than old hag Led Zeppelin, which is what it may well have become.

1979. Quartz keyboardist Geoff Nicholls leaves to join Black Sabbath, as an unofficial member.

Quartz drummer Malcolm Cope on the heavy metal resurgence:
Well, we noticed it when... one of the big surprises for us was when we started touring with Sabbath, and all of a sudden the kids were coming out of the woodwork. You weren't seeing the type of kids the way they were dressed particularly on the streets, but all of a sudden you get to a gig, and it's a fantastic following as a gig. You know, we're talking about 4000, 5000 seaters. All of a sudden you're seeing all these kids that are quite young. That was a major attraction, to get into this mould of music and to see this following, this fan base—it was marvelous.

1979. Zeeb Parkes and Phil Cope form Midlands doom revivalists Witchfinder General.

Witchfinder General guitarist Phil Cope:
I was in the school band playing pop music. Me and Rod Hawkes did form a rock band called Rabies, in '77, but it never got off the ground. But basically we just used to do club things, something on the weekend, just find some equipment, learning all the time. But Witchfinder General started in 1979, broke up in 1984. It saw the rhythm section change three times, at least, but Zeeb and myself were there right from the start to finish.

1979. Neat Records is founded by David Wood of Impulse Studios.

Tygers of Pan Tang vocalist Jess Cox:

I was there when it started. I mean Dave Wood, the owner, basically wanted to start two labels and he was going to call one Neat and one Tidy. So he had Neat and Tidy, because he was Mr. novelty man. He was always looking for a stupid angle; he liked novelty records and he used to work with novelty bands and novelty records prior to starting Neat Records. I mean Neat Records was only started as just another label. He got around to starting Neat and didn't bother with starting Tidy, basically. And he had a couple pop songs on there. I mean Neat 01 and 02 were just pop acts. One was called Motorway, which is like a working man's club band who'd go around here playing cheesy songs, and another one was a girl vocalist who they signed up. Then we came along, and we were Neat 03 with "Don't Touch Me There," and then of course the NWOBHM kicked off and just went ballistic, and he just kept signing rock bands to the label.

Obviously we got signed onto MCA in 1980. I kind of disappeared, but I kept coming back to Neat for various projects. In '86 we had a Tygers albums, a compilation to put out called *First Kill*, which I was involved with Neat. And Robb Weir and I did an album… we were kind of doing an album there as a band called Tyger Tyger, which was supposed to be like the main two Tygers of the band, because we were the songwriters getting back together to do something. So I was almost kind of involved with them, but I went away and did a degree, in fact. But when I came back, after the degree I was actually doing journalism, to tell you the truth. I was a music critic for the daily paper here in Newcastle, and I went back and interviewed Dave Wood, and he asked me to stay and work with him, so I did.

We took over Neat Records; well just re-launched Neat Records. It was Neat Metal Records, and started to reissue all the albums— Raven and whatever, Blitzkrieg—and sign some other bands like Savage and Sweet Savage and whatever else. We did a thing called *The Metallic-Era* which was all the tracks Metallica covered from the NWOBHM bands, by the original artists and put that together, and that sold phenomenally well at the time, I remember. So we kind of re-launched the label and did it mainly the '90s. Through the '80s I was kind of doing my own thing because I had a solo career as well. But I did the solo career at Neat, too, so I was always involved with Neat.

1979. Rip Off Records puts out their very collectible *Belfast Rocks* compilation.

January 1979. UFO issues their well-regarded *Strangers in the Night* live album, considered one of the greatest live hard rock albums of all time. It is particularly well embraced by UK metal fans, making UFO yet another example of an old guard band suddenly benefiting from the NWOBHM. The band is also seen as "buddies" of the movement through their sociable and partying ways about London town. The guitarist who replaces Michael Schenker (who sprouts his own fine band) is Paul Chapman, from Cardiff, and a barroom raconteur on par with the likes of Phil Mogg and Pete Way.

January 1979. It is announced that Ronnie James Dio has left Rainbow. The situation allows for headline-grabbing news to come in both the Rainbow and Black Sabbath camps. The shakeups prove healthy for the profile of heavy metal in general, in that it gave headbangers something to gossip about.

January 1979. Def Leppard issue *The Def Leppard E.P.* (also knock as the *Rocks Off* EP or *Getcha Rocks Off* EP) in a run of 1000 copies. It will be reissued with a 15,000 run later in the year. It is a significant batch of songs, each squarely NWOBHM in its own way, or more accurately, addressing specific yet different characteristics of the genre.

Def Leppard vocalist Joe Elliott on press reports that they were a Thin Lizzy cover band in their formative years:

Well, we did do a gig once where we played three Lizzy song, within 50, 55 minutes of all our other stuff. We would have done something like this. We would have opened up with "Jailbreak." We would have done "Rosalie" as an encore and about halfway through the set, we would have done "Emerald." But at the same time we were also doing "Only You Can Rock Me" by UFO. We did "Hot Blooded" by Foreigner once and we also did "Pretty Vacant" and "Suffragette City."

When we first got going, we started learning covers just to give us something to do until we'd written something. For every old song that we worked out, somebody was coming in with a new one and we'd work on that, so we could play both. So we'd have "Suffragette City" or "Misty Dreamer" or something (laughs). "Emerald" was always a challenge, because once we had two guitarists, we thought, well it would be daft not to utilize the same kind of thing. And of course in 1978, even amongst the punk thing, there were bands, actually through punk, that were actually starting to get heard, almost like a more commercial version of punk. I remember it never really took off in a big way, but you had to think like, "Take on the World" by Judas Priest, with all the drums, which was nothing like Priest really were. It was a complete sell-out for them. But there were minor hits. They were going to like #18 in the singles charts with stuff like that and there was UFO just sneaking in there and Lizzy were having lots of hits. So it wasn't so alien to have the twin guitar thing.

January 15, 1979. Scorpions issue their sixth album *Lovedrive*. Arguably due to the presence of Michael Schenker on the record, but also arguably due to the era, the album represents the last of the band's purist and European sound before a step toward Americanization with *Animal Magnetism*. In this respect, it is a classic that was embraced by NWOBHM fans and musicians alike.

Scorpions guitarist Michael Schenker:
The thing with *Lovedrive*…my brother found out that I split from UFO and it was a perfect opportunity for them to ask if I would help out. Matthias Jabs had just joined and wasn't ready. I was kind of in limbo land not knowing what my next step was going to be. When I did the *Lovedrive* album, everyone was so impressed and they really persuaded me to join the band and they got rid of Matthias, basically. I did a little bit of the tour and I realized that I could not do this. I had done this, and I had been there, but there was something else that I needed to do but I couldn't figure out yet what it was.
I was invited to audition for Aerosmith and stuff like that. I kind of disappeared from the tour because I couldn't talk to them as I knew they would try to persuade me to stay. I just couldn't. Matthias freaked out and he left again and they asked me again and I said, "I can't do this, honestly, I can't do this." They said, "Please, please, please." I tried again but I just couldn't do it. I couldn't stand on stage, night after night, copying other people's lead breaks.
Eventually, in 1980, I understood what was happening. My

brother's vision was to make it all the way to the top with a band. It was his dream, but it wasn't my dream. I am a lead guitarist who needs musical freedom. Matthias eventually joined for good and they found somebody who was pulling on the same string and that was important. I always tell my brother that he would have never been able to experience what he experienced because I would not have been pulling on the same string, as I have a totally different dream than he has. It would not have really matched.

Early 1979. Money issue a full length LP called *First Investment*, on Gull, Judas Priest's early days label. Aside from this, Money are most known for their "Leo the Jester" track on the well-traveled *Metal Explosion* compilation. *First Investment* was produced by Chris Tsangarides, who also plays some keyboards on the record. "(Aren't We All) Searching" was launched from the album as a single.

Early 1979. Girlschool issue their first single, "Take it All Away"/"It Could Be Better," on City Records, after which they would switch to Bronze Records. Definitely not much NWOBHM awareness here, as the music enclosed leans both boogie and punk. Next up came support from (and for) Motörhead who collar the gals for their *Overkill* tour, followed by a leg up with Ted Nugent.

Girlschool guitarist and vocalist Kim McAuliffe:

Basically people were fed up with what was going on. At that point, me included or the band included, the fact is, we were missing heavy metal bands coming out. Obviously you had all your great ones, didn't you? You had all your greats, but there wasn't any more coming out, if you know what I mean, so we decided to do it ourselves. As for getting signed to Bronze, what happened was obviously they had Motörhead at the time. It was Lemmy, basically, that came along and saw us at rehearsal. We were literally touring around ourselves, doing everything ourselves. We got our own little single out, "Take it All Away," which, because of the punk era, everybody at that point could actually do what they wanted.

What happened was me and Enid, since we were little, we used to play at this little club, and so we stared off there and we got to know this guy at the new club and he started his own little record label with a punk band called UK Subs, who were fantastic and great mates of ours. So of course we started out with them for the first single. And then Lemmy heard about us, and then they wanted to get out with our band, support them on their very first major tour. And of course they thought, oh yeah, girls, a bit of a laugh, whatever. So he came down to see us play at rehearsal, and we were all really frightened. He looked really scary. Of course he came down and he was lovely.

February 1979. Midlands act Jameson Raid issue the "Seven Days of Splendour" EP. The band would appear as The Raid on the second *Metal for Muthas* compilation with the track "Hard Lines."

February 7, 1979. Sex Pistols bassist Sid Vicious dies of a heroin overdose. Punk, long dead, is now officially gone cold.

DJ Neal Kay on punk:

Punk, the movement inspired by the Sex Pistols and many others of their ilk, appeared in the sort of aftermath of Purple and prog rock bands and the rest of it, and to be perfectly honest with you, they became the number one hated enemy. Couldn't write, couldn't sing, couldn't play, shouldn't have been there. The stage is reserved for artists, not idiots. Terribly sorry about that, old boy, but I'm a little bit old-fashioned too. Part of the reason for that is my family have a history that goes back to music hall on my mother's side. The father was a music hall entertainer and I have stage and theater entertainers in my family, and it's always driven me to prove the truth. I only believe in real artistry and those that can't shouldn't be there.

You know the old fashioned thing in those days, both sides of the pond, if you were useless and the audience hated you they used to extend the pole from the wings with the hook on it and they used to hook you off the stage. Well I'd like to have done that with just about every punk that stuck his head up about the earth. I'm very factual about it, I've never hidden it. I hate them to this day. All they did was help to try and destroy music for me. I'd rather listen to classical music, and I do sometimes; my tastes are probably verging on the edge of boring for a lot of people, but I know music.

February 10, 1979. Harry Doherty, writing about UFO in *Melody Maker* speaks of the fans as young, shaking their heads, playing imaginary guitars and wearing denim jackets "splattered" with band patches. Nick Kent said much the same six months later describing the crowd at a Van Halen show, additionally pointing out that he also saw The Godz and Angel patches on these often sleeveless denim jackets. In NWOBHM parlance, this indicates punters' thirst for digging deep to find their hard rock fix.

February 15, 1979. Iron Maiden play The Bridgehouse, Canning Town, a show Paul Di'Anno's believes to be his first with the band. The famously punk-hating bass player and leader of Maiden now has a punk fan as his new front man.

> Iron Maiden bassist Steve Harris on getting the band's personnel straight:
>
> There was a period of time when we didn't have two guitars because we couldn't find a guitar player who fit in right at the time. We went out basically, like musically, a three-piece. So I was playing on the bass the harmony figures a lot of the time that the second guitar would have been playing, and then going back to try and hold the riffing down. So even doing it like that, you know, we knew that we needed to get back to the two guitar thing because we felt it was restricting us a little. And it felt right having two guitars.
>
> At one point we had second guitar players in and out like you wouldn't believe. God knows how many. It was really a trying time, to be honest, because it was just going back before the first album. But even with the first album, as well, people in and out. They'd join and they're in the band for like, effectively a week after rehearsing or something, do a couple of gigs or something and just, you know, girlfriend wouldn't let them come rehearse, things like that or whatever.
>
> So it was a pretty frustrating time to try and get people worked back in again. It was a very trying time. But we knew what we wanted. We knew we wanted the two guitar thing. We even had a keyboard player for a little while but that didn't work. I think it would have worked if he was a rhythm guitar player as well. Some songs, songs like "Wrathchild" or whatever, just didn't need keyboards.

March 1979. Bernie Torme issues a four-track EP, followed by another couple of singles focusing on novelty covers. Bernie, in his own quiet way, suggests somewhat of a bridge between punk and metal.

March 1979. Samson issue their second single, "Mr. Rock 'n' Roll."

March 1979. Everybody's favourite band that could have been, Trespass, play their first gig.

March 24, 1979. Motörhead issue their groundbreaking second album, *Overkill,* which reaches #24 in the UK charts. Also in March comes the first single from the album, pairing the seminal double bass-drum classic title track plus non-LP b-side "Too Late, Too Late." *Overkill* is arguably the heaviest album of all of the '70s.

Motörhead bassist and vocalist Lemmy on preferring a faster form of heavy metal than Black Sabbath: They didn't play a role in my life. I never listened to them, really. I only met Ozzy after he left them. I don't know man, a lot of people get off on being depressed. I always thought it was kind of depressing music because it was so slow. The faster ones were okay, but then you got another two dirgy ones. They were just too dirgy for me. I haven't got time to be that slow. We certainly helped a lot. I say again, Deep Purple started that, with "Speed King." That song really started all that shit. I realized that there was at least five other people that felt the same way.

April 21, 1979. The *Sounds* magazine Heavy Metal Chart puts Iron Maiden at #1 with "Prowler," with "Iron Maiden" reaching #11. A week later, Maiden play the Soundhouse for the first time.

Iron Maiden guitarist Dennis Stratton on the punk credentials of Paul Di'Anno and the band's subsequent experience of punks: I just think he was a little bit lost in some kind of fashion or whatever. When I joined the band, he was totally with Maiden and then when we did gigs, he would wear a porkpie hat or he would dance around like a bit of a mod or whatever. The band still stayed the same; there was no problem with the actual Maiden set and the Maiden outlook to the way we recorded the album. I just think Paul liked to be a bit different and I can't really answer for that. Steve Harris was always a very big leader and still is, so he wouldn't stand for that. But I remember when we took Paul to Japan in '95, he had dreadlocks put in, hair extensions. It was just an image thing, I think. But the punk scene was more messy, more—excuse me for saying—but more out of tune, more messy than anything else. It was nothing to do with the metal scene; it was different audiences.

But I used to go down the pubs to watch different punk bands. I even used to hire out a PA and do PA hire for Siouxsie and the Banshees and things like that. But the two audiences would never be at the same gig. You would never have a punk band on with a metal band, although it has happened since. In them days, you had either a soft rock band or a heavy rock band or a punk band, but they were different audiences.

May 1979. Michael Schenker tumbles out of his short-lived and always tenuous gig with Scorpions. Silver lining is that he goes on to create a pan-world honourary NWOBHM band in the capable Michael Schenker Group. Given MSG's British parts, it's slightly less NWOBHM than Gillan, but on equal status with Ozzy Osbourne and his band.

May 4, 1979. Margaret Thatcher and the Conservatives take over the governing of the UK, ousting Labour. Years of strife and confrontation ensue.

May 8, 1979. The apocryphal Camden gig featuring three metal "baby bands," which generates the lengthy review that would give birth to the term New Wave of British Heavy Metal—see entry for May 19, 1979.

Angel Witch bassist Kevin Riddles on the significance of the Camden gig on the careers of Angel Witch and Iron Maiden:

We had a really wonderful rivalry with Maiden back in those days. We used to play the same pubs, the Ruskin Arms, the Dutch House, all in London. And the Music Machine situation, it was being put together by a heavy metal DJ called Neal Kay, and we used to always play his club up in Kingsbury in London called the Soundhouse. And Maiden put out what was called *The Soundhouse Tapes*, and it was a semi sort of bootleg that they kind of did themselves. So they had some recordings done there. I'm not sure how they did it, whether it was off the desk, or whether they had brought in a mobile studio, but it was good rock 'n' roll, rough and ready, live tapes.

Anyway there was a bit of a competition between us and Maiden, and Maiden won. As it is, quite deservedly. But with Rod Smallwood being the clever man that he is, he knew at a certain point, for that one gig that we were all doing, we were going to be the headliner for Music Machine, and Maiden were going to be in the middle slot and Samson was going to be the opener. But he knew that EMI were coming down that night to see those bands and sort of make the decision who to sign for an album. And of course Maiden pulled out all the stops and it worked brilliantly for them. And I've had nothing but adoration for them ever since. And I'm not sarcastic. You know how some people are sarcastic. I'm not sarcastic — I think they did absolutely brilliantly.

But Rod had obviously got wind that this was going to happen, and he'd obviously been over to research it better than we could, had his finger on the pulse much better than we did. We were literally out on the road all the time. So we didn't have a proper manager, as such. We didn't have a management company behind us. We were too busy gigging.

So we didn't know anything about it. Should've, thinking about it. We should've felt there was something up, or else we might have gone in the middle slot. Because it's a quirk at the time of the British underground — the tube, the Metro, whatever you want to call it — but at the time, the headline band went on at about 11:15 in the evening. And the last tube left the station right outside at 11:45. So generally, people saw the first three or four numbers of the headline band and then went home. So if Maiden had been on the headline slot, then 15, 20 minutes into the set the place would've emptied — because that's exactly what happened to us.

But we knew that was going to happen. We said, well, our name's on top of the poster; that will do for us. But please, please, don't think I'm arrogant enough to think that if the boot had been on the other foot that Angel Witch would've got that deal, or that we would have anything like the success Iron Maiden had had. Steve Harris is just a phenomenon as far as I'm concerned — in a good way. The guy is one of the first ever bass players to not only front a band, but write pretty much everything and write all their big songs, and just keep it going. I think he's an absolute phenomenon.

May 19, 1979. The May 19, 1979 issue of *Sounds*, featuring Ted Nugent on the cover, includes a detailed (and not particularly glowing) review of a three NWOBHM band live bill—Angel Witch, Iron Maiden, Samson—by Geoff Barton, called Deaf Barton. Editor of the newspaper, Alan Lewis (and soul and Motown fan, evidently) adds a few words of intro sub-title that includes the saying New Wave of British Heavy Metal for the first time. The full range of headline text reads:
"If You Want Blood (and flashbombs and dry ice and confetti) You've Got It
The New Wave of British Heavy Metal: First in An Occasional Series By Deaf Barton
The Page for Idiots Who Play Cardboard Guitars"
The cover also includes a banner at the top that says "HEAVY METAL …THE NEW BRITISH BANDS". Interestingly, the text for the Ted Nugent cover story reads: "YEEEAAARGH!" which is a bit like "Kerrang!"
Additional to this issue is an ad for a Judas Priest and Marseille gig (and then later a Marseille ad). Thin Lizzy's *Black Rose*, at #5 on the Top 75 Albums chart, is the lone heavy record until we see a Deep Purple compilation

way down at #47. Also in this issue, there's a Rock 'n' Roll chart and lots of post-punk and a fair bit of reggae coverage. There's the big Ted Nugent article but no heavy metal albums or even singles reviewed. There are a few concert ads in the back for the likes of Iron Maiden and Samson, plus something called the Heavy Metal Crusade with Samson and Angel Wytch (sic). There's also, however, a Heavy Metal Chart which reads in full:

1) AC/DC – "Let There Be Rock," 2) Led Zeppelin – "Whole Lotta Love," 3) UFO – "Rock Bottom," 4) Dire Straits – "Sultans of Swing," 5) Free – "Alright Now," 6) Deep Purple – "Smoke on the Water," 7) Rush – "Xanadu," 8) Rainbow – "Stargazer," 9) Pink Floyd - "Money," 10) Status Quo – "4500 Times," 11), Black Sabbath – "Paranoid," 12) Supertramp – "The Logical Song," 13) Ted Nugent – "Cat Scratch Fever," 14) Bad Company – "Good Lovin' Gone Bad," 15) Yes – "Yours Is No Disgrace," 16) Deep Purple – "Fireball," 17) Meat Loaf – "Bat Out of Hell," 18) Def Leppard – "Getcha Rocks Off," 19) Scorpions – "Another Piece of Meat," 20) Motörhead – "Overkill."

The chart is "compiled from record requests at the Penthouse HM Disco, Dixon Lane, Sheffield 1." the list of bands and their songs seems to be a reflection of the "good music" Neal Kay would enjoy personally and promote, namely old school hard rock and prog rock. Note the scant two actual NWOBHM tracks way down at #18 and #20.

DJ Neal Kay on the fateful Music Machine gig that gives rise to the term "New Wave of British Heavy Metal:"

I was invited by the manager of the Music Machine. It was the old BBC TV theater in Camden. It held about 1500 people, which was a fair size for London then. It had two or three step-up platforms at the back, levels, floors. It had a whacking great stage bar. The stage was real high, and it was a big stage. And Mick phoned me up and said look, I've been reading all about you and what you've been doing, and your fans and followers and all this.

By then the Soundhouse was getting people coming in from all over the place. South London, North London, hell, they were flying in for weekends, and the locals were putting them up. It was just unbelievable. And Mick said, "Look, how would you like to put on your own like three-band show during the week and compare it?" And I thought yeah, what a shot. It's going to enable me to present to the industry in London new bands, and they don't have to come out to Kingsbury to the 'wagon. Because back then the business was notorious for not wanting to go anywhere. Hell, you had to do the damn thing on their desktop, if you could have got it there. They didn't even like leaving their own office, you know? Go to Wembley? You must be joking! It's like darkest Africa back then. Back then they didn't want to do it.

But I thought the Music Machine was a great expansion. It was a big place and it didn't bother me that much—it gave a stage to the bands. I put myself in the auditorium and on the floor somewhere, out of the light, just my discotheque console and me and my microphone to compare the evening, and I arranged and did everything, really, I suppose. Did the lot.

But if it was that particular night you're talking about, I suppose it could have been a mixture. If Iron Maiden played that night, it could have been Samson, it could have been Praying Mantis, it could have been Toad the Wet Sprocket, it could have been Angel Witch; I don't know because I don't remember, other than saying that if Maiden were there, then that was the night that they were obviously seen.

You see, I still found myself very much on my own back then. Things were kind of getting out of hand in so many ways. I found myself having to drive all this on my own. The 'wagon, the Music Machine, the organizing of all this stuff and the staging of stuff, and it was like there was no one to help me do anything. There wasn't. I did all the business myself. I got into the Soundhouse in the early afternoons, I got on the phones, I went to the record companies, I did the whole lot. Because if you don't... if there's no one else, you must do it. And you find out your mistakes and you do it properly, and then you do it professionally, and then you do it so that people respect you for doing it. And that's the only way to be, and if you're going to upset someone you may as well upset someone, but get on with it.

By then, it was always an unofficial thing. I don't think they'd ever have liked to have thought of themselves as a movement, but what I would have called it was a brotherhood. I would have called it a band of brothers if I can use that overblown phrase, because that, to me, is what it became. I actually called the members of Soundhouse the Soundhouse Nation. That's what they were to me, and that was in print all over the place. They weren't just punters, they weren't just people, they were the Soundhouse Nation, and for me, they were the finest club audience in rock on earth. Because they could move mountains, and they did.

Iron Maiden bassist Steve Harris on Neal Kay and the importance of The Music Machine:
Well he was obviously very sort of evangelistic about the whole thing; he totally believed in it. And you know it was great. He was great to us, which is why we liked to repay him, later on, when we were doing headline tours and stuff—we took him out as a DJ, as a thank you. Because he really did help us. But he helped us because he liked our music. He wouldn't have helped us for no reason. But he really loved the demos and it just went from there. We did like two or three at the Music Machine, so not sure which one you mean. But they were all really quite key. Because it was like a real gathering of the hardcore fans. The Music Machine became this kind of thing, every now and again, and you know, Motörhead played there all the time as well. So all of them were really good.

Diamond Head guitarist Brian Tatler:
Apparently the title, the term, was coined by Alan Lewis, but I think it was Geoff Barton who was the reporter actually going out to watch the bands and do the reviews. And there was a big piece with Iron Maiden, Angel Witch and Samson, possibly. And then there was also then a big spread on Def Leppard, who got front-page and about three or four pages inside, where Geoff Barton had gone to see Def Leppard in a working men's club in Sheffield. So to me, reading that, all I was doing with Diamond Head was playing little pubs around Stourbridge in the Midlands, and we thought, "Oh, Geoff Barton has gone to see Def Leppard; maybe he'll come to see Diamond Head." So we did a little four-track cassette and sent it off to *Sounds*, and it appeared in Geoff Barton's playlist. You know, Diamond Head demo, and that was such a result, that you could do that, send it off and there it was—Geoff Barton liked it. Awesome (laughs).

Journalist John Tucker on when the NWOBHM starts:
    It's always dated from the byline that Alan Lewis put to Geoff Barton's feature in May 1979. And the bands that were featured on that bill that he reviewed that night were Angel Witch, Samson and

Iron Maiden. Angel Witch had been noodling around London for some time as a four-piece. Samson, as you know, a lot more bluesy in their early incarnations. Maiden had always been pretty much straight down the line. So these bands had been playing from about '76, inspired by the old guard and taking a nod from the likes of Priest who, yeah, maybe were the bridge between old, new and punk, and looking to break out and do something new.

But I think the one that everybody claims to be at was this one in Camden, in terms of stand-out gigs in the early days. As I say, you've got Samson, Iron Maiden, and Angel Witch. These are all London-based bands, and you've got this thing about territory. It's hard to break out of territory; they're all known in London, which is your big market.

Three band bill, coupled together, and *Sounds* is asked to review it, so Geoff Barton goes down and sees these three bands. And all of a sudden you've got something quite, quite different. Samson is still fairly bluesy at this stage, but you've got Angel Witch who... they're rough. At the end of the day, Angel Witch were never very polished. They make a hell of a racket and they do it very well.

Then you've got Maiden, who must have been the first band to marry a metal band with a bit of an early punk singer. I saw Iron Maiden before I heard Iron Maiden. I saw them at a local gig, and I could not believe it when the vocalist walked in wearing a pork pie hat, and had his hair cut really short, and the rest of them looked like what you'd expect a metal band to look like. Very odd. So that was a bit different. This was the one that was reviewed, this was the one that was given the byline of New Wave of British Heavy Metal and this is the one that everyone wishes they were there.

I think it's the 8th of May, 1979; that was one I'd like to have gone to. I'm sure like most of these things, it wasn't particularly brilliant or particularly different—it was just three bands doing their thing. But it was the combination and the culmination of a lot of people's hard work, and on the night someone saw it, and someone reviewed it, and face it, things were never quite the same again.

May 21, 1979. Saxon issue their self-titled debut, on Carrere Records; it sells about 15,000 copies in the UK. *"Stallions of the Highway," "Backs to the Wall"* and *"Militia Guard"* are indeed fully formed NWOBHM proposals, as is the warmongering cover art.

Saxon guitarist Paul Quinn:
For us, it was just we were not pretending to be working class. We still are, in a way. We're still working in that it was kind of us against the world; it felt like that. It got marginally easier as we got more

famous. We got signed in '78, but we didn't release until '79. The idea that we were harbingers of the metal scene was right for Britain because we were basically the first of that new wave to make any success. We did a tour after we changed our name from Son of a Bitch and played basically the same set with a few new songs that would end up on the first album, and with a new backdrop, which was the first album warrior instead of the Hulk, the Incredible Hulk coming through the backdrop on the Son of a Bitch one.

The warrior... oddly enough, we got that from Frazetta, his style. We had English artists who could do a nice job and they were the ones that came up with the logo as well. Frazetta had a book out of what he'd done with all his bands actually (laughs.) He had a really good compendium, omnibus book. Oddly enough, the fact that Britain was overrun... it was kind of an aggressive name, as long as it's not the Anglo-Saxon detrimental meaning. But fans were just manic. There was a working men's club concert secretary—the guy that booked us in the first place, in Wales—trying to hold this audience back. Y'know, half-heartedly 'cause how can one man hold back an audience from a stage? It was extremely funny and great times.

Saxon vocalist Biff Byford:
    The two bands that joined together were myself and Paul. I played bass at the time, and sang. And we were more into prog rock, actually. We were more, I wouldn't say jazz but it was in the more musical end of prog rock, more melodic passages and highly melodic choruses. And the other band were a bit like Free; just a riff going around and around endlessly. So when we joined together, those two styles sort of clashed in a great way, really, and that created our sound. And thrown in that mix was obviously the other influences we had.

    I think we got the sense of the end of an era, but yeah, we would go see the big bands. We were massive Sabbath fans and Purple fans; Uriah Heep, Thin Lizzy, Black Oak Arkansas, Wishbone Ash... I could go on forever. These bands were influences in our early songwriting. I think those bands were still big and they were still household names, but I just think that the members were moving onto different things, so in that sense it was the end of that era.

    On the first record, though, we could have gone one way or the other. If you listen to the first album, *Saxon*, it's very mixed. There are some very heavy metal tracks on there and some very melodic tracks. But the producer was into doing all the backing vocals and things, so he did a big backing vocals job on all the ballads and stuff, and we sort of had our full reign on the heavy metal stuff. But probably the choice of producer wasn't great and so that first album was a very mixed bag. It wasn't until *Wheels of Steel* that we actually got our act together.

Saxon guitarist Graham Oliver:

When we did the debut album, it was pretty much directed by a guy named John Verity from Argent; he was instrumental in getting us our album deal. And the people who signed us up... Norman Sheffield and Dave Thomas and Trident were the organization that had Queen at the time. And John didn't really have the vision. Great, talented guy, but he's very much like an early Mutt Lange, all glam and that kind of thing. A really good engineer and good producer, and a good singer in his own right. But we were like angry young men, and the tracks calmed us down on that. Things like "Big Teaser" were influenced by the Heavy Metal Kids, Gary Holton. That's why it's twangy like that, big Cockney-type. I think there's some good moments on there, because when we did those songs live, they were a lot more in-your-face. "Militia Guard" is fantastic; Paul Quinn did a fantastic guitar solo on it. Very much, I believe, in advance of the time.

Journalist John Tucker:
Saxon are very different from Motörhead in their approach. Theoretically, Saxon would be, I suppose, a rock band. They'd been doing this for a long time. By the time their first album came out, they're 30; they're not young. But the thing about Saxon, amongst other bands, was they embraced heavy metal, and they not only went along with it, but they promoted it and pushed it, and they had no problem being a heavy metal band when so many other bands hated the term and didn't want to be a part of it.

June 1979. Saxon issue as a single from their debut, "Big Teaser," backed with a convincing NWOBHM rocker called "Stallions of the Highway." There's also a version that pairs the a-side with the down-wound rote NWOBHM balladry of "Rainbow Theme"/"Frozen Rainbow," as part of a singles series.

Saxon vocalist Biff Byford on signing with Carrere:
Our early years were totally by accident, by lucky accidents. Because one of our first demo tapes ended up at EMI. The guy left EMI and went to work for a French company and took the tape with him. So the deal we were offered was from that company, who were an independent company. But we could have easily signed to EMI, and maybe Iron Maiden wouldn't have been signed to EMI. But that's how history goes, isn't it? But Carrere had their own office, a big office in Mayfair, actually. It was really un-rock 'n' roll. But yeah, they had a whole place, full-on. And don't forget we were distributed through Warner Bros., which were absolutely massively powerful in the '70s and '80s. They had Van Halen and all those bands, and they certainly knew the market.

June 1979. Samson issue their debut album, *Survivors*, sometimes cited as the first NWOBHM album (especially for discounters of Motörhead as a NWOBHM act), although the band's sound is still tentative and unfocussed. Of course, Saxon's self-titled debut must qualify as well.

Samson bassist John McCoy:
The first album completely, I wrote the songs with Paul. I played bass on the album as well, and produced it. The second album I only wrote a couple things and played on a couple of tracks because by that time Paul had taken in Chris Aylmer on bass, and I was working with Gillan, so I wasn't able to continue with the Samson project. To be honest I don't think Paul was really that aware of it until after the event, that he was a part of the NWOBHM. We were just playing in a band. We weren't really thinking hey, we're doing something special here. We were just playing what we played. We had musical references going back to the '60s, to things like Chuck Berry and Bo Diddley, to not so obvious things like the Pretty Things or the Incredible String Band. We shared influences, and I don't think Paul ever saw himself as some sort of standard-bearer for a movement. Maybe he should have jumped a bit more on that bandwagon. Oops, Neal Kay again.

June 7, 1979. Def Leppard record a session for BBC Radio 1, which airs just after Geoff Barton's piece on them for *Sounds*.

June 16, 1979. Geoff Barton, having only recently seen Def Leppard, writes a positive feature on them for *Sounds*.

June 19, 1979. Blue Öyster Cult issue *Mirrors*, which is considered to be another poppy album on the pile of records from previously heavy bands that now disappointed.

Blue Öyster Cult drummer Al Bouchard:
When we were making the record, I hated it. I really didn't like it. I thought this was going over the top in terms of trying to make a commercial record. I thought it was very sterile, I thought that his technique and his recording of the album was the kind of thing that you would do with a band that didn't know what they were doing. Where a band wasn't so good.

You know, his Twisted Sister album was brilliant, absolutely brilliant, but I think with Blue Öyster Cult, we were such a tight unit, I felt like he made a very sterile record with us. And one of the things was he wanted just the bass and drums to play together, no other instruments, and of course I didn't play to click tracks for years, so that wasn't a big deal, but he didn't want us distracted. It's hard enough to do a song without the vocal, much less without any other instrument other than my brother playing the bass. So I rejected that.

I think most of us in the band were not happy with the result. I am told that people had changed at the record company, and there was different management, and all of a sudden it was time for us to have another hit, Godammit! And, "Tom, make it a hit! You did it before, and you did it with Nugent!" So that's what happened.

Raven bassist and vocalist John Gallagher:
A friend of my brother said, "You're going to the city hall?" I said, "Who's playing?" "Blue Öyster Cult? Oh, who the hell are they?" "Oh, they're American, they're great, you'll love them, come on down." We went and saw them and I was blown away. And wow, they're sliding their guitars against each other just like we'd been doing for four years (laughs). And they had the full show; it was the *Tyranny and Mutation* album, so they were a great band. We used to do one or two of their songs back in the late '70s.

June 30, 1979. Motörhead issue "No Class," backed by the non-LP "Like a Nightmare." Offering non-LP b-sides and even non-LP a-sides is soon to be a regular occurrence, and one that breeds excitement with the punters.

July 7, 1979 – August 31, 1979. Motörhead work on *Bomber*, at Roundhouse and Olympic studios.

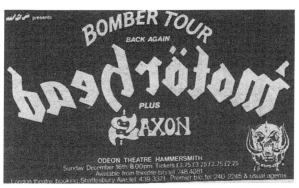

Motörhead drummer Phil Taylor on what made Motörhead metal:
I think it was the fourth bar, second crotchet of the second... I don't... it was the music! I really don't know. It wasn't us that gave it that name. It was the media that comes up with these names. I mean Lemmy came up with the name Motörhead, and that was the name of the band, and the title that one is given, or the pigeonhole that you're put into, that has always been created by the media. So it was a heavy metal band we were, and a heavy metal band we remained. And then of course it became just metal, and then after all, who thought of names like thrash metal, death metal, wooden metal, trouser metal, tripod metal, door metal—I've got a good idea that it was probably the press. So I refuse to answer that question on the grounds that I'm a drummer.

July 28, 1979. Sledgehammer issue their debut single "Sledgehammer"/"Feel Good." The track will be featured on the first *Metal for Muthas* compilation, in a revised version.

> Sledgehammer producer John McCoy on the band's influences: Oh wow. Lots of drink, lots of drug, lots of volume. They were good guys, but Mike Cook was a strange guy. He had a specific idea of what he wanted to do and he didn't really take anybody else's opinion at all. He wanted to do what he wanted to do. I really don't remember that much about it, which probably said something about the state I was in at the time.

August 1979. An early five-piece version of Venom now includes both guitarist Jeffrey Dunn (Mantas) and drummer Tony Bray (Abaddon).

> Venom drummer Abaddon:
> We all grew up influenced by the same bands: Judas Priest, Kiss, Deep Purple, Motörhead, these types of bands, even Black Sabbath, but we didn't think they were extreme enough, and we thought there was room for a band that… we didn't particularly set out to be more extreme, it's just that's the way we were. Guys in the North of England at that time, it's a very industrial area and guys tended to be kind of street rats. And when you got in a band, you were either playing punk or you were playing heavy metal. Or you're playing variations of both.
> We were still influenced quite a lot by the punk movement. It was a very London thing but we were very aware of it. And the punk thing was about not necessarily being great musicians, but being kind of fantastic band members and really putting across a message and really being pretty extreme. And we liked that and we thought it was a good crossover between the more extreme heavy metal bands—which were still kind of staid—and the more extreme punk bands. And we fit it in there really easily. And because of the way we were and the way we'd grown up, there was no hardship. It was really easy to be an extreme band right from the first rehearsal.

August 1, 1979. Rainbow issues *Down to Earth*, which is quite a heavy, NWOBHM-ish album, and quite well regarded at the time. Replacing American Ronnie James Dio as lead singer is Graham Bonnet, a Brit, and on keyboards, replacing Canadian David Stone is Don Airey, a Brit, making the band completely British for the first time. The album scores two hit singles in the UK, the band play *Top of the Pops*, and Rainbow headlines Donington.

Saxon vocalist Biff Byford, on supporting old guard bands like Rainbow, Nazareth and Slade:

Well we had all our own fans by then. It was like two lots of fans. Ours were young; not all young, really, but you could definitely tell the difference. There was definitely badges on jackets with our audience. And don't forget, we were probably a cult band, a band that people were discovering—a generation change, really.

August 3, 1979. AC/DC issue *Highway to Hell*. The album finds the band blowing up, with AC/DC becoming increasingly an inspiration to NWOBHMers.

AC/DC guitarist Malcolm Young:

I think *Highway to Hell* was the easiest for us to make. We sort of knocked that up in about three weeks, that album. At that time, we were just about to be dropped by the label. So they said, you can't have these rock 'n' roll producers in there. You've got to get a more commercial-type producer. So we worked with this guy for maybe two weeks and it was going nowhere. He was trying to turn us into a disco outfit. This was the old label trying to get a big hit, and it was all disco at the time.

After a couple weeks we just pulled the plug on him. We just said, "Look, we're taking tomorrow off" and we went in and in one day... because anything we wanted, we thought it was the right stuff and he was like, "No, no, no, this... go back to the disco" crap. So anyway, we got rid of him. We just told him to take the day off and we went in and knocked out nine tracks in a day, put it together with the stuff, just banged it up. And then we found Mutt Lange, and sent him the material and he said, "Well, we can do this pretty quick." So we finished that album in four weeks. And that was the best, the fastest we've done an album. Except for the early days—the very first album took four or five days.

AC/DC manager David Krebs on signing the band:

I hired Peter Mensch to go out as Aerosmith's road manager, or tour accountant, rather. Tour accountant—that was always a training ground. If you went around the world as a tour accountant, you sure understood what was going on. In order to sign AC/DC, who we toured without representing them, even though I saw AC/DC in '77 in London, from the first moment, I tried to co-manage them. I tried to make a deal, but I was just so in awe of how good they were. Because I really believed in this hard rock thing. I really thought it was a good form of entertainment for kids.

But in order to sign AC/DC—they lived in England at the time, and we were the first Americans, to my knowledge, to open an office in London—we had to agree to having a maximum of four acts. We sent Peter Mensch over there, and Cliff Burnstein came to work in our New York office. And I think the first label we had, which Cliff ran, was called Word of Mouth Records, which I always thought was the most important ingredient in the game.

But AC/DC, I think they did much more touring in Europe than they did here. They were on Atlantic Records, but I think at that time when we signed them, maybe they hit 25,000 sales here. They were much bigger there, because when I saw them in London in '77, they were headlining a sold-out theater, I think 2000. Did you ever see AC/DC with Bon Scott? If not, you missed something special. Not that Brian Johnson isn't great, but Bon Scott had something extra.

Journalist Garry Bushell:

We'd also claimed that AC/DC were half British anyway because two of them were born in Scotland, so we're having them (laughs.) Very much an English mentality, AC/DC. And not only that, hugely influential to bands we revered, especially Rose Tattoo, who managed to cross over into hard rock and obviously played to an audience of skinheads, punks and rockers. They were definitely one of the important bands in the early '80s for that mixing of the scenes.

Saxon vocalist Biff Byford on why AC/DC is an honourary NWOBHM band:

Because the family emigrated, didn't they? They emigrated from Scotland, I think, AC/DC? The Young family? So I thought they were first generation Australians, or maybe they were born in England. I don't know, really. I think maybe they were born in England and then emigrated to Australia when they were young. That's the only claim that people would have, I suppose. I don't know about the drummer. I don't know what generation he was Australian. It might not be of British heritage. But I think one of the claims is that obviously the Young brothers were English. I think it's a bit daft.

Plus England was one of their biggest major markets in the early days. They had a massive following here. I went to see them a few times on the *Highway to Hell* tour because we had the same promoter. But yeah, a bit like Airbourne, really, now—they have a good following in England. I think AC/DC broke in England first.

Raven bassist and vocalist John Gallagher on whether the UK adopted AC/DC as their own:

Definitely. I was very lucky, I got to see them four times with Bon. I've never actually seen them with Brian and Brian's from my hometown. But yeah, we did see them, and at the time I was very into a lot of progressive stuff. My brother would be playing AC/DC— "Oh what's this? This is so simple; what is this?" Went and saw them, it was '77, *Let There Be Rock* tour. And when you experienced it live, you're like, now I get it. It doesn't need to be anything else than what it is. It's just like getting hit over the head with a sledgehammer.

As for England loving AC/DC, it's one of those things where... especially the further north you get, in England, they're getting more passionate, I think, about their music. Not to knock the south, but definitely if they love you, they're going to love you for good. And it just grew every time you'd go to see them—it got crazier and crazier.

Plus they toured non-stop in the UK, and I guess the generation of bands before them, like say the Zeppelins and whatnot, they either had their own difficulties or they weren't touring. I mean, Zeppelin did Earls Court in '75, and then I think the next gigs they played were the two gigs at Knebworth. I mean they were the biggest band in the world, but they were too big to play England. You had an opening for a lot of other bands to say, "Hey, we're good as well."

Tygers of Pan Tang vocalist Jess Cox on who was hot and who was not:

Well, yeah. I remember *Highway to Hell* was just like wow. We were kids, the early Tygers, and *Highway to Hell* was like Jesus. It was phenomenal. And the first Van Halen album was going on before we kicked off in '79 or '80. Great albums. And they still kind of kept going. I mean Whitesnake was still doing really well, Lizzy was massive. So these bands… a lot of them didn't really take a back seat, and none of them really got that hurt by it. A lot of the American bands fell away in Europe, like Foreigner and Journey, although they were a pretty big deal in '82 and '83 and stuff like that. Into the middle of the '80s they kind of died away, but the English bands still stayed really popular, but… well they split up, I guess, most of them.

I think we just added into the pot. The NWOBHM bands just got added in, but I think probably more for the younger kids than the older guys. I mean I remember being affronted by punk, initially. Because I was into these whatever you want to call them, dinosaur bands. I mean Led Zeppelin and Sabbath and all them—my whole world ended. I remember being absolutely gutted at the time and annoyed and furious at punks. I thought absolutely awful.

But then as I got into it I started listening to The Clash and I started to get it a bit. I mean there was a lot of rubbish. The punk movement was some really quite horrific garbage, but some of the bands were just… they just all switched some lights on in people's heads, I think, and you can be a bit more free thinking. So hold on, there's a world out there. And some of the metal bands picked that torch up a bit and we weren't just singing about shagging and God knows what. Some more thought went into the songs, lyrically, and so it wasn't as banal as some of the early rock bands.

August 5, 1979. Def Leppard sign with Phonogram, less known as a NWOBHM-friendly company than, say, MCA or EMI.

Phonogram executive David Bates on signing Def Leppard:
It was probably two things. It was a local reporter at the *Sheffield Star* called Keith Strong, and he picked up on them, and he told me about them, and there was a DJ, a rock DJ, who also had been playing their independent released stuff, and he told me about them. So that's how that came about. And then I went to see them, at the Porterhouse in Redford, which was a tiny little gig, and yeah, that was it. And then the next day I went up to Middlesbrough, at The Rocket and saw them play there as well.

I had grown up with Led Zeppelin, Cream and that kind of stuff, and when I started working as an A&R scout at Phonogram, punk and new wave—well, punk at that new point—had just kicked in. And that was quite a lot of gigs I used to see. Not all of them, because I also saw quite a few other styles of music as well. But it was going against the grain at that point. To be seeing a band like Def Leppard, and to sign them was definitely going against the grain, because the press was not really about that at the time. I mean, *Sounds*, yeah, they were into both camps, punk and rock. But the *NME* was against it, and *Melody Maker* was moving against it, so it was definitely going against the grain.

Def Leppard were clearly into Led Zeppelin, Judas Priest, bands like that I think, rock bands. But deeply, they were into Sweet, which was a glam pop rock band, and I think they liked Bolan and Bowie. They were into quite a lot of stuff, but yeah, they had the rock thing which they liked, but equally, they were just as big on Sweet as they were on anything else.

Diamond Head guitarist Brian Tatler:
I'd been listening to, and reading about it every week, and I do remember it being announced, that Def Leppard had been signed by Phonogram, and again, that gave me a bit of a kick, thinking, "Wow, Def Leppard's been signed. We've got to get on with this, got to get signed, get a record deal, got to do more gigs, do more songs." But once one band was signed, it just seemed that that was the way forward. And then Girlschool got a record deal and Iron Maiden signed to EMI, Angel Witch signed to Bronze, and so we didn't really want to sign to a little label. There was Neat Records and there was Heavy Metal Records, things like that, but I obviously thought, if you want to be Led Zeppelin or something, you want to sign to a big label, a major. And so we had our sights set on the top, if possible. Just wait for a large label to sign us.

August 15, 1979. Led Zeppelin issue what will be their last album, *In Through the Out Door*. It is by far their most lightweight and light-hearted album, featuring quite a bit of keyboards. A corrective swing toward the guitar is quietly called for, and the NWOBHM bands will answer that call.

Tygers of Pan Tang vocalist Jess Cox on the idea of out with the old, in with the new:
The whole idea was that your younger brother didn't want to listen to his older brother's records. He wanted his own scene, and something new coming along when you're young. That's what you're like—that's mine, that's my music. You latch onto that. They're all your age, they dress like you, they think like you, and they

captured a whole generation, basically. The NWOBHM didn't want or didn't care about UFO or whoever it might be. They saw this as their music and I think that's what carried on.

Because it was the real flavour of the month for a while; the NWOBHM was the sort of main music within the charts. You still had your sort of really horrible chart things as well, obviously, but Iron Maiden was on *Top of the Pops* and there was Def Leppard and Saxon, and you could see these bands, high profile, and it was throughout the papers, then, which was *Sounds* really.

Remember, there was no internet. There was none of this technology that there is today, and sites where you can just find out about any band. It was literally people writing to each other or ringing each other up or reading… our newspaper. That's how you found out about music. But it caught a generation of kids, basically. Some of the older bands, of course, were still going. I mean, God, AC/DC, *Back in Black*, 1980—that was right in the middle of the NWOBHM and that album still stands out today as a phenomenal rock album.

Led Zeppelin expert Dave Lewis on the changing of the guard:

I think what people wanted, what the kids wanted of that age group, they wanted to grow up with something that was theirs, and Led Zeppelin hadn't been, really, because they'd been around ten years, along with Sabbath and Deep Purple. But suddenly the likes of Def Leppard and Diamond Head were speaking to these guys because they were their peers. They were the same age group, and they were easily accessible as well. Let's face it, they weren't playing 200,000 at Knebworth; they were down the local town hall or wherever. And I think that gave it a good feel, no doubt about it.

And Zeppelin had gone. It's interesting how quickly Zeppelin in the early '80s got forgotten. They really did. They only came back later in the mid-'80s when bands like The Mission and The Cult were beginning to cite them. Led Zeppelin became unfashionable almost by default because of this new movement, there was a lot going on in it, and this new heavy metal was being embraced by a new audience that hadn't grown up on Zeppelin.

So Zeppelin wasn't, certainly, the iconic feel that it is now. It was to change, and again it was to last much longer than we all felt. But there was a period where those bands were mildly unfashionable, and the reason was there were other bands filling that void. Not to say they were going to last, and many of them didn't, and not to say they were as good as what Black Sabbath or Led Zeppelin were doing, but the good stuff lasted and that movement took it further and then it took it into speed metal and thrash and everything we know today. All the different factions of metal that became very clear and sort of defined.

So I think there's a turning point after Zeppelin in the '80, '81, '82 period, where you are getting kids suddenly identifying something that was theirs, and I don't think that age group felt Led Zeppelin was theirs. It was mine, but they needed something, and those bands came along and filled that void. Particularly, as I said, now that Zeppelin had split, Purple were no more, Sabbath was off the rails, all the iconic acts were doing something else or were gone. So there was something screaming out for loud rock music played in the right way to be seen and heard by a whole new movement, and that new movement certainly gave the kids what they wanted.

August 17, 1979. The release into theatres of *Monty Python's Life of Brian*, a major cultural touchstone for UK youth and young males in general.

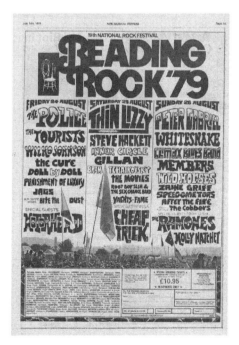

August 24 – 26, 1979. The last *Reading Rock* festival before it goes predominantly heavy metal the following year. One of the reasons cited for its turn toward metal was the confrontations between new wave and metal fans at the 1979 fest. *Reading* 1979 included, at the heavier end, Motörhead, Thin Lizzy, Gillan, Whitesnake, Wild Horses and Molly Hatchet.

September 1979. Steve Zodiac and his Quo-alikes Vardis—actually originally called Quo Vardis—issue their debut single, "100 M.P.H."

September 1979. Sammy Hagar issues his considerably bright and somewhat heavy *Street Machine* album. With very little heavy rock being produced out of the US, Hagar becomes a favourite of NWOBHM fans and musicians, aided by the prolific ad campaigns for his records courtesy of Capitol, and aided by the goodly reputation of Hagar's two records with Montrose in 1973 and 1974.

Raven bassist and vocalist John Gallagher:
Oh, absolutely. I mean, Montrose are huge in Newcastle. We all loved them. There was some music magazine had a flexi disc, I remember, and they had snippets of four or five songs, like who the hell are these guys? They're incredible. And when Sammy Hagar finally came over,

he used to do wonderful. Those songs were staples of the heavy metal discos. Like "Bad Motor Scooter," "Space Station #5." And that used to be our finishing number when we played the clubs for years. Until we finally turned around and recorded it.

September 1979. Polygram reissue Def Leppard's "Ride into the Sun," originally a three-tracker (*The Def Leppard E.P.*, also known as the *Getcha Rocks Off* EP or *Rocks Off* EP). The band had issued it earlier in the year themselves in a 1000 copy run; Polygram printed up 15,000 copies. Also in September, the band enter the studio to record four new tracks.

September 20, 1979. The UK Subs issue their debut, *Another Kind of Blues*. It is produced by Gillan's John McCoy. The album, arguably, represents the influence of all of this UK heavy metal upon punk. For quite a spell, punk becomes post-punk and loses its focus on guitar, oddly crowding around prominent bass lines. But the UK Subs are one of a few new acts that bring back the guitar, take a bit from metal, and begin to forge something soon called hardcore as well as Oi!.

September 30, 1979. A memorable early NWOBHM battle royale at the Music Machine, Camden Town finds Sledgehammer and Iron Maiden backing up "Iron Fist & the Hordes from Hell," a.k.a. Motörhead.

October 1979. Judas Priest issue their classic *Unleashed in the East* live album, which sports an album cover that further solidifies and underscores this idea of a heavy metal uniform and look, specifically based around leather and studs. Biker imagery, a soon to be recurring NWOBHM theme, is also emphasized here.

Judas Priest guitarist Glenn Tipton on the band's evolving heavy metal look:

We actually never sat down and said okay, we're going to become a leather and studs band. And we never have actually sat down and said, you know, how are we going to portray ourselves? Even choreography onstage, the way we move, we never really worked... we sometimes have to be careful that we're not in a certain place when explosions go off on stage, but other than that, we just fall into the routines on certain songs, where we're going to be. If me and Ken are playing leads together, we actually just fall into that. We never sat down and worked it out.

And we never did, with our image, really. If you go back to the early days, you'll see our image was different, obviously. But 'round about *British Steel*, we decided to slide into the leather and studs, with tracks like "Hell Bent for Leather," and again, we never say okay, you wear this, I'll wear that. Everybody wore what they felt comfortable in, to the point where, I mean, if you ask me now, "Okay, do you feel comfortable in leather and studs when you go out on stage?" The answer would be, "I couldn't wear anything else."

Judas Priest tears off the cloth and puts on the leather.

That's what we've become. We've become an entity, as Priest, and the leather and studs is part of it. It's all about that energy on stage, the excitement, the visual excitement, the show, how comfortable we feel, and it's something that we've all fallen into. I mean, Rob has five or six costume changes or more, but they're always appropriate for the song you sing and the way he wants to portray himself. But it's very metal, it's very leather, it's very studs, and it's something we fell into over the years.

Judas Priest vocalist Rob Halford, on identifying with heavy metal, a key element of the NWOBHM:

I think that again just from the experience of *Sad Wings of Destiny*, we basically said to each other, well this is it, isn't it? We are without a doubt, this is Judas Priest, we are very proud to be known as Judas Priest, this heavy metal band, *the* heavy metal band. So it's true, I think, that right from the beginning we were just sending the message out in the press especially, this is who we are and this is the music that we want to be known to represent heavy metal music.

Again, in terms of press and media, there was a push-back right from the start. Immediately people were going, heavy metal? What is this? This is like whatever, you know, if that's what you want to call yourself. K.K has got this wonderful scrapbook with clipping from a British music paper. I think they talk about *Sad Wings of Destiny*. It was something to the effect of, well if this is heavy metal, guys, keep your day jobs because you ain't going anywhere.

You know, that's the kind of push-back that you were dealing with. So when you do that to Priest, you do that to most bands, you go, what the hell are you talking about? You know, don't talk about us like that. Don't push us under the carpet. We are who we are. We believe in ourselves. We are strong about what we feel we want to do, and we already got this great fan base of support that is extremely important for any band obviously from day one, if you can get that type of topical connection. So there were already Priest fans going hey, this is my band. They are a metal band, don't talk about them like that, you know. So yeah, right from the very beginning that's all we wanted to be known as in Judas Priest was, "We're heavy metal."

Diamond Head guitarist Brian Tatler:
Priest were definitely part of an earlier movement. There's no way I would lump Priest in with New Wave of British Heavy Metal because to me, it started in '79, and Priest started in '69. So no, they were more like Sabbath, and they were from Birmingham as well. I used to think, right, Sabbath are from Birmingham, Priest is from Birmingham, Diamond Head is from Birmingham—there's a connection there and we could follow that line.

Primal Fear bassist Mat Sinner:
I think Judas Priest had a lot of very important basic musical things. They have great guitar riffs, great hook lines, they had two guitar players that played together, even harmony solos, so they combine a little bit of the spirit of Deep Purple and Thin Lizzy and some other bands, and make their own sound and make an even harder sound. So they got the leather, they got the looks, they got the mean things, and

they still have a commercial approach to their music. So I think Judas Priest, in their way, was a unique band, and a really, really outstanding band. I think they played very, very tight together. Those riffs were based for two guitarists—both guitarists played the same riff. With other bands like Thin Lizzy, they don't play a lot the same. They play different kind of guitar parts.

Journalist Garry Bushell:
Priest was a big influence obviously. A huge influence. Them and Sabbath I would say were the main... you could hear Sabbath's riffs in punk and you can hear some Priest in punk as well. People would just nick riffs from anywhere. Amongst what I would call the rock snob end of punk, they looked down on bands like Priest, but that wasn't necessarily shared by everyone in the audiences. Although Sabbath more defined heavy metal, Priest were more... they added the image. I'm just thinking about that for the first time. I think they did. I think they were the first to get the image. Even some of the hard rock bands used to laugh at Priest trying to cop that look. Bands like UFO would frequently... they were not entirely respectful of Priest's image (laughs).

The basic thing I liked on Judas Priest was that the riffs were written for two guitarists. If it was written for only one guitarist it didn't give you that power and that extreme metal approach they have. The songs were that good because they have two guitarists playing the same riff in a very tight way at the same moment. That was Judas Priest.

Raven bassist and vocalist John Gallagher:
Incredible influence obviously. I think there's a band named after every song. Sinner, Running Wild, Exciter, Killing Machine... crazy. Yeah, they were a huge influence. I remember I read a review, when I was a kid, of *Sad Wings of Destiny*. This sounds great. I went and bought it and converted everyone in my school to be a Priest-head, before we'd even seen them. And they just had that thing where it was the twin guitar, they were heavy, the guy had an amazing voice and stage presence.

I mean when we first saw Halford he was scary. He went through different incarnations, but at the time he just looked pissed-off, miserable, really weird. And they were incredibly loud and just a great heavy band. They had this gothic sensibility about some of the riffs and construction of the songs that was very different from a lot of other stuff. I just think they were very influential. Down the line, I've got to say Iron Maiden over Judas Priest—although it was pretty funny because they looked like they were just trying to be Judas Priest at the time.

October 5, 1979. New York's Riot issue their second album, *Narita*. Not quite as revered as 1981's *Fire Down Under*, it was nonetheless a huge improvement on the 1977 debut, *Rock City*, helping Riot to become embraced by the UK's new generation of metalheads.

Early October 1979. Iron Maiden manager Rod Smallwood and graphic artist Derek Riggs meet, bringing into the metal world a band mascot called Eddie. The era of overtly heavy metal illustration is born. Later in the month, Iron Maiden make the cover of *Sounds*, further suggesting an excitement level for metal's new baby bands.

October 12, 1979. Gillan issue their second album, *Mr. Universe*. As alluded to, *Mr. Universe* might be considered one of the earliest of NWOBHM albums, along with records by Saxon, Samson and Motörhead. The album enters the UK charts at #13, peaking at #11 on November 3, 1979. Also in October, Whitesnake issue their third album, *Lovehunter*, which reaches #29 on the UK charts. The last two Deep Purple singers are both working, both fronting hard rock bands, and both doing brisk business, at least in the UK.

Gillan bassist John McCoy on Ian going "heavy metal" again:

I think it's a personal opinion. You say heavy metal to people and they think… my impression of what heavy metal means is Black Sabbath's *Paranoid*—that's heavy metal to me. And for somebody who doesn't like heavy metal to wind up his own band and then go and join Black Sabbath, he doesn't like heavy metal? My God, you know? Ian's a strange guy, and it depends which way the wind is blowing as to what he wants and what he likes. But the thing is that it was proved by our album and singles success in Britain that it was the right direction for him to be in. By the time we got to the *Glory Road* album, all the albums were top three and all the singles, a couple were Top Ten, Top 20—it was a big band.

So consequently it was obvious to him that this was the right thing to do. And I strongly believe that the material we had, the songs that we wrote at that time, are some of the best performances he's ever done. I've worked in the studio with a lot of great singers and Ian is still in my top five singers. He's still incredible, but I think that period, the Gillan period, was when he was at his best, when he was at the peak.

I'm absolutely sure that he wanted to rock out. Because the thing about Ian Gillan Band, the band that he had before, these were super-talented jazz rock players, and maybe Ian felt, I don't know, that he had to prove himself to those guys. It wasn't a rock band, it was kind of an impressive musical band. But you know, you couldn't bang your head to it too easy, because the tempo suddenly kept changing. I think when we got to the final sort of Gillan lineup, the strongest lineup I believe with Bernie, I think he relaxed and realized, yeah, it was okay to rock and have a good time and enjoy the basic rock genre. He's a very complicated guy.

October 13, 1979. A study in the evolution of the NWOBHM takes place when Iron Maiden, Nutz and Saxon play the University of Manchester.

October 19, 1979. London act Girl issues their debut 7", "My Number," on Jet, the Don Arden-run label that also signed Quartz. Girl would distinguish themselves as one of the few glammy hard rock bands of the genre. As well, Phil Collen (ex Lucy, Tush and Dumb Blondes) would move on to Def Leppard and Phil Lewis to LA Guns.

October 27, 1979. Motörhead issue their third album *Bomber*. Also in 1979 comes exploitation compilation, *On Parole*, old Motörhead songs repackaged.

Motörhead guitarist Fast Eddie on the airplane lighting rig concocted for the *Bomber* tour:

I seem to remember sitting in the office and we were all talking about what we could do. And it was like, well, why don't we have some sort of wings across the stage? Across the stage, with lights on, in amongst the equipment, the back line. We were talking on those terms. We hadn't really got into the flying idea. And then the lighting guy, Pete Barnes, and them started to come up with an idea of why don't we make a lighting truss out of a wing? So that all the front spotlights and everything would be on these sort of wings, in front of a plane.

And then of course it went from there to a whole plane, and then it was, why don't we fly the fucking thing on chain hoists? Which was actually quite dangerous, really, because there was no safety in them days. We didn't have a safety thing on it. Sometimes they said they did do a safety, but they never did, I don't think. So it was just on four chain hoists, well, three chain hoists, one at each wingtip, and one at the back. And they were hand-operated. The fucking... you'd be standing under the bomber thinking, fucking 'ell, you know.

But it was the most wonderful thing, I'd have to say. I think it gave me more pleasure than anything else, was seeing the kids when that bomber used to... we used to start the show with it. Of course, this is like 1979. Things hadn't really been done like that. You know, this was for our kids. We could get it in Hammersmith Odeon or anywhere. It was just something spectacular. You've got the fucking aircraft lights going at the beginning and the Lancasters flying over, and it added a whole thing to the show.

The Damned drummer Rat Scabies on the punks' and NWOBHMers' shared qualities over the old guard:

Well, nobody could play any of that! You know, when you're 17 and sitting in the bedroom and you got just a pair of sticks and a drum kit, the last thing you can do is master *Pictures at an Exhibition*, or any Yes song. It was a little bit—for me anyway—it was try as I might. I couldn't play the drums like the guy could on *Blow by Blow*, and so I just played as much as I could, and tried to be as good as I could, and when I ran into Brian, we just had kind of a natural affinity going.

And the hard rock of the day, none of it really had that kind of energy. And also, none of them had really anything to say. You know, there were none of those bands that sounded like they were talking to me when they sang lyrics, including The Who. It was all about fucking goblins and girlfriends and pixies some kind of fucking bullshit about a sculptor. It was just a million miles away from where the real world was for me, which was living on the fucking streets and trying to hustle through and maybe one day I'll be able to join a band.

So when it turned up, it wasn't like a preordained, well, those guys were going to do this. It was you know what? Hang on Captain, we don't play like those people and we never will do, but we can do *this*. And there were some other guys who'd done it their own way, and does it really matter that it's not mainstream? I think what punk did is it kicked everyone up the ass. It was kind of like, "Listen here guys, you're getting fucking old and lazy. And you're not communicating anymore." And again, I think Lemmy is the main kind of guy in that. He was unashamedly metal, but the speed that Motörhead played at was kind of the guiding light.

October 27, 1979. Liverpool's Marseille issue their second album, a self-titled, to general indifference, given the band's arrival before their time, and an inability to then capitalize on the changing times. Two singles are on tap, namely "Over and Over" and "Bring on the Dancin' Girls."

Late 1979. Praying Mantis issue their debut single "Captured City"/"The Ripper"/"Johnny Cool," under the name, *Soundhouse Tapes Part 2*. "Captured City" can be found on the first *Metal for Muthas* and a live crack at "Johnny Cool" can be located on *Metal Explosion*. A 7" version omits "The Ripper."

Praying Mantis guitarist Tino Troy:
Peter Mensch from Leber Krebs approached me at a post-show Iron Maiden party and said, "Tino, fantastic band, the Mantis. Get yourselves a front man and I'll sign you dudes!" By the time we found someone, that NWOBHM runaway train was just rolling into its terminus... arrgh!

DJ Neal Kay:
After EMI finally signed Iron Maiden in 1980, I got a knock on my front door one night about half nine in the evening and there's these two dudes standing there, and they introduce themselves as Peter Mensch and Cliff Burnstein. Cliff Burnstein was the head of A&R for Phonogram LA at the time, and of course Peter Mensch was with Leber Krebs, and they already had Ted Nugent, Boston, AC/DC, every heavy metal band and hard rock act in the world, for agency/ management over the pond. And I didn't know either of them to be honest with you. Never heard of them.

And they almost forced their way in and said, "Look, what else have you got? We're here to listen to your tapes." And I played them a tape by another Soundhouse band who I thought really could do so much. They were called Praying Mantis. Praying Mantis were... well their music was more accessible than Iron Maiden's, commercially speaking. They were melodic rock, sort of Boston but with more balls. Very, very fine band, great songwriting, big ability, two brothers, Chris and Tino Troy. It was their band, half Greek, half Spanish, quite amazing. Very strong talent.

And I played the tape to Cliff and Peter, and they asked me to set up some meetings at the Soundhouse, unhappily while I was working onstage, on my stage. Which is really weird. I had Mensch and Burnstein in one ear and I had the two brothers on the other side and I was trying to work to an audience as well, which is fucking ridiculous if I think about it now.

So basically, Mensch offered the two brothers the gig of a lifetime. He said, "We'd love to sign you, take you to America, put the money in, get the albums out, tour you, do the whole bit, but we want you to get a front man." Because the two brothers did the singing, the bass player. "And we want you to get a keyboard player," which for their kind of music was not unreasonable and I could see that.

Then we hit a snag. Unfortunately, the folly of youth, they thought they could do it without them. Mensch and Burnstein were trying to get me to persuade them to change their mind. The battle went on for a week, and I'm afraid the two brothers were adamant they were not going to do that, they didn't want to, and they threw out the chance of a lifetime. And ever since then they have been so sorry about it.

The next thing I know I get a phone call from Peter. Would I meet them down at Phonogram? He'd latched onto the tape from Def Leppard, and I got a shout, would I go down there? And when I get down there the Leppards are in there with the local record shop owner manager Frank Stuart Brown, looking wonderful in a brown flared trouser suit and a tie so wide I could have put a 747 down on one end of it and spun it around and got off again without any trouble. And they went into that meeting with Frank Stuart Brown as their manager, and they came out of that meeting signed to Phonogram with Peter Mensch as their agency manager.

Late 1979. Witchfynde issue their debut single, "Give 'Em Hell." It marks the arrival of the genre's first Satanic-leaning act.

Witchfynde guitarist Montalo being amusingly vague:
We live sort of the centre of England, in Derbyshire, which is on the edge of wilderness. Me personally, I'm mostly out in the wild when I'm not sort of playing with the band—I'm out in nowhere. For us, the witchcraft side of it... it did extend to a large part from all of the people in the band, who were interested in various aspects of that sort of thing. But with me, it's more a way of life. And so obviously, you draw your inspirations for whatever creative thing you're involved in from your way of life. And so that's where the lyrical side of the songs come from. It's one thing to try and make people aware that there's a different side to life, and how it all works. I guess we were fairly well read. The other members of the band, Andro and Gra and Steve, they were read in various aspects of the occult, and in on the practical side as well. We used to get involved in various sorts of creative aspects of it.

And it got some press, but it wasn't really a big deal, to be fair. That was just something that we were involved with, exterior to our band. On a creative level, that's all that was. We were just involved in something that took up our time. And it was in a very notorious place, on the outskirts of Manchester; we were working on some sort of project there. And that's all that was (laughs). It was a natural magic type of thing that we were involved in. Again, it was trying to put it in some sort of creative context, for a future plan of ours. But that's all that we were involved with. There's nothing sinister about it. We're not really involved in that type of thing. It was probably a magazine called *Sounds*. You know, they try to latch onto things. We don't really make a big deal of it, to be honest.

On a personal note, Sabbath, Tony Iommi, he helped a little bit with us. He used to listen on the production side, to the songs that we were doing, and he used to advise us a little bit on the business side—well, me, that was; I used to speak to him quite regularly on that side. He also helped Quartz, who we also knew.

Saxon were friends of ours as well. We came from not too far away. Saxon came from probably, what, 40 or 50 miles down the road from us. They're from sort of Barnsley, Yorkshire. And also, of course, Def Leppard lived very close. And in fact, Def Leppard used to come and see us; we used to play in a little pub in the wilds of Derbyshire, and Def Leppard used to come there and watch. And in fact, I think, one time there was some sort of fight broke out in the car park, and Def Leppard got involved with it all, to help out. But because of that, when Leppard got their first big break, they asked for us to go on a tour with them. Because we came from the same area, they knew what we were like.

Late 1979. Bruce Dickinson joins Samson, after Paul Samson and Thunderstick poach him from his current act at the time, Shots.

Late 1979. Trespass issue their "One of These Days" single, recorded in October. The band is, arguably, regarded as the best NWOBHM band of a most purist type—the kind who had independent singles only, never recording an album. A deal with Chrysalis almost ensues.

Journalist John Tucker:
Trespass always said they were big on UFO and Rush. I think Rush have got an awful lot to answer for. Whether they'd like that or not, I don't know, but everyone liked Rush when I was at that age. Clever song structures, pushing things... they could do your three-and-a-half minute's worth if you'd like. In fact some of the longer songs are a load of three-and-a-half minute songs glued together. But it was all there. They were very good at what they did. Certainly Thin Lizzy and the older UFO stuff was quite inspirational; these were bands that stuck to their guns and did what they were always doing.

November 1979. Cronos joins Venom, the band at this point consisting of Clive Archer on vocals, Mantas and Cronos on guitars, Alan Winston on bass and Abaddon on drums.

Venom bassist and vocalist Cronos:
We didn't want to be any regular heavy metal band. Because basically, Venom came out of the big back end of the punk explosion in England. And we've always been basic rock fans—Deep Purple and Led Zeppelin and bands like that—but the thing for me was

bands like Sex Pistols and The Damned, the real hardcore element. I really wanted to combine the two. I didn't want to be another Lynyrd Skynyrd or another fuckin' Journey or Boston. They were cool bands for what they do, but it wasn't what I wanted to do. I wanted to kind of look like them but a lot dirtier and swear a lot. So the Venom thing had to sort of fit into a new category. And we had to call it black metal because calling it heavy metal didn't describe it.

But we realized the kinds of riffs we were playing were influenced by Black Sabbath and Thin Lizzy and Judas Priest. Yes they're our influences, you can't escape that. You can't get to 20 years old and not heard any music in your life. But we did not want to rip these bands off. We wanted to sound like we sound. We used to have this concept called, "Heads down, meet you at the end." And that's how we used to treat some of the songs. It was like, "I don't know where the fuck I am right now, but let's see if we can all stop at the same time" (laughs).

November 1979. Wild Horses, a slapdash marriage of Jimmy Bain to Brian Robertson, issue their debut single, "Criminal Tendencies."

Wild Horses bassist Jimmy Bain on the NWOBHM:
    We got signed to EMI at the same time, I think, as Maiden got signed to EMI; '80, '81, around that time. And there was a big buzz about all these bands that were just coming up. We got to play a lot. We played a lot of festivals together and in England, I was living there at the time, and it was a good time. You could see that there was a real buzz amongst the musicians themselves, that they were onto something. They didn't quite know where it was going to go or how far it would go, but they kind of had this... there was a kind of optimism, in London especially, like you see with Saxon and Iron Maiden, especially. Bruce Dickinson was playing in Samson, got the gig in Maiden, and I knew him from Samson because we'd done some shows together, and followed him through into the Maiden days, and he was another guy who just had so much enthusiasm for what he was doing. He just loved it and it kind of went over to everybody, just him especially. He was just a super guy.
    Generally speaking I'm not sure. Just everybody felt there was something good about to happen, and sure enough it did. Everybody had a good run at it, from what we can gather anyway. Maiden, certainly, are still going at it really well. I kind of pat them on the back for the planning they did. They never lost touch of their audience and the records have come far enough apart that they get enough time to go and tour all the places they want to tour, and everything's worked out really well for them. They've been well-managed and well-directed.

November 1979. Saxon issue a second single from the debut album, namely "Backs to the Wall."

Saxon vocalist Biff Byford on the NWOBHM's heavy metal brotherhood:

I noticed it on our first major tour. We hit that straight away. The fans wanted us to play great and write great songs, and they were with us. That's how it felt. It never felt to me like, "Look at me, I'm a fucking smart-ass rock star in front of all these people." It always felt to me as if we were very, very lucky and privileged to be popular and people come to see us, you know? For us it was more than people coming to see us. It was a fucking event. It was an absolute physical fucking transformation that took place for us, and still is. When we hit the stage it's not about running around like prats looking good. It's all about connecting with the audience and putting that passion across.

We used to shop from Oxfam shops and things. I mean we used to dress ourselves in things we found in shops for three quid. We weren't really aware of any sort of image. I went into a shop in London in '79, '80, and Bob Dylan was in there buying a leather jacket, a black and white one. Actually bought three. The guy had got one left so I bought it, so that's the jacket I wore through all them early years, really. It was just a jacket. That's the one jacket that people associate with those early looks. We never had anything planned. It was just a random thing. We used to wear tight fucking clothes because we liked it, basically.

November 1979. Def Leppard issue their "Wasted"/"Hello America" single—two choice rockers—which reaches #61 in the UK. By the end of the year, the band will have supported Sammy Hagar and AC/DC on separate tours.

Phonogram executive David Bates on whether he noticed a desire in the band to break in America:
Yeah, from day one (laughs). Yeah, I think they just had heard all the stories weekly of bands touring America. You knew about the legends of Zeppelin and the other rock bands that toured America, and I think their ambitions in the early days were, a) to make an album, and b) to go on tour, and to go and play... the other circuit that existed in the UK was the City Hall circuit which a lot of bands did as well, but big was the idea of going to America, hence the song, "Hello America."

Def Leppard manager David Krebs on the AC/DC connection:
AC/DC had specified in their contract that in order to manage them, we could only sign a maximum of four acts. I had sent Peter Mensch over there to sign some bands. Peter was from New York but was good friends with Cliff Burnstein, who I had hired. They

both went to the University of Chicago. Anyway, I knew Aerosmith and Ted Nugent had peaked in 1979, and we were looking for a next wave. So we signed AC/DC in 1979 and then in 1980 Peter signed Def Leppard, plus we had Scorpions and Michael Schenker. But that was smart of AC/DC to put a limit on the signings, because we had 25 acts in New York, and it's a good way to make sure you get management attention.

Led Zeppelin expert Dave Lewis on the birth of the NWOBHM, and Def Leppard's ties to Zeppelin:

That began to rear its head about '77, '78 over here, particularly. There was a guy called Neal Kay who had this disco night. When you look at that term, you think a disco is going to be *Saturday Night Fever* or funk and soul and all that. But he had this pioneering heavy metal disco, and that's where you get the audience going and doing air guitar and enjoying the music for what it is, which was quite ground-breaking at the time.

I think the one thing about this music is it wasn't very expressive outside of going to concerts. It didn't have its movement, really. It was a bit insular. As a fan at the time, you didn't really have a lot of contact with other fans, other than when you went to the gigs. So to have something like that, to have a central place where people could talk about this music and feed off it and inspire each other and turn each other onto different bands, that's when you begin to get the beginnings of the NWOBHM.

And significantly I think the like of Leppard were seeing Zeppelin as a standard-bearer and wanting to take their music in a similar direction and be like Led Zeppelin. You've only got to look at the name Def Leppard. You don't need rocket science to find out what they were thinking of when they came up with the name. And there's always that significant moment when Joe Elliott tells of being in the Knebworth audience. There's a fantastic thing, actually, in *Sounds* magazine. The week that Zeppelin's album, *In Through the Out Door*, and the Knebworth gig was reviewed, there's a half page advert for *Rocks Off*, the first Def Leppard single.

So you're almost seeing the new and old wave of what was going to be—the old wave's there and the new wave's there. And I think Def Leppard definitely took that music and it became more accessible. And again, if you go to look at the movement of radio in England, which is very insular again, there was a movement becoming much clearer. We had *The Friday Rock Show* with Tommy Vance, which was quite significant where people could clue into this music again and where Def Leppard probably got their first airplay. So that movement was beginning to come into play in '78, '79, and then flowered very much in '80 and '81, and then just went on from there.

So there were beginnings, admirable ones, where this music was suddenly being shared. Because before it had been guys in bedrooms with their posters and their record players. It wasn't communal, so it didn't have a feel of a movement. I don't think, even if you go way back, Zeppelin was a movement. It only really reared its head when you went to concerts. Again, they didn't have fan clubs and stuff like that, which is where I came in with my magazine. But there wasn't a lot of interaction.

So for that movement to get its identity, it had to have things like Neal Kay's disco, like the fact that Def Leppard had been to Knebworth and were beginning to come into play and offer some new music that was fresh and at the same age group of the people it was being aimed at. Where Zeppelin were older guys who had been around a while. Zeppelin were much older than Def Leppard at that time, and I think Joe Elliott, his audience were teenagers. They were able to grow with the music which happened in the '80s. I know it felt like a movement in that newspaper, *Sounds*, and in sales. It definitely felt like a movement, and lots of kids wanted to be part of that and identify with it, they really did.

November 7, 1979. Punk heroes The Damned issue their third album, *Machine Gun Etiquette*. It's the last album credit for bassist and vocalist Algy Ward before he goes on to form Tank. Previous to The Damned, Algy had played with similarly hard rocking punk act The Saints.

The Damned drummer Rat Scabies: We liked Algy's playing, because he was a really good bass player, kind of in the world of bass players. You know, there weren't as many that were fast and furious

as he was, and he was good at it. He used to play in The Saints, and he also came from where Captain lived, which was Croydon, and so when we needed a bass player, Captain said, "Listen, we want somebody who can really play good. So let's get this guy." And then I guess somewhere later on, Algy decided that he was going to be a metal boy (laughs), and that's what he did.

Heavy Metal Records' Paul Birch on whether punk and metal mixed:

I don't think they were oil and water. In 1977 punk was in a pure form, but by 1982 there was a sort of convergence. With The Rejects, we did an album called *Quiet Storm* and it was a heavy metal album, but The Rejects had been a punk group. So it wasn't inconceivable that a group could cross over from one genre to the other, at least to some extent. A case in point, but there were many other groups that displayed a sort of combination of the two. And then of course, a later incarnation would have been Oi! music, which was kind of like lavish punk. Looks lavish, anyway.

But in its own right, the NWOBHM was quite a pure genre, and there were groups that were in it, like Diamond Head, and there were groups that were out of it, like UFO. So you were either one of those NWOBHM bands or you weren't. But then again, you see people like Geoff Barton who lead opinion in heavy metal. He created *Kerrang!*; it's a pity he didn't retain the copyright to the brand name, but he was the creator of it, and widely acknowledged. Geoff was a big fan of Jim Dandy and Black Oak Arkansas, and they could hardly be described as being NWOBHM.

November 9, 1979. Iron Maiden issue *The Soundhouse Tapes*, consisting of "Prowler," "First Invasion" and seminal NWOBHM anthem "Iron Maiden." Back cover features testimonial from NWOBHM articulator Neal Kay.

Iron Maiden bassist Steve Harris:

We made a tape, a four-track demo tape, basically, and we took it down to Neal Kay's Soundhouse, and it was like the other end of the earth for us, because we were in East London, and it was right 'round the other side north somewhere, London, in the darkest depths of Hinden way, that sort of way. So we took the tape to him, and left it with him. Just to try get a gig; not for any other reason, really. We knew it was a good place for cool fans, rock fans.

And he started playing the tracks off the tape. He had a set chart in *Sounds*, from the weekly *Sounds* magazine. Obviously people like Rush were in there, and then all of a sudden, our track started going up the charts until #1, along with all this stuff. And so me and Paul, actually, went down there one night just to see what would happen, you know, when they played one of our tracks. Of course we weren't known then or anything like that, so we'd just stand at the bar watching what was going on. And the whole place just went crazy when the Maiden tracks come on. So we went and saw Neal again and said, "Look, you obviously really like the tape. Can we now get a gig?" and all that.

He was like, yeah, definitely into taking us on. And so when we played there, straightaway, the first time we played there, it was sold-out and everything. It was pretty amazing, really, to see... for us, you know, a) being in the chart anywhere, Top 20, and to actually start moving up, and at one time we had two or three tracks all in the Top 20; and b) for them to be freaking out over our songs, and they're not even released yet. It was really an exciting time.

DJ Neal Kay:
    There were two main sources of these demo tapes, demo cassettes. Either they arrived by post, or members of bands would bring them in and see me at the Soundhouse. Uninvited, they'd turn up in the evening show and cautiously come up to the stage, and say, "Hey mate, here's our demo tape. Would you take it and give it a listen? And if you like it, do us a favour, give us a ring, will you?" I mean my heart used to go out to them. I was the only one it seemed at the time who had the guts and the bollocks to do anything about it. And it's the thing with me, and it always was. I don't like seeing people repressed in any way—I do not. And when it comes to music, it's the most important thing sought out in my working life. And this kind of music is absolute. And when no one cares and no one wants to know and no one wants to do anything, then someone has to stand up.
    I think it was Steve and Dave, actually, who came by. I seem to remember it was Steve and Dave, but you're asking a lot of me now. I'm sure it was Steve. Actually I believe I was very rude at the time, I do remember. They came up to the stage and in their east-end Cockney voice, which is where they come from, they presented the tape and I'm sure it was Steve said to me something like, "Do us a favour, mate. Take it home and give it a listen, and if you like it give us a ring." And I probably swung around—I'm absolutely convinced I did—and said, "Oh yeah, you and about five million others. When I get the chance, pal, I will do it. Thanks."
    Oh no! I mean how can I have done that? But it was just another approach made by another small band, and you've got to remember all business took place in front of the Soundhouse audience. We did business, and it got so elevated at one stage that I had Peter Mensch on one side of me from Leber Krebs and Cliff Burnstein from Phonogram LA on the other side, trying to get me to convince Praying Mantis to sign a contract with them, while I'm working an audience at the Soundhouse.
    I took the Maiden tape home that night with a bunch of others— went mad! Went absolutely berserk. That's it. There it is. That's it. Fait accompli. Checkmate, for it's there. It was there. That's it! I couldn't sleep that night. I had to phone Steve. The next morning...

well I just couldn't stop playing that tape. It was fresh, powerful, key changes, great chord progressions, incredible flowing melody, speed, performance to the level, everything that all the others hadn't. And to top it, they went to a studio to do it as well. The quality of the tape was miles higher than anything else. The only other band that ever came up with anything as good was Praying Mantis, and they were actually five or six months before Iron Maiden. The dates on their demo tells me. But the Maiden tape was awe-inspiring. I don't know how else to put it. Here's a band waiting to smack the world, basically.

And I feel the same about those guys today as I did over 30-something years ago. I am delighted and pleased and happy that they have conquered the world, toured the world, and still are doing so to the Nth degree. Though I knew they would back then, though. That's the thing.

But they did not play the club. Not at first. Basically what happened was this. I got this tape, I took it home, I listened to it. I was jumping around my lounge, swinging the old air guitar over me shoulders, and thinking this is really exciting. And it's about 3:00 in the morning and my first wife's trying to get some sleep. And I can't calm down because there's no chance. All I know is I've got to get this out to the public, and I've got to get it to the industry.

Now I'd made some serious contacts by then. The first thing that helped me on the way was a personal appearance arranged with CBS and Epic of Ted Nugent and his whole band. He came to play London Hammersmith Odeon, I went up to the record company and said I want to try something real unusual. I don't know how you're going to go for this, and they finished up talking about it. You know what? They gave me Ted Nugent and his band on a Tuesday night up at the Soundhouse for a guest appearance. After then no one could refuse me. How could they? I've had Ted there.

So the record companies wanted more. They wanted a lot more from me, and that was great because then I could get a lot more out of them. We exchanged white labels, they made sure I had the very latest stuff, transatlantic, anything I wanted within reason. And I got more personal appearances: Sammy Hagar came to the club, as well with his band, members of Rainbow did, I had loads of stuff happening. So by the time I got the Iron Maiden demo tape, I had already made some very firm friends in reasonably high places in the record companies and I could go up there and take tapes up and say listen to this, listen to that.

As for the crowd reaction to Maiden, we had a system developed by then between me and the audience because they were a respected audience by then. It was known that if you were a shit band, don't play the Soundhouse because the audience will give you the silent treatment. And I used to have this thing. I'd get on the mic and say, "Look, evening Soundhouse, nice to see you here. We've got some new stuff to play tonight, and in the time-honoured fashion and tradition, you tell me afterwards if it's thumbs up or not in the usual manner." And they'd whistle and stamp their feet and go mad and make terrible noises if they loved it. If they didn't, you could hear a pin drop. And they didn't need that with Maiden. The floor was full. It was just happening. It was happening straight away. It went straight in the charts, two or three of the tracks off there just went. And that told me even more what I needed to know. I knew anyway that you couldn't deny it. I said it on the back of the EP. I said here's something that must not be ignored. Of course convincing the labels, that was a different story at first.

The Maiden demo, they named it after the club, we knew that. And Rob Loonhouse did the pictures. It was an honour, I suppose. A thing to say thanks. I mean the Soundhouse was an amazing club. Because of all these antics, we had people who used to perform acts. I'd do certain numbers like "Planet's On Fire," Sammy Hagar. There's a chorus in it. A bunch of guys and girls got together and started doing this sort of doo-wop shit in the middle of it, just like the old stuff, and then go straight back to the air guitar again. You had to see it to believe it.

Gradually the media cottoned onto this lunacy that was sort of growing. They came down, and even the *Times* sent a bloke down, poor man. He kind of came in a human being, but actually I think they melted him somewhere about the fifth number. We found his jacket and shoes, broke shoes, on the stage. Don't know what happened to him. We destroyed him. We used to take this old Focus track, "Hocus Pocus," and when you get to the little twiddly bit, I used to whack the faders down and everyone would scream, "Fuck off!," and I'd whip them up again, and it was like the Soundhouse thing. And when we didn't like someone that was like invited to do an article on us or someone who had besmirched the fair name of the club, I'd play "Hocus Pocus" and bellow, "And one for…" and point to him. "Fuck off!" they all screamed.

We had a hell of an audience. And they were, I think, respected by the industry, because although they could play all these games… I used to take them to the coast, as well. I hired three coaches once and ran the Soundhouse down to the south coast for the day, and because I was a member of a bike club at the time, I also used to do bike runs for the Soundhouse members. One bike club member, one Soundhouse member. I took 114 bikes, one time, down to Hastings, and we finished up back at the Soundhouse. I ran it like a social club for heavy metalers. I wasn't interested in normal things. Anyone could do normal things. It's nothing.

And they were rock fans. As I say Rush, these sorts of people, Aerosmith, a lot of progressive stuff as well, but mainly sort of rock stuff, classic rock stuff. So they were there. Well, they never went away; it's just that punk... the press weren't writing about these people, and because they weren't, it became more of an underground thing again, a real roots thing. And it was actually a really good feeling to be part of all that. It is just amazing, because we would go up to somewhere like, I don't know, North of England, Blackpool or even up into Scotland, Aberdeen for the first time, and we would have 300 people coming to the gigs without ever having seen us before, mainly because they had checked out... they couldn't get the EP or anything because it wasn't out yet, but they were checking out the tracks, and the fact that they've got the profile of being in the Top 10, "Who is this band?! Iron Maiden—never heard of 'em," sort of thing. And they're top of the chart. So people were coming to check us out, and I've always said, when you've got people in, then that's it. You're there to prove your point. And we did (laughs).

Raven bassist and vocalist John Gallagher on Neal Kay:
Yeah, he got a very popular heavy metal disco down in the London area and he'd be playing all those songs, and he'd team up and have bands play with him. Iron Maiden, obviously, and Samson, and I think maybe Witchfynde. People were card-carrying members of the NWOBHM. There was *Sounds*, which was the most popular magazine at the time, like a newspaper. There was three: *Sounds*, there was *Disc*, and there was the *New Musical Express*, and I think the *NME* is the only one that's still out there. And we used to call it the *Enemy* because they hated anything to do with rock. And *Sounds* and Geoff Barton was championed the heavy music. I mean that was the famous cover: Blackmore smashing the guitar with *Kerrang!* written on the front. And that's where they got the name for the magazine.

Journalist John Tucker:
By '78 the Soundhouse was well enough established for the young Steve Harris or the young Dave Murray, actually, to take the Iron Maiden demo in the tail end of '78 and say, "Give this a spin, will you?"

When the revolution actually started is the interesting question. I mean it's sort of the name—we can date the name to a particular magazine. But when did things actually start happening? When did record companies actually start saying, hey, we need to have one of these on our books? It was a chicken and egg situation. What came first? Explosions of bands filling a void, or loads of people scouting around to find bands that were already doing their thing, but doing it very locally?

I think one of the things about NWOBHM was it was all over the country but in isolation. Even now you have bands not knowing anything, really, about their peers. The guys in Bitches Sin up in Cambria knew nothing about Diamond Head—two big bands, two contemporary bands—and knew nothing about each other. Because even though it's a small country, there's not a lot of communication apart from *The Friday Rock Show*, no great radio play apart from two hours Friday night.

So a lot of bands think they're working in isolation and they're really doing something, and then they find out oh, there's another band doing a similar thing. And those things come together at the same time, the likes of me sitting here, and you're reading about all these bands from an external point of view, a fan point of view. And you're seeing things happening and you are seeing a pattern, a network almost. It wasn't the easiest acronym or name to come up with that joined all those dots together.

Late 1979. Ethel the Frog's new label, EMI, issue a second version of the band's "Eleanor Rigby" single, this time backed with fine and early NWOBHM scorcher "Fight Back."

December 1979. Iron Maiden signs with EMI. It seems that the majors might have an appetite for stronger stuff beyond Def Leppard.

Iron Maiden bassist Steve Harris:
I know why they signed us, because they'd come down to the Soundhouse and saw it was jam-packed and they couldn't get in. In fact, they were stuck in the back. They couldn't see properly or anything like that. I think whether they liked the music or not, they thought bloody 'ell, what's going on here, we better sign these before someone else does. There was obviously something going on. There was a real buzz, and so whether they understood us musically, I suppose, is debatable, but I suppose it didn't really matter. They just knew that there was this thing going on and they signed us on a three album deal, which at the time was unheard of, really.

DJ Neal Kay:
Well the thing was that Maiden wanted to put out an EP. See they didn't sign initially. I mean I had a lot of trouble myself trying to get record companies to hear it. I suddenly realized amongst all this madness and cacophony that we were really comfortable in the Soundhouse, and that we understood our world very well, and that

others that came to us did too. But you know the old bowler hat brigade of the '40s and '50s, and those that held the power in the industry, they had lost power when the Beatles actually happened.

Up until that time you couldn't do a damn thing if you were an artist. You were told exactly what you'd record, you were told how to record it. In some cases you didn't even play it, you just sang it. The industry had total control over your product, your output, and how you did it. The Beatles happened and changed all that shit forever, thank Christ. Okay. And of course stateside Buddy Holly must take the ticket for that as well, because he was one of the first to record, unofficially put down arrangements, and he worked in a very freelance way.

So that all changed everything, but it hadn't changed stuff enough. That was all right for the concept of normal music, but when you're working outside of normal music, we were considered a counterculture, I feel, back then. My dream was to get it to mainstream. I didn't want it to be seen as counterculture or a fashion or anything else. The problem with the media is that I was afraid they would try and turn it into a fashion. And it's not—it's a way of life. You can't turn a way of life into a fashion. It's rubbish.

And it worried me a lot at the time. But the big problem was that these guys high up in the record industry, the established ones, still couldn't hear it. I took Maiden's demo tape… I can remember clearly taking it to CBS, and I knew them all out there, at that time. I really did. And they were not bad guys. They'd helped me a huge amount before with the Soundhouse promotion and stuff. And they couldn't hear it. They wouldn't sign it. They didn't understand it.

Well, first of all A&M passed, and that really surprised me. I knew Charlie real well up there, and he'd been the man who'd been feeding me Styx stuff and all sorts of stuff, and it was loved at the club. But A&M are not really a sort of a hard rock label. I actually fancied Phonogram, because at the time, with Cliff Burnstein operating in the UK on attachment, and Peter Mensch from Leber Krebs sniffing around for management… between the two of them they had 90% of the established acts anyway. They really did.

All these bands were signed to Leber Krebs management at the time. And Burnstein had signed a hell of a lot to Phonogram. Of course Atlantic was the other. And it seemed like the Americans were just miles ahead in understanding rock. The troubadours of the folk rock era and the businessmen lead by David Geffen opened up everything into a more free, more cool, countercultural way of making things mainstream.

But yes, EMI were the only ones that would bloody well listen. And also Rod Smallwood, by then, was on the scene. And Rod obviously signed Maiden to management. Actually that critical gig did take place at the Soundhouse. Brian Shepherd was the name of the guy who came from EMI to check out Iron Maiden. I'd put the show on and it was a sellout. You couldn't move. Sheppy came late. He was short, like me. He shoved his way into the Bandwagon and he couldn't see anything. He couldn't see a bloody thing. And in front of him there was a bunch of kids holding up a big banner, Iron Maiden, so he couldn't even see the stage that night.

And I think Ashley Goodall was with him, but Ash had been a friend of mine who'd asked me to help put together *Metal for Muthas*, which preceded the Maiden thing. So they came down to the 'wagon, they couldn't see the band, but the place was really jumping. It was rocking. And I understand at the end of it, Rod turned to Sheppy, Brian, and said, "What do you think?" And Brian said, "Well I can't see anything, that's for sure. But everyone seems to love them and I've heard it, so yeah, I like it. We'll have it."

And apparently it was signed that way. I'm delighted it was done at the Soundhouse. There's a lot of people actually accuse me of being a bit jingoistic where Iron Maiden are concerned, I suppose, and see it as a pet project. No, they're wrong. I didn't see it as a pet project, I saw it as a special project for the world. I never saw Maiden in any other way, and all the bands that I've ever listened to that I've looked at from these demos, I only ever consider them if I can shut my eyes and see them onstage at the Odeon or any of the big outdoor fests. I'm not looking for pub bands. There's no money. And that's what Mr. businessman wants. Hell, we need the spirit. We need the rock 'n' roll, man.

December 1979. Tygers of Pan Tang issue, on Neat, their debut single "Don't Touch Me There"/"Bad Times," which gets reissued my MCA in March of the following year.

Tygers of Pan Tang vocalist Jess Cox:
In the UK it was just a natural progression. There was a big melting pot going on at the time with new music from the punk thing. The next generations weren't into Genesis and Yes and whatever else. They wanted something a bit more street. So when the Pistols and the Clash and whoever came along, it kind of knocked everything else to the ground for a while, really. All our old metal or whatever you want to call it, well, we thought it was destroyed, but it was just sort of put on the back burner for a while. But then the rock thing came through. As all movements will come and go, the punk thing obviously ran its course.

Some people helped created it. There's your Geoff Bartons and whoever in the world, decided to rope in a few rock bands that were starting up. I think it literally was a natural thing as well, it seems. I remember when we got sort of tagged by Geoff, he'd already found various rock bands. Well, obviously you got Def Leppard in Sheffield and Saxon and Iron Maiden and Angel Witch. There was a lot of young rock bands out there. And I guess he just sort of capitalized on it, really, and started the ball rolling.

And once he started it, it just went ballistic. I was up here in Newcastle involved with Neat Records and so many tapes started to come into the studio, and that's where all the other bands—White Spirit, Raven, Satan; I mean the list goes on—they all come from my area. I think Geoff Barton started to call it the northeast NWOBHM or NENWOBHM because there were so many bands.

Even Venom was thrown in there, although what was a NWOBHM band was quite difficult. These days when you split the genres down, it's quite obvious what a band is. But the NWOBHM… do Dumpy's Nuts sound like Iron Maiden? I don't think so. Girlschool, Magnum or Venom… I know these are extremes. Magnum were kind of thrown in there as well, but weren't really from the new wave.

But yeah, so where it came from and how it happened, I guess it's possibly down to journalists as much as anything else. But the bands were out there. They were definitely out there because people realized, hold on, I could do that. Because we'd seen other bands that couldn't particularly play or sing or whatever pick up a guitar and start playing gigs and it was acceptable. And there were many small labels that jumped up—Ebony, Heavy Metal Records, Neat Records—and released product from these acts outside of the majors of course, which had snapped up the first five or six bands.

Tygers of Pan Tang guitarist Robb Weir on finding Neat Records:
We played at a high school and Dave Wood, his two sons were at the high school, and they made their dad come down because they heard that we were playing at their school. And he stood at the back and after we finished playing, he came up and said to us, "Listen lads, would you like to come and record a couple of songs? I've got a recording studio." And that was the start of it.

We were Neat 03. The two releases before us, I think one was a football chant and one was some sort of pop band, so we were the first rock band to record on the Neat label. And we did one single and we left, and then I think Raven followed us onto the label. But we were then signed to MCA and touring around the world, so I can't really tell you a sort of historical content of what happened after that.

Neat was in Newcastle and Newcastle City Hall was one of the old fashioned city halls that was built with a huge pipe church organ at the back of the stage, which is still there to this day, and was always renowned for fantastic acoustics. And a lot of bands, through the '70s and '80s, if they were doing a live album, would choose to record it there because it had—and still has—such good acoustics. So a lot of bands, if they were thinking to themselves, well, we'll record a new album, they'd say we'll do it in Newcastle. Newcastle produced a few good hard rock/heavy metal bands. I don't think as many as Birmingham, but we've done all right.

December 1, 1979. Motörhead issue the title track from *Bomber* as a single, backed with non-LPer "Over the Top."

Saxon vocalist Biff Byford:
Our first tour, actually, was with Slade, and we did half the tour and Def Leppard did the other half. After that we supported Nazareth, and that was right on the verge of releasing *Wheels of Steel*, yeah? And then we toured with Motörhead, on their *Bomber* tour, which obviously changed everything—that was when it really exploded, at that point there. We were just a support band and about to release *Wheels of Steel* but we weren't playing those tracks. We were playing some tracks off the first album, but we never toured with anybody on the first album. And then in-between that we played a few shows with Rainbow, the "All Night Long" period with Graham Bonnet. Yeah. We went down a storm and they kicked us off. So we liked that—it's all part of the rebellion, you know?

Motörhead bassist and vocalist Lemmy:
Saxon were great. We took them out on the *Bomber* tour with us. Anvil from Canada, were really good. We took them out on tour back in the '70s... Tank we took out on the whole European tour; they were great. The first incarnation, because that was after Algy left The Damned. I don't know, we've always had pretty good support bands, except we had this bad few years in the late '80s where we seemed to get all these bands who went "Arrrrgh!" and couldn't play. So then we started specifying which bands we wanted and it's worked very well so far. We never toured with Raven. Tank, yeah, sure. Like I said, I feel a kinship with every band, whoever they are, even jazz bands. Because we're all doing the same shit; we're all overcoming the same bullshit to do what we do.

Recap

The last hurrah of the '70s, 1979, is considered by most to be the first year of the NWOBHM. Singles came flying out of the woodwork by all manner of baby band, but most significantly, 1979 was the year for key singles from Girlschool, Trespass, Samson, Tygers of Pan Tang, Witchfynde and most notably Def Leppard, who rise quickly, over the course of the year, from the endearingly independent *The Def Leppard E.P.* through to a major label deal with Polygram.

As for bands getting their act together but not issuing product yet, there are none finer and more ill-winded than Venom, Grim Reaper and Witchfinder General.

More significantly still, 1979 gives us additional candidates for first NWOBHM album, in Motörhead's *Overkill*, Gillan's *Mr. Universe*, Saxon's *Saxon* and Samson's *Survivors*. It's a debate that can never be settled. I mean, sometimes these things can be settled to some level of satisfaction (*Black Sabbath* as first metal album; *Kill 'Em All* as first thrash album), but in this case, forget it. Wrapped up in concepts such as the Gillan question (two actually, age and the presence of a decent '78 album), the dirty sounds of Motörhead (let's not forget their record in 1977!), *Survivors* maybe being not heavy enough, with similar charges leveled against *Saxon*... it's a mess, but a delightful one to debate o'er beers.

And our favourite rumblings from the dinosaurs? Well, in 1979, Judas Priest and UFO issue fine live albums, *Unleashed in the East* and *Strangers in the Night* respectively. Scorpions rock us like a hurricane with *Lovedrive*, as does AC/DC with the hugely beloved *Highway to Hell*. Rainbow participates as well with *Down to Earth*, as does Thin Lizzy with *Black Rose* (no entry; not all these need entries) and then Led Zeppelin, not so much, offering the effervescent and ethereal *In Through the Out Door*, which throws the guitars through the out door, slamming the lock on 'er before any power chords could creep back in.

Neat Records opens for business in 1979 as well, with Tygers of Pan Tang rocking there first before exiting for the bright lights of MCA. And let's not forget, the very name "New Wave of British Heavy Metal" innocently sneaks into the lexicon, through a *Sounds* feature from May of this year.

Finally, if one brash band of a new-ish sort dominates, that's got to be Motörhead, who issue two instantly classic full-length rounders in the same year, *Overkill* at the entry and *Bomber* at the exit. Whatever one's hair-splitting over to what extent the band belong by virtue of their frantic and punky dirtball metal alone, one can't deny how much they physically were everywhere in and about the NWOBHM, touring, drinking and drugging with all our favourites, issuing non-LP singles, looking the part, propping the bar, basically raising the spirits of their fellow rockers by dastardly demonstration.

Tantamount to these 12 months, however, if unarguable relevance is the prime factor, must be the unleashing of *The Soundhouse Tapes* from the doggedly determined Iron Maiden. The NWOBHM now had a flagship act, a cream of quite a crop, a fierce unit purely NWOBHM to the heart and soul, haters of punk, proudly prog but only with egregious force. Before the year was out, Maiden would find themselves snatched up by EMI for worldwide dissemination of their demon seed, the result being that a sharp focus would take hold as all our youthful rock heroes took to heart the Maiden experience by proxy and cast their bloodshot eyes toward a new decade of heavy metal hope.

1980 — "Black Sabbath's done all right; let's find another new Black Sabbath."

1980. Many more obscure NWOBHM singles arrive over the course of 1980. Some of these minor releases, for which exact dates within 1980 are not known, are as follows:

The female-fronted After Hours, with "All Over Town;" Midlands-based Arc issue "Tribute (To Mike Hailwood);" Avalanche – "The Preacher;" Berlin Ritz - "Crazy Nights;" Big Daisy - "Fever;" Brooklyn – "I Wanna Be a Detective;" a second band named Chainsaw issue "Lonely Without You;" Cheeky - "Don't Mess Me Around;" China Doll - "Oysters and Wine;" Cryer – "The Visionary," on Happy Face, Diamond Head's label; Dawn Trader - "Dawn Trader;" Dawnwatcher – "Spellbound;" Denigh - "No Way;" Dragonfly - *E.P.*; Energy – "Energised;" Gemage - "The Story So Far;" High Treason - "Saturday Night Special;" Hoggs - "See It Now;" Kraken – "Fantasy Reality;" Lightning Raiders - "Psychedelik Musik;" Limelight - "Metal Man;" Lone Wolf - "Cash for Candy;" Marz - "Lady of the Night;" Metal Mirror - "Rock an' Roll Ain't Never Gonna Leave Us;" Manchester's 100% Proof issue "New Way of Livin';" Overload - "Into Overload;" Scotland's Penetrations - "Coming to You;" West Midlands act Ricochet - *Double B Side*; Rokka - "Come Back;" Shock Treatment – "The Mugger;" Slender Thread – "I See the Light;" Slowtrain – "Ronnie;" Dick Smith Band - "Way of the World;" Starfighters - "I'm Falling;" Stryder – "Forcin' Thru';" Titan – "East Wind, West Wind;" Toad the Wet Sprocket - "Reaching for the Sky;" VHF - "Heart of Stone" and Weapon - "It's a Mad Mad World."

1980. The well-regarded Crucifixion issue "The Fox." "The Fox" also shows up on Neat's *All Hell Let Loose* and *60 Minutes Plus* compilations, albeit re-recorded.

1980. Requiem issue "Angel of Sin." Drummer Karl Wilcox would resurface in a later reincarnation of Diamond Head.

1980. Warrior issue a rare early full-length indie called *Let Battle Commence*.

1980. Lautrec issue "Mean Gasoline." Lautrec were lucky enough to tour with Saxon, also having backed up Def Leppard and Magnum. Both Reuben and Laurence Archer would move on to NWOBHM mid-marketers Stampede, with Laurence further distinguishing himself with a stint in UFO. The single was white label only.

1980. Midlands act Mayday issue "Day After Day." Recording for Reddingtons Rare, a store/label renowned for releasing cool early Quartz product, Mayday actually had this single produced by Quartz's Mick Hopkins.

1980. Welsh rockers Crys issue "Lan Yn Y Gogledd." The band would also manage two full-length albums.

1980. Axis issue "Lady." B-side "Messiah" showed up on the *Lead Weight* compilation, with the band's only other output being "Flame Burns On" on Neat's *All Hell Let Loose* and *60 Minutes Plus* comps.

Axis guitarist Mick Tucker:

A lot of these bands, the bigger they get the less touring they're doing. You look at Zeppelin, that was it, I think one gig in the '80s. I think it's a case of all these young bands just thinking we can do the independent thing. The first band I put together, Axis, we just paid for it ourselves. We went and just kept going down the country, put a bit of money together, went to Neat Records, recorded three tracks with them, and then we went out and got a thousand copies printed up and we just gigged. I think a lot of bands were doing that.

I remember when I was recording, the actual tape operator was Cronos. I said what are you doing? He was doodling around, drawing the Venom album cover. When you look back you think, hmm, pretty strange. Neat was in Newcastle. I'm originally from Middlesborough, about the next town there to Newcastle. There's a lot of musicians there and it's a pretty good breeding ground for musicians. There used to be a big club circuit up there, so I think you used to get a lot of the guys could go out and play the working men's clubs where you'd go and just play covers. They used to have rock nights and stuff in there, so you did get a lot of musicians coming from the northeast.

At that time when it was all kicking off, my first band Axis, we had a big tour bus and we'd just drive around the country playing gigs and sleeping, eating in there. Just a great time, you know? But there was a circuit and you could go out and get gigs. That's long gone now. We played with Raven, Trespass, Witchfynde, Angel Witch... I'd seen Def Leppard pretty early on, as well. But they signed a major, and so they didn't really do the club circuit.

1980. Charlie 'Ungry issue an indie LP called *House on Chester Road*.

1980. Ethel the Frog issue trouncing Beatles cover "Eleanor Rigby" backed with classic original "Fight Back."

1980. A band called Trojan opens for business, in Birmingham; they would eventually become AORists Shy.

1980. Hellanbach issue their debut single "Out to Get You," on Guardian. Journalists locked onto this band as a cross between the NWOBHM and Van Halen, mostly because of vocalist Jimmy Brash's often spoken patter.

1980. Speed issue "Man in the Street," on which Bruce Dickinson guests on lead vocals.

1980. Tank forms, the band featuring Algy Ward, ex of The Saints and The Damned, along with brothers Mark and Peter Brabbs.

Tank bassist and vocalist Algy Ward on whether his punk past influenced the Tank sound:

No, no, no, those things... not those things. You're trying out Americanisms now (laughs). No need to apologize. No, no, no, all I did was stuff that was edgy. So that's it, really. To myself, well, me, personally, there's no difference. No, no, no, I'm 55 years old, and the first single I ever bought was "My Generation" in 1965 by The Who. And I was listening to jazz and blues when I was in my mother's womb (laughs).

I don't listen to heavy rock, or I don't listen... I listen to the stuff I want to listen to. I was listening to all sorts in the mid-'70s. Oh, no, Deep Purple, Led Zeppelin... you've got to realize, I can't be confined by what I listened to. I'm esoteric, I suppose. But I like what I like, and if I don't like it, well then I won't fucking listen to it. No point, in those days.

Tank drummer Mark Brabbs:

My brother and I were into '70s heavy rock, with Black Sabbath, Deep Purple, all that sort of thing, a bit of Led Zeppelin thrown in. Algy was always a ZZ Top man, and even when he went through his punk period, he was still into ZZ Top, and obviously, Motörhead and Deep Purple. So we were all pretty much rockers. I mean, I got into the punk thing. I hated when it first came out.

I remember going to see The Damned before Algy joined them, in Croydon. And Rat Scabies came up, and they were supporting someone like Stray, some heavy rock band. Rat said come up and jam. And I said, "Well, I don't know what you're playing." And they're like, "It doesn't matter. Get up and make a noise." And I thought, this is a bit childish. And I didn't really get it until I heard, actually, "New Rose" from The Damned and when Stranglers put out "Peaches." And then *Never Mind the Bollocks* came out, the Sex Pistols, and that really kicked the whole industry in England right up the backside.

But the punk element of the band mainly came from Algy, and actually, my brother, he liked some of that. I wasn't into that. I was more into sort of dinosaur rock bands. But then, obviously, when we started jamming the songs, it just became what it was. We didn't aim to be anything other than what came out, when we got together. So it wasn't preconceived, like, let's do this, let's do that.

And it kind of reflected our lifestyle. Because when we were young, we were party animals. We lived life in the fast lane. So it's kind of safe if you listen to the early demos of some of those songs that made it onto *Filth Hounds*. Some of the playing is almost subtle, you could say, compared to what the finished article became, which was a lot faster, a lot more aggressive. And that was probably down to more lifestyle than musical influences, if that makes sense.

Jess Cox on the ties between punk and metal:
It was a huge melting pot of music at the time. I know all the guys in the Tygers, for instance, were all into anything and everything. It wasn't just like metal or die. It's like the Tubes, the Pistols, plus I was a big Clash fan. We were all influenced by different things. We loved classic metal, of course. I mean, Led Zeppelin, you can't get any better. Deep Purple, Sabbath, Lizzy, Ozzy, even Journey and Foreigner, so some of the American stuff. But we all had our punk albums in our collections as well, with the Sex Pistols and the Clash being the main two.

I mean, it was kind of inseparable in a way. I know, for instance, Phil Lynott with Thin Lizzy did a few things with various punk acts, and of course you've got Algy Ward who stormed across from punk into metal. Half the time it was just a uniform you had on. The sound was probably quite similar. I mean, we even called ourselves punk metal, the early Tygers—we were a punk metal band. We weren't a sort of classic heavy metal band, although that's what it turned into. We would even dress that way. It's crazy when you think back—it's laughable—but at the time we wore like straight pants. I used to wear a shirt and a tie with a cord. So we'd dress sort of punky; it was very much out the punk movement, really.

Damned drummer Rat Scabies on whether anybody ever suggested they adapt and become a metal band:

Yeah, I think somebody from a record company said it once. We used to think of it as a joke, really. Because the truth is, if you're not that thing, it's very difficult for you to be it. You know, sometimes we would do stuff that was kind of like heavy metal-sounding riffs, almost to set the whole thing up and make fun of it. But actually we weren't any better at it (laughs). We couldn't do it. We're not made that way. You kind of have to be the real thing.

1980. Bernie Torme, now no longer operating as The Bernie Torme Band, issues a single, "The Beat"/"I Want"/"Boney Maronie." The band is essentially Gillan without Ian, namely Bernie, John McCoy, Mick Underwood and Colin Townes.

1980. It's a great year for heavy metal compilations, previously a phenomenon almost unheard of. Even K-Tel get into the game, issuing *Axe Attack*, which includes tracks by Girlschool, Motörhead, Iron Maiden and Gillan, amongst more established acts.

1980. Northeast England's well regarded Hollow Ground issue their classic and highly collectible 7" four track EP, on Guardian. Vocalist Glenn Coates would move onto Fist for their second album, *Back with a Vengeance*.

January 1980

January 1980. Girlschool issue "Emergency"/"Furniture Fire." A-side "Emergency," from the debut LP, features the familiar refrain "999 emergency," soon to be more familiar when Motörhead would send it up on the *St. Valentine's Day Massacre* spit-swap EP.

> Girlschool guitarist and vocalist Kim McAuliffe on the band's biggest influence:
> Well, obviously Motörhead, really; that's the main one. Right in the beginning we were just writing our own stuff and it was influenced by Black Sabbath and Deep Purple. I mean obviously we were into heavy metal when we were young. But then later it was punk and Motörhead.

January 2, 1980. Ethel the Frog offshoot band Salem have their first meeting, at a pub in East Riding of Yorkshire. The Hull act's first demo would emerge a year later.

January 11, 1980. Girl issue "Do You Love Me"/"Strawberries" (a.k.a. "The Single") from their forthcoming debut album *Sheer Greed*.

January 23, 1980. Saxon record a BBC session that is broadcast three weeks later on *The Friday Rock Show*. Three selections from the debut are joined with the much more risible "Motorcycle Man" and "747 (Strangers in the Night)."

> Tygers of Pan Tang producer Chris Tsangarides on Saxon:
> Surprisingly, they wrote great pop tunes, and I mean, I fell off my perch when I saw them and Iron Maiden on *Top of the Pops*. It was always a hip hooray when you saw a rock band playing on that show—it was great to see. And they had quite a few hits back in those days, which goes to show how many people were buying their music. Although the name and the image, if you never saw them, but just saw it, you would think, it would be some doom-ridden metal stuff, but it was far from it. It was very, very tuneful, great melodic pop songs, with heavy backing.
> They knew what the fan—people like themselves—liked. And the way I see it, you have to be a fan of the music that you were doing, because when you are working with this stuff, you think, would I buy it? If not, then something is wrong. "We better sort something out here, boys." But that's kind of how you approach things. Anyway,

that's the way I do. You're a fan of it—do I like it as a fan? If I don't like it as a fan, why? That really is the root behind it all. They all are the same as their fans, and it's with the same people, except one lot plays it and one lot listens to it, that knows just as much about listening to it as they know about playing it (laughs). When the New Wave of British Heavy Metal bands came out, at the time, most of them looked like the fans. They wore the same cut-off denim over their leather. They looked the same—there you go.

Saxon bassist Steve Dawson on his band's links to biker culture:
    Well, in the first instance, both myself and Biff had motorcycles. And obviously that came through in songs like "Stallions of the Highway" and "Motorcycle Man" and stuff like that. But, really, the connection to the motorbiking world didn't come from us. Because the bikers in the Hells Angels and people like that, they picked up on it and sort of made it their anthem. And they approached us to play lots and lots of their shows, and we still do now. We played loads and loads of concerts for the motorcycle people.
    We've never ever had a problem with any Hells Angels or motorcycle shows—they've always been fantastic. And they've always treated us with utmost respect. The only bit of trouble we ever had with anything to do with motorcycles, we did a motorcycle festival in the southern part of Italy and they insisted on taking us to the stage on five Harley-Davidsons. But trying to ride on the back of a Harley Davidson holding a bass, you can't do it. It's quite difficult, because you can't hold on. And a lot of those motorcycles are made for two people. And there was nowhere to put me leg—me right leg was on the exhaust pipe (laughs). So by the time we got to the stage, which was about a quarter mile ride, I had burned through my trousers and scorched my leg.

February 1980

February 1980. Marseille issue their "Kites"/"Some Like it Hot" single.

February 1980. Def Leppard issue an advance single from their forthcoming debut, a new recording of "Hello America," backed with capable non-LP fast-tracker "Good Morning Freedom," which peaks at #45. *Sounds* pans the song, beginning the backlash against the bounders from Sheffield. The band embarks on a northern UK tour, supported by Witchfynde, who Def Leppard used to go watch play, in the Peak District.

February 1980. Saxon records what will be their seminal second album, *Wheels of Steel*, working at Ramport Studios.

Saxon vocalist Biff Byford:

It's a very large sound, *Wheels of Steel*. If you listen to it, it's all about performance, really, and the guitar sound is very, very British. I think we created a British guitar sound on that album, definitely. And it's the one album that everybody had to beat, actually. Don't ask me why. I mean, I don't know why magical things happen in studios. They just fucking do, yeah?

And you know, sometimes they don't and sometimes they do, and if the performance captures it, then it doesn't really matter how good or bad it sounds. If you've got a great song, it's a great song, regardless. I just think a lot of it's in the songwriting, the magic of the songwriting. So we just went into the Who studio, actually, in London, which was quite good; I quite liked that. It's got a good vibe, and we just played everything at full volume, recorded it at full volume, listened back at full volume, and put it out. And it just went nuts, really.

Saxon guitarist Paul Quinn on the magic of *Wheels of Steel*:

Right place, right time, I think, is a lot of that. It wasn't particularly focused; it's still as diverse as we are now. It had really fast songs on it, and songs about driving fast or "don't let the bastards grind you down" type lyrics. A lot of our stuff is really either anti-war or something historical.

As far as production goes, Pete Hinton was a very positive ideas man in that he'd give us a kind of insight into what was more economic and he did a lot of edits for singles. Like the "Wheels of Steel" chorus became half of what the original version was. Sound-wise, he occasionally helped with EQ-ing the amps, although his engineer was good. He'd worked with Lizzy anyway, Will Reid Dick. Our soon-to-become manager at that point was Nigel Thomas and he tried anything that we put forward to him. We recorded guitars in a shower room for the brightness, and had a PA running as well so that we didn't wear our headphones in the studio. That was wild (laughs). Imagine trying to keep the sound of the PA away from the microphones that the guitar was using.

Saxon bassist Steve Dawson:
Somebody might come up with a title, like, "Oh, 'Wheels of Steel,' what's that going to be about?" Originally it was going to be about steam engines, because I'm a fanatic on those things. Then you go, well, that's not really heavy metal enough (laughs). So we transposed it to a car, a '57 Chevy.

Saxon guitarist Graham Oliver:
By the time we got to *Wheels of Steel*, what happened is, we finished with Norman Sheffield as management; he didn't really work out. So we were picked up by Carrere Records, and we were put in the old studio in Battersea. And when we were in that studio, we were pretty much left to our own devices.

And what we did is we just hammered those songs down more or less live, and we didn't do the kind of recording where you put the drums down and then you put the guitar down and then you layer this and that—pretty much that's what happened with the first album. What you got with the second album, it was just us being us, and being allowed to do it with no direction. In fact Pete Hinton was just there to sit in the control room and say that was a good take, that works, do it again. But that's all he did; he wasn't like a producer that kind of stamps his own ideas on how he thought we should be.

February 1980. Iron Maiden works on their debut album, at Kingsway Studios.

February 1, 1980. Jet issues Girl's debut album, entitled *Sheer Greed*, which rises to #33 on the UK charts, buoyed by tours with Pat Travers and UFO.

Girl producer Chris Tsangarides:

As the punk was going on, I went over to a band called Girl, who were, for want of a better word, glam rock. Makeup-wearing, rock 'n' roll era, Aerosmith-style, and we were making this record with them when the Sex Pistols were in the charts. And people didn't know quite what to make of them. It was one of those wrong time or wrong place or whatever. But it's quite a few people from that band went on to much bigger and better things. Phil Collen, for example, in Def Leppard, and Phil Lewis in LA Guns, etc.

But that was an interesting marriage; there were punk elements in there, and they were very into the band Japan, and then Phil was into Gary Moore and so on. And it was a really interesting project. I really liked it, but I got a phone call from the managing director of the record company, asking me whether the band they had signed and put in the studio with me, were they heavy metal or not? And I really didn't know what to say to the guy. I said, "Well, do you remember the rehearsal?" And he went, "Yes." "They're just like that." So they didn't know what they were signing or were doing or whatever. They did have relative success, but audiences didn't know what to make of them. They were neither punk nor heavy but this in-between thing, and they just kind of disappeared and didn't do much.

February 1, 1980. The *Metal for Muthas* tour kicks off, headlined variously by Samson, Saxon and Motörhead. The none too specific tour featured, at various times, 22 different NWOBHM bands, including Iron Maiden.

Iron Maiden bassist Steve Harris on first hearing the phrase New Wave of British Heavy Metal:

I remember it was put in *Sounds* magazine, and it was all part to do with the Neal Kay thing, the whole tie-in, and all these bands; it was an underground movement going on, and it was just this term that had come up, the New Wave of British Heavy Metal, and it really stuck. It became this whole movement.

And you know, it was great to be part of that. You know, we didn't think of that, we didn't come up with that, but it was nice to be lumped in with it all, because it was a whole vibe going on. The unification, was again, against the punk thing. It was a reaction against that. The punk thing was a reaction against the big rock bands, and we were a reaction against that as well. Because we were trying to get gigs and the whole thing, it was just the whole feeling of a togetherness, of this. We've got this good music here and we need to get out and sort of show it to people.

DJ Neal Kay on the *Metal for Muthas* tour:

I mean, Maiden, Mantis and meself toured *Muthas* in our own right. Before then we did the "heavy metal crusade." That was—and I love the title of that—that was like taking it to the people. That was crusading for justice, for me. And people hate me talking like this. They always did when I was working in the industry, but fuck 'em. I don't care. I think that when you mean something, and it matters that much to you,

if you're going to stand for it, then to hell with everything. Nothing can get in the way. Nothing. No part-timers, no stupidity, no people who don't understand. They don't belong, so just go around them or through them.

And the crusade did all this. It took two, three bands at a time, with myself in the usual comparé/DJ role, out to a circuit of universities, colleges. It was arranged by Paul Samson's manager, Alistair Primrose. The only problem with that was Samson headlined all the shows, and by about the fourth or fifth it was clear that Iron Maiden in the middle section should have been the headline band.

And I'm not being cruel, I'm not being rude, and I certainly wouldn't besmirch Paul Samson's name, because the guy died a couple years back, and he and his wife were very close friends of my first wife and I outside of music. We liked Paul very much, but Paul's idea of… to him there never was a New Wave of British Heavy Metal.

Iron Maiden guitarist Dennis Stratton on the *Metal for Muthas* tour: Praying Mantis had been in the same sort of scores as Maiden and Tygers of Pan Tang and Saxon and everyone else. We were all mates and the situation was that Praying Mantis would support Iron Maiden on the *Metal or Muthas* tour because that was put together with Neal Kay doing the DJing. So it was just two bands touring around England—England, Scotland and Wales—just doing the first tour because, sooner or later, very shortly, the Maiden album was gonna come out.

Producer Chris Tsangarides on the gathering storm that was the NWOBHM:
I think it started actually from that compilation album *Metal for Muthas*, that we suddenly had that phrase, New Wave of British Heavy Metal. I was still getting started out as a producer then and these bands were coming to me, like Tygers of Pan Tang and Sledgehammer and God knows what, and they were just bands. I didn't even realize that we were New Wave of British Heavy Metal or anything like that.

And it's only after a few years that I suppose we were. Because if you actually knew, when you went into the studio with a band today, you could make a record, and you're not thinking, "Oh, I'm making a classic that everybody is going to buy and it's going to sell 25 gazillion." You never know what's going to happen with it, and when it does, I'm more surprised than anybody.

February 2, 1980. Saxon headline London's Electric Ballroom, supported by Angel Witch and Sledgehammer.

Angel Witch bassist Kevin Riddles on the band's sound:
When people ask me what Angel Witch were like in those days, I always refer them to a quote from journalist Geoff Barton, who was the key journalist for *Sounds* magazine at the time and was very instrumental in bringing the whole New Wave of British Heavy Metal thing to fruition in the '80s.

He saw us when we supported, I believe it was Samson and Iron Maiden at the Music Machine in London. And he did a huge article, where they got the phrase New Wave Of British Heavy Metal. In the article was sort of like, 'If you want blood, and then in brackets, flash bombs, lightning, smoke and mirrors and everything... you've got it.

And when he came to describe us, he said, Angel Witch seem to me to sound like Black Sabbath played through a cement mixer. And it kind of stuck with us. I mean it was one of those things. It was like, okay, I'll go with that. I'm quite happy with that. For the simple reason being, because we were

of that genre of bands, that sort of Black Sabbath sound which nowadays, of course, you would call it doom metal.

But we weren't aiming for that, particularly. It was just the way we sounded because of the way Kevin played, the way I played; it was hard, it was fast, it was loud. That's kind of what came out. In a lot of ways, it was the same way with Motörhead—the fact that Lemmy plays chords on the bass nearly all the time, it's almost inevitably going to make the band sound heavy. You can't have it any other way. Motörhead are never going to do a love song. or if they do, it's not going to sound happy and melodic and lovely. They're still very heavy and very loud. It's the way Lemmy plays.

And it was the same with us, really. It developed because we were a three-piece. We weren't going to be. In the early days we were a four-piece, but that rhythm guitar didn't stay with us that long, with Rob. When we became a three-piece, we had to fill things out. But we didn't want to be, to use the Canadian example, Rush. We weren't technically that proficient anyway, but we wanted it to be harder than that, and louder and stronger than a normal three-piece would've been.

February 5, 1980. Venom play their first gig, at the Meth (Methodist Church) on Station Road, Wallsend, UK. With their bassist Alan Winston abruptly quitting before the gig, Cronos moves over from second guitar to bass. The band now consists of Cronos, Mantas and Abaddon, with Clive Archer (also, like the others, with new mystical name, Jesus Christe) on vocals. With Cronos newly playing bass, plugged into a guitar amp and conjuring the very devil in heavy metal, suddenly Motörhead don't seem quite as irascible. Also, incredibly, the scariest-looking member of the band was soon to be departed—vocalist Clive Archer sports what has to be called an early version of corpsepaint.

February 7, 1980. *Rolling Stone* reports that record sales in the UK were down 20% in 1979, which corresponds, abstractly anyway, with the idea that there was a vacuum in the industry after punk. This made 1979 the worst year since 1973. A similar lament was taking place stateside, with 1979 turning out to mark a pronounced depression over recent previous years.

February 8, 1980. Iron Maiden issues their "Running Free"/"Burning Ambition" single, which coincides, essentially with the release of *Metal for Muthas*, both records being on EMI. In May and June, Maiden embarks on a short tour with Praying Mantis and Heavy Metal Soundhouse DJ Neal Kay (which Steve considers to be, essentially, the *Metal for Muthas* tour). Touring as support to Judas Priest follows.

Iron Maiden bassist Steve Harris on the band's instant acclaim:

I don't really know, because we had a following right from the start, literally from the first couple of gigs that we played. You know, we just got a following. They just started coming to the gigs, and making their own shirts and stuff like that; we didn't have any shirts to sell or anything yet. It was just too early days. And they started making their own things, and really following us about. I mean, it's not very far, but it's difficult to get from one part of London to another. It's the same just playing like Stratford, and just going to Ruskin, or Harrow Road in Barking. It's quite a way, and difficult to get to, but yet they still used to turn up there, and it was amazing, really.

And I think right from that early thing, we just had this hardcore following. And so it just gave us an edge over a lot of the other bands. You know, we would go play the Music Machine, where there were three or four or five bands on the bill and we would get such a reaction because it was almost like a rent-a-crowd coming as well. We would pick up new people as well, but the hardcore fans followed us about. Just as they do now, but, you know, now it's a more massive scale.

DJ Neal Kay on *Metal for Muthas*:
I helped Ashley Goodall from the label put that together. It was like a sampler of the NWOBHM cassette bands, and it was put together just as a sampler in mind. It wasn't meant to be a $10M production or anything like that, although I was absolutely fucked off to death with the artwork. I thought it was absolutely horrible, to be honest with you. It sold us down the river, man. Down in Mississippi. Without even a paddle. Awful, you know?

Journalist Goetz Kunhemund:
    Iron Maiden have influenced all kinds of heavy metal that we know today because they're the core of heavy metal. They are as important to power metal as to speed metal; even black metal has a lot of Iron Maiden undertones. Hard rock, everything. Maiden just took hard rock from the '70s into the '80s and they founded a genre that didn't exist before because there weren't any rock magazines, there weren't any metal record companies, there weren't as many bands.
    They brought in this do-it-yourself attitude into rock music—Maiden started it all. They are a big part of power metal as well. In Hammerfall you can hear a lot of Iron Maiden as well as you can hear a lot of Accept or Rainbow or Helloween. Power metal bands would pick up on the guitar harmonies that Iron Maiden didn't invent but made very popular within heavy metal. We all know they took it from Wishbone Ash and Thin Lizzy—there used to be bands before Iron Maiden who had twin guitar harmonies. Judas Priest as well, of course. But many power metal bands that exist today have two guitarists and they use twin guitar harmonies and they use the Iron Maiden way of playing twin guitars.

February 15, 1980. *Metal for Muthas* is issued, on EMI. The album reaches a surprising #12 on the UK charts and spawns a NWOBHM tour (actual start date was February 1), variously headlined by Samson, Motörhead or Saxon. Maiden's "Sanctuary" was a featured track on the album, the song inspiring the name of Maiden-associated company Sanctuary Records. Acts on the album were: Iron Maiden (two songs), Sledgehammer, EF Band, Toad the Wet Sprocket, Praying Mantis, Ethel the Frog, Angel Witch, Samson and Nutz.

Iron Maiden bassist Steve Harris:

We had two tracks on there, and we were opening side A of the disc as well, so the profile for us was really good on there. And then after that we went out and did the *Metal for Muthas* tour with Praying Mantis supporting, and again, it was just this whole movement going on. It was really quite exciting to be part of this whole thing.

Obviously there were a lot of bands around, Toad the Wet Sprocket and people like that, strange name. But there were all these bands; there was just this whole movement going on. So if you were a fan going to the gigs, it was pretty obvious what was going on. It was this underground thing, but for someone outside coming in, they might not have realized straight away what was going on. It was obviously there, and it was proved when he put that record together and it did really well.

DJ Neal Kay:

The actual idea was Ashley's, not mine. He didn't have a name for it. I named it, and that caused a lot of trouble up north, which I will explain in a minute. His idea with EMI was to take all these demo tapes, I was to put them together, and come up with stuff, and he gave me some tapes to listen to that had been sent in to EMI, because everyone knew by then that EMI was listening, because *Sounds* told them they were. Which is good.

And Ashley represented the new, younger generation of A&R men. His attitude was different. I mean Sheppy, Brian Shepherd, was one of those as well. EMI had a pretty good A&R department, actually, at the time, as opposed to some of the others that were just cloth-eared and weren't going to listen. They became the enemy as well, you know. But Ashley was good. He was very young at the time. He may only have been in his very early 20s—I'm sure he was—but he kind of believed in me and I believed in him.

He phoned me up and said, "I've got this idea for this compilation thing with all these new bands. Why don't you come up to Manchester Square and we'll talk about it?" And I did. I came in to London, and by the end of the afternoon we had an idea that we were going to do it. He gave me a load of tapes, I took them away, I came up with some tracks and stuff I thought were good. Bands were encouraged to record their own stuff for the album, which I thought was a terrible idea, because the recordings were not all that, some of them. Maiden got two tracks on the *Muthas* thing, which everyone knows, and Praying Mantis were on there too.

Journalist John Tucker:

There were a number of compilations but *Muthas* was the king. The MCA one, *Brute Force*, had some lovely stuff on it. And again, I go into this in my book *Suzie Smiled* because there were bands on that that never went anywhere, and that's the only place you'll find them. And it's interesting because MCA tried to jump on the bandwagon and put out an album called *Precious Metal*, which is pretty much classic and American rock and realized they completely missed the point. So the second time around they got it dead right. But *Metal for Muthas*, February 1980, that was when things were happening. And that was a good showcase. That was a good way of getting all these bands from wherever in the UK to actually helping the likes of us who were spread out a bit, find out what's new and what's happening.

Nutz were on there, Toad the Wet Sprocket. They were a kids band — they were 14. Their moms and dads drove them everywhere, and they had such little combos when they played live at the 'wagon, they had to put their little amps on chairs. And their moms and dads were there. The lead singer was a milkman from Luton, I remember, but they were so damn good. And I'll tell you what, they could play "Blues in A" better than anybody.

I mean it was a great idea. It suddenly woke everyone up, both sides of the fence, to the fact that the record companies were suddenly listening. If they'd put out a compilation of all these unheard-of new bands, then something was finally moving. And it did inspire a lot of others to get more actively involved on different levels.

Angel Witch bassist Kevin Riddles:

The way that *Metal for Muthas* came about was because EMI, in their wisdom, decided they wanted to jump on that bandwagon, to get one or more bands on the label because they never really had that. I think they had their successes with other genres and never really did that much with heavy rock. They missed out on bands like Zeppelin and Black Sabbath and they were looking to get involved.

Basically, Ashley Goodall came up with the concept of putting together a compilation of all these New Wave of British Heavy Metal bands. So ourselves, Maiden, Toad the Wet Sprocket, Praying Mantis, Samson, everybody who was around on the circuit at that time. Admittedly, it was very London-centric sort of based. They were mainly southern bands. But there was the odd ones from further afield.

We were asked to go and record, which we did, and everybody had the same deal. It was you're going to have one track, or maybe two, on *Metal for Muthas*, with an option for a follow-up single. There was no money involved, but they paid for the recording. We thought, great, okay, and we're all gigging solidly at the time. There was a great circuit in England at the time. You could be out three or four days a week, and that was our jobs, basically. That's what we were doing.

And we went and recorded the tracks, and from that, it went so well, EMI decided to pick up the option on just two bands, and that was Maiden and Angel Witch. So we were the only ones that had that option taken up, and that's where "Sweet Danger" came from, if I remember rightly.

February 15, 1980. Long-time home country hard rock favourites Nazareth follow up their dark and heavy *No Mean City* album with the light and thoughtful *Malice in Wonderland* record. Gone is the band's celebrated slashing logo, and gone is the pubby grit of the band, replaced by a form of California "avocado mafia" sophistication.

February 19, 1980. AC/DC's Bon Scott dies, in London, freezing to death in a car after a night of heavy drinking.

DJ Neal Kay:

I was at the Music Machine the night Bon Scott died. I was with Lemmy, we were drinking, Bon was there. Lemmy and I were on a rare night off playing pool, right upstairs, right at the very back. And I don't know what happened exactly, but I got home about three in the morning. My wife woke me up about a quarter to nine, and said, "Have you heard the news? Here's the newspaper." And it said, "Bon Scott dies on the *Highway to Hell*," which was the album of the day, 1980.

And I couldn't believe it. Could not believe it. He was there just a few hours ago! And I remember phoning up Peter Mensch, who I knew, and I just said, "Hey Peter, is this real?" He said, "Yes, Neal," in his whiny way. And he was so blasé about it I couldn't believe it, because Bon Scott, to me, was AC/DC. Brian Johnson came from a pop rock band from Newcastle called Geordie. They had success in the '70s with a few 45s and that was it. And I don't dislike the bloke, but he's certainly not Bon Scott. Actually, AC/DC were booked to do a personal appearance at the  Soundhouse when Bon Scott died, oddly enough, which is another reason why I was in touch with Peter Mensch.

Early 1980. Firebird issue "Change." The sound is keyboardy Christian pop metal, produced by Ian Gillan at his own Kingway studio. As well, Welsh act Night Time Flyer issue "Out with a Vengeance" while Stormtrooper put forth "Pride Before a Fall" while Sunderland's Warrior morph into Battleaxe, who will be good for two albums.

March 1980

March 1980. Diamond Head issue their first single "Shoot Out the Lights"/"Helpless." By May, the band had completed the mixing of their forthcoming debut album.

Diamond Head guitarist Brian Tatler on the NWOBHM's indie culture:

It did seem like all the New Wave of British Heavy Metal bands were doing their own records, making their own singles, going to little local studios and making cheap records, really. We kind of got the idea from punk rock. Because indie labels came out around the time of punk rock.

It'd never been heard of before. It was always, you'd aim for a record deal, a big record deal. You had your EMIs and CBSs. But certainly with Rough Trade and all these tiny labels, it gave it a different idea that you can make your own record and get a distributor. You can sell it yourself and sell it to specialist record shops. And I think all of that was taken from punk who already said we could do this. You've just got to make the product in the first place, and then just go and sell it.

I mean, the indies, at least they were signing bands and making releases and all that. Maybe EMI were inundated with tapes, you know? They might have had 200 bands trying to get on board, and they made a wise choice in signing Iron Maiden, didn't they? But once EMI have got a band, they're not really looking for another New Wave of British Heavy Metal band, and you do get that sense that each label wants a token band, and find the best one they can of this new style. And then the rest of you are left to scratch around and sign to Rondelet or whoever's left. Years ago you wouldn't have got a record out unless you would've got signed. It just hadn't really been invented, had it, indie, until punk rock. And that was do-it-yourself.

But you had to make your statement. When *Sounds* picked up on the New Wave of British Heavy Metal and gave it front cover, everybody was like, oh, this is something different. That kind of alerted the UK record industry to the fact that there's something new here, that there's a metal movement going on. And I think record companies realized metal fans are very faithful. I'm going to buy every record and go to the concerts and buy tickets and all that. So there must be a market and there's a lot of money to be made there. It's not like pop music, which is instant, isn't it? Whereas metal, you could build it at the time to sell a lot of records. So you know, Black Sabbath's done all right; let's find another new Black Sabbath.

I just know that bands were making them themselves, almost as cheaply as possible. They would just go into the studio in one day and make the record, and set everything up, and record it almost live, and probably just overdub the vocal, do a new lead vocal, and possibly another lead guitar solo. So it was very limited budget, very limited time, get it all down as quickly as possible.

I can remember our drummer complaining about the drum booth. Because they had a really, really good drum booth in the studio, just in a corner, heavily carpeted, and then you shut the door behind you. And he used to say it felt like claustrophobia; you almost felt afraid to breathe deeply, and you'd be expected to give this performance, in nothing bigger than a phone booth (laughs). Whereas now, you set up the kit in a large room to get the ambience. But then the kit sound was just dead (laughs).

We paid for them ourselves, our demos. Obviously we recorded everything ourselves in our bedroom, or we had a little office we could rehearse in on a Sunday. The bass player's dad worked there, so we would just use the office and record there. But we would only make these little cassettes with our new songs, and I actually think we learned our art of arranging by recording straight into the cassette and listening back to it thinking, that doesn't really go to it does it? No one explained it to us, but it just felt natural—it was all complete instinct and intuition.

March 1980. Jet Records puts out the *Metallergy* compilation, budget priced to cash in, including defunct non-metal band Widowmaker, plus some three-year-old Quartz songs, selections from progressive rock band Magnum, plus Gillan guitarist Bernie Torme as a solo act.

March 1980. *Sounds* issues its 1979 reader's poll results and metal dominates. Def Leppard wins best new band with Iron Maiden, Samson and Saxon making a showing. Rush, a major NWOBHM influence, wins best band. Geoff Barton, however, elsewhere in the issue, slags Def Leppard at length, for a second time in as many months.

> Diamond Head guitarist Brian Tatler:
> Suddenly there were lots of bands all over the UK. And nobody was aware of each other until *Sounds* kind of tied it all together. But you could read this newspaper—it was a broadsheet—and find out, whoa, there's a band from Sheffield, New Wave of British Heavy Metal, and then there'd be someone from Newcastle or Bristol or whatever. It seemed to be everybody's doing this thing, and I suppose you'd be competing to see who is the best, and you'd listen to their new single and their new EP, and you would try to see where you were in the pecking order. And being as arrogant as a young man can, we felt we were the best. We're better than these. We'll probably get a record deal because we're better than this band.

March 1980. Def Leppard embarks on their first major national tour, with Magnum as middle act preceded by one local band at each stop, including Jameson Raid in the Midlands.

> Def Leppard drummer Rick Allen on the NWOBHM:
> Well, we were all coming in 'round about when punk was just turning the whole thing on its head, and the three-minute exciting song came about. And we had been used to—no disrespect to any of these

bands—but long-winded performances by Emerson, Lake & Palmer. It was all very clever and everything, and lovely, and they could jam and whatever, but it was a little bit self-indulgent. Especially for 14, 15-year-old kids. So what we did was embrace the immediacy of punk, with a similar sort of chordal structure of rock. So the combination to us was great. And then of course when Queen came along, we basically ripped off everything they did.

March 1980. Judas Priest issue an advance single from the forthcoming *British Steel* album, namely "Living After Midnight"/"Delivering the Goods;" there are additional tracks for the 12" version, but the a-side was a clear shocker in terms of its simple and commercial direction.

Can you take 12 inches of "British Steel"?

"British Steel"—the metal monster you've been waiting for from Judas Priest. Including the songs "Living After Midnight," "Metal Gods" and "Breaking the Law." "British Steel." The Priest takes rock 'n' roll to the hilt—and then some.
Judas Priest. "British Steel." On Columbia Records and Tapes.

Buy it once. Enjoy it a lifetime. Recorded music is your best entertainment value.
"Columbia" is a trademark of CBS Inc.   © 1980 CBS Inc.

Rob Halford on the birth of the NWOBHM:

I think we felt that the New Wave of British Heavy Metal was creeping up through like '76, '77, '78, '79. You could read little bits and pieces in the paper about this band and that band, or a pub or a club or whatever. You could sense that everybody was going, "Hey, have you heard about this new sound? It's called heavy metal, you know. It's going to be great."

I mean, this generation of music fans has got something to run to and identify. And as we know in rock 'n' roll, everything happens at the beginning of a decade—I don't know why it's that cycle but it is. You look at music and that's how it's always been. So without a doubt I think it's fair to say that the New Wave of British Heavy Metal—including Priest, which is part of the old wave—we all came together and that was just like the dynamite going off. 1980, bang, we're here, let's go, we're going to grow. This is now going to be a worldwide event, and it was.

It was just tremendously exciting because suddenly you are surrounded by the bands and the fans that are feeling the same way you have felt for a number of years before that moment, before 1980. You just feel, I guess, satisfied, maybe a sense of relief that it's not just us. This is great! Look at this band, there's Maiden, there's Motörhead, like we're all in it now.

We believed in it in Priest right from day one. We knew something was going to happen but we didn't know exactly when. But when all these other bands started to connect, then it was tremendous. I think we all felt it was probably worthwhile more than anything, you know. We knew that it was going to happen and now it has happened.

So it was tremendous excitement and energy, and you are able to check each other out and be inspired, and to some extent influenced about where we're all going together as bands within the heavy metal scene. So yeah, it was a tremendous moment, a great boost.

I think it was a great boost because there were still those detractors. Everybody was trying to crush it. Metal sucks, metal is rubbish, you know, it's going nowhere and we're like no, no, no. We're going to stick through this. We're going to get through it and we did. Just before that new wave of heavy metal thing exploded, we had to deal with the punk and the new wave, and then the new romantic moment, because suddenly everybody said, "See ya! We're going over here now."

So a lot of bands like Priest left to get on with it by themselves. I mean it's very important to remember that media and press, any kind of exposure, is vital to a band's growth and development. Suddenly we were left with nothing. Nobody was interested. Couldn't get an interview, couldn't get a photo shoot, it was like whatever. But we sensed that punk moment was going to be very turbulent and very short-lived. Some great things happened at that time but that's the thing I love about metal. It's like the blues, it's like jazz, it's always gonna be here. It's not like a music that is going to fade off into the sunset. It will always be here and that's how we felt through a bit of that turbulent period with the punk, new wave thing. We knew it was gonna survive and so yeah, '80 was the start of the match.

Judas Priest bassist Ian Hill:

The punk thing was just starting off at the time, but we were never here to see it, per sé (laughs). We were always out on the road or in the studio. The thought of us going out and catching a show in those days was alien to us. Obviously, it was in the music papers at the time, *New Musical Express* and *Sounds* and *Melody Maker*, and things like that.

But the direction of our music attracted a certain audience anyway. We didn't attract girls for instance (laughs). We used to at one time, but with the leather and the studs and the actual power, the raw aggression of the music, it was not something that is that attractive to the female audience. So most of our audience were teenage boys, really. Which we all were ourselves at the time. We were sort of in our mid-20s at the time, maybe 30, but yeah, that was when the typical heavy metal fan, if there was such a thing, started to evolve.

I guess up to that point *British Steel* was the definitive heavy metal album. It also crossed over into other areas. There was, as you know, a couple of very good radio-friendly tracks on there, in "Living After Midnight" and "Breaking the Law." So the radio station started to pick up on those songs, and it started to gain us fans from areas we wouldn't necessarily pick them up from. Maybe people who'd never go see us live, or bothered to be into the things we were into at the time (laughs). So it probably started heavy metal on its way to its popularity.

March 1980. Whitesnake issue *Live at Hammersmith*, in Japan only, on Sunburst/Toshiba. The album would become sides three and four of the double version of the widely issued *Live... in the Heart of the City*.

David Coverdale on the NWOBHM:

My illegitimate children. I would joke about it. I know the guy who invented it. I'm still working with him—he's the editor of *Classic Rock*, NWOBHM. What it was, though, like any other thing... when you had the punk explosion the cream rises to the surface— The Police, the Clash, all these things. But the bands that rise to the surface are not the ones who are just fashionable. They're the ones who write songs. Songs is what lasts. Musicians get old, images become amusing, but songs can live forever, and that's always been my driving force, is to focus on songs. I was too old.

But of course you had the great Def Leppard came out of that, some great stuff, and Maiden, still flourishing, Priest. Let me give you a different perspective. A different perspective is Vanilla Fudge was the heaviest band I'd heard, which is significantly before that. Purple were called heavy metal and I can understand that. To me, I'll hear old blues stuff, when Muddy Waters, like when he started to play electric guitar through distorted amps, those riffs were putting horn sections out of business.

But it's much more of a media thing than an audience thing. It's a media title, it's a media categorization. I don't think any people who came to my shows thought I'm part of the New Wave of British Heavy Metal. For one second this was an entirely media-driven thing. As stuff is today. They try to make things posh and fashionable in order to accommodate themselves. You'll get your Biebers and all that, and God bless him and good luck to him, but that's very impressionable. The hard rock fan can tell shit from shine-ola.

March 1, 1980. *Live Quartz* is issued by Reddingtons Rare and then soon reissued by Logo. Reddingtons Rare also issue Quartz product in the "Nantucket Sleighride"/"Wildfire" single and the "Satan's Serenade" 12", into June of 1980.

Quartz drummer Malcolm Cope:

At the time, you see, we'd done extremely well with the record sales. Reddingtons Rare Records... well, Reddington and Danny who ran the shop, and one or two of the guys got friendly with him, and he suggested funding our recording. And through his shop, we were actually selling thousand of records. Released off of what was the live album. I don't know the exact figure, but he'd done thousands of records on that live album, and then we leased it to Logo, and of course they started to sail across Europe with that.

And then we did a cover of that Mountain song, "Nantucket Sleighride," which sold a phenomenal amount, because the television program called *Weekend World*, that was the theme tune to that. And also *The Muppets* used it on one of their shows; only a few seconds, but it pushed the sales of that like crazy.

And so MCA signed us and was trying to follow up on all those sales, you see? Because the reason was, we were not hot on the idea of doing anything. We were capitalizing on this underground independent thing, which was going all our way. And then this deal comes out of the blue with MCA. Well, honestly, we wanted to go sort of more international than what we could do with just with Danny. So we fell into it, and I think that was one of our demises, to be honest with you. Because once we teamed up with MCA, I think the kids were all quite keen on this indie thing, and it seemed to sort of knock the cherry off the top of the cake.

Quartz guitarist Mick Hopkins:

We were riddled with bad luck over the years; you could take the wrong path with decisions. But with Reddingtons, it was so different. We'd sold quite a few thousand albums around our area, and probably sold more than what we did on *Stand Up and Fight*. Because you need to have a lot of publicity; we got a certain amount, but we could've done with more. And they were having problems, MCA. They were bought up by Universal, if I remember right.

So the live one was out in 1979 and that was on Reddingtons. The debut is on Jet. And the high point, the original, was on Reddingtons. And then a company called Logo, who were part of RCA at the time, they put out our live album as well.

March 2, 1980. The last of the *Metal for Muthas* tour dates take place, a total of 30 of them in one month.

March 7, 1980. The start of Judas Priest's *British Steel* tour, the significance of which is that the support band was Iron Maiden, who boldly bragged about blowing Priest off the stage, and according to witnesses, often did. There were 19 shows, ending on March 27, 1980.

Iron Maiden bassist Steve Harris:
Well, let's just say that a lot of our fans turned up again, and we were a bit surprised, because obviously they were a British band, and nobody expected us to be... you know, I think a lot of people bought tickets that were Maiden fans, without a doubt. And so it definitely showed in the reaction—it was fantastic. I still think they're a great band, but we did really make it hard work for them. They had to work really hard every night, and maybe they weren't used to that, I don't know.

UK journalist Garry Bushell:
Maiden had already come through. They'd obviously been signed by EMI by then and they'd had *The Soundhouse Tapes* and that, but that was a very important tour for Maiden. It was a chance to play to an audience who hadn't seen them before. And, of course, Priest have not got the pace—obviously very heavy—but they've not got the pace that Maiden had. Maiden were much faster, if I recall.

DJ Neal Kay:
  They may have been giving them a run for their money, but Iron Maiden went behind Judas Priest on their first major tour with the release of their album. I mean I knew them well; they were friends at the time. They'd come to the Soundhouse for me. We did a video for them, "Living After Midnight," in which I loaned them Rob Loonhouse and the Headbangers. And there's a scene in that

video where they come to the solo and Rob Loonhouse replaced K.K. Downing, and plays it on his hardboard guitar.

I knew the Priest camp real good, and I went along to see some of those shows, and as good as Maiden were... look, you suddenly don't become a rock 'n' roll hero overnight. You need to learn the profession. You need to tread the boards, learn the ways of rock 'n' roll. Priest were brilliant, and probably still are. They were a very experienced band back then. They'd replaced their drummer Les Binks—he'd gone. They had a new twin guitar-driven fast feel. Their earlier stuff had been a little more stodgy, but well-put-down, well-driven, well-respected.

The newer stuff from Priest was dead heavy metal. You know, there's no question, and they were the perfect band for Maiden to support on tour. They let Maiden on board without any tour fee. They trucked their stuff. I mean it was a nice relationship that was going on. I went to see them, I'd just come off tour with April Wine, I think, in Sheffield. I'd been with April Wine, the Canadian band, and some others, and I knew that Priest and Maiden were playing the city hall or somewhere and I was there and I went that night and saw all the boys and everybody. The thing was that Maiden were very good, but Priest, for me, were still the more polished because they had more time at it.

Tank guitarist Mick Tucker on Iron Maiden:
I'd seen them at a club in Middlesborough, a tiny little club which holds about 200, and you had Eddie the Head behind that used to spew blood. That was with Dennis Stratton, the original lineup there, as the first album was released. Then I'd seen them at Newcastle supporting Judas Priest. They were actually getting their own gear off the stage. I think Paul Di'Anno said they're going to blow them off the stage, apparently, from what I read. And the Newcastle May Fest, pretty big stage, but obviously Priest had just said you've got three foot of stage across the front. They had no room at all, and no lights, nothing. I think they got a pretty rough day. But I thought they were great; it was loads of attitude, heavy, twin lead guitars—absolutely brilliant."

March 14, 1980. Def Leppard issue their debut album, *On Through the Night*, on Polygram, which peaks at #15. Oddly, even if there are all sorts of reasons to exempt Def Leppard from the ranks of NWOBHM bands, *On Through the Night* is in possession of a central NWOBHM sound, possibly more uncommonly completely NWOBHM than most records, given the wide variety of acts considered part of the movement, and their varied sounds from prog metal to AOR to thrash to nascent black metal to doom.

Def Leppard vocalist Joe Elliott:

The first album was a lot of fun to make and a lot of torture to listen to. We were at Ringo Starr's house, which used to belong to John Lennon. This is the place where he shot the "Imagine" video, Titttenurst Park, in Ascot. We were 18, 19-year-old kids let loose in a candy store, really. It was Christmas time almost. We had three weeks to make the record. We got all the backing tracks done in one day and spent 21 days ruining it by doing too many overdubs (laughs), and not enough time on the vocals. So we had a great time doing it, but it was a good lesson in like... that's what a record sounds like if you enjoy it too much. Whereas later on in our careers, we've made records that were absolute torture to make, but you could listen to them ten years after the fact and think, that was well worth it.

The first album had great intentions. It did show what we were trying to do with the vocal harmonies. But unfortunately it was only me and Sav who could sing in the band. So I had to handle nearly every vocal part on it, and I just didn't have the character of Freddie Mercury when he does that. And the other thing was, it was like, "My God, we're making a record," and I'm jumping up and down and getting drunk and running around John Lennon's bedroom. It's like,

"You've got to sing," and it's like, "Fuck off, I'm playing some video."

We were just playing. We were just totally playing. We hadn't woken up to the fact that this was really hard work, get on with it. We didn't have a producer that was prepared to grab us by the hair and throw us in and say, "Look, stop fucking around." He'd join in with us — nice guy and everything...

But the first album is shite. I immediately didn't like it. I was 21 years old. We had just been signed to the

Three debut albums from Mercury which may deeply affect you.

record label three months earlier. You compare it to Van Halen I and tell me it's competent (laughs), or the first Montrose album.

Def Leppard drummer Rick Allen:

We were never really too keen on our first record. We'd been playing those songs for years and years, before we recorded them. And quite honestly, I thought the songs sounded fine in a more raw sort of state. They didn't necessarily need any kind of production, and the production that eventually went onto those songs, I don't think did the songs as much justice as we gave them live.

I mean, most of the songs, you do them in the rehearsal room and that's one thing, and it's kind of like, "Wow, we're doing this again, for the umpteen thousandth time," but when you put them in front of an audience, they really take on a different personality. For instance, "Pour Some Sugar," "Rock of Ages," they just seem to take on this anthemic quality about them, and people really dig that; they really enjoy it.

Martin Popoff

Tygers of Pan Tang producer Chris Tsangarides on Def Leppard's early sound:
It was very typical of what most of the bands were doing. It really was quite rough and ready. Most new wave bands in those days were pretty rough and ready—on the first album, at least—and then as they got better, it got more polished. But my favourite Leppard album they ever did was *High 'n' Dry*. I really like that; it was more an AC/DC style, in their groove. After when they started with their more poppy approach, that was a lot to do with Mutt Lange, the producer, who had a vision; they liked his vision, luckily for them, and they went with it, and they went on to sell gazillions.

Judas Priest bassist Ian Hill:
We were just finishing mixing with *British Steel*, and Tom Allom, our producer, came in with a young band, which was his next job, and he said, "Do you mind if these guys have a look around and maybe sit in on the final mixes?" We're, "Oh, no, fine," and it was Def Leppard (laughs). And I think right after that, they toured with us, and I think Maiden toured with us twice. So we were quite aware of the new wave coming up.

Late March 1980. Girl, ahead of its time as a sort of pioneering hair metal band, issue their "Hollywood Tease"/"You Really Got Me" single, with the a-side reaching #50 in the UK charts the following month.

April 1980

April 1980. Bitches Sin is formed.

April 1980. Wild Horses issue their self-titled debut, which yields single releases for "Criminal Tendencies"/"Dealer" and "Fly Away"/"Blackmail," all album tracks. Wild Horses doesn't feel like a NWOBHM band, however their existence demonstrates the favourable conditions set by the NWOBHM for record deals being available to old rockers without very good songs.

Wild Horses bassist Jimmy Bain:
Yes, for one thing, the bands got record deals. I got a record deal, Maiden got a record deal, we were happy just to be able to go into

the studio and record some songs and get some kind of product out there so we could move onto something new. So that was great in just getting a record deal. So it felt good that the labels were interested in that kind of music for a change, because normally in Britain they would only be interested in it if you were Top 10, Top 40 kind of stuff. They weren't interested in heavy rock music, per sé.

But something was happening. In '83 we came over with Dio and did *Monsters of Rock*, and the patches were everywhere. It was just a sea of Saxon and Maiden and Priest and everybody. And then we quickly became successful, and the red Dio patches were soon there as well. It was a sea of denim, and it looked great, too—it was cool.

Even during punk, you still had your metalheads there that were sticking to their guns, whether the punk thing was going to be there or not. They just ignored it, almost, and carried on listening to the things that they listened to, and they just ignored the punk thing and hoped it would go away. And it stayed quite a long time—some of it is still there—but that was the feeling amongst the metal guys: I hope it goes away, because it's not cool. But live and let live. Anything can make money in this business. It doesn't matter if it's good.

April - May 1980. Girl follow up a co-headline tour with well-respected Canadian axe hero Pat Travers, with 34 dates through April and May.

April 1, 1980. Iron Maiden embark on their first headlining tour, broken into two legs, to allow for a campaign supporting Kiss on their *Unmasked* tour. The first leg ends August 23rd. The pairing couldn't be more telling in terms of "out with the old, in with the new," given that Kiss was promoting their poppiest album to date, and yet deriving zero commercial benefits from the commercial ruse.

Iron Maiden bassist Steve Harris: Well, the Kiss tour came toward the end of 1980, as the record came out in February or March. So by the time we get on the tour it's toward the end of the year, and the album had been out for a while. And it had been selling well in England and these other places that we just didn't expect to be any sales, really. And we went on the Kiss tour, and all of a sudden we were playing from 8,000 to 10,000 people to 25,000 people in a couple open-air gigs, huge crowds. Again, there were a lot of fans turning up getting right down in front early so they could see us, which was amazing, which gave us confidence and gave us the people to actually feed off of in front. And it just spread to the rest of the crowd. It was amazing.

UK journalist Garry Bushell on Paul Di'Anno's ability to unite punks and metalheads:

Absolutely, absolutely. That's exactly what it was like. Paul used to come onstage and he'd wear a porkpie hat, which is what the skinheads and the two-tone bands had re-popularized. It was very much that "rude boy" look. He'd come on and he'd have the leather jacket and the bullet belt and the porkpie hat. He would go out and he'd talk their language, absolutely the same.

The difference between them and, say, a band like The Cockney Rejects, who were the more violent end of the punk scene, was the Rejects would come out and say, "We're West Ham and if you're not West Ham, we're gonna attack!" (laughs). "We'll see you outside," sort of thing. Whereas, Paul Di'Anno would come out and say, "We're West Ham, you're Leicester, you're Liverpool, tonight we're gonna have a party." And that was the difference in that issue. The aggression that was there was channeled into the music; it wasn't aimed at any of the people.

So it absolutely brought people together, yeah. Motörhead co-existed, and they were playing with bands like that. Certainly between the upper class punks, there wasn't a big rift between them and the rock bands. The Sex Pistols, Cook and Jones in particular, were huge, huge fans of Thin Lizzy and there was a huge respect. And then they did the band called Greedy Bastards with Phil Lynott.

April 12, 1980. Fist issue, on Neat, their first single "Name Rank and Serial Number"/"You'll Never Get Me Up." It is reissued two months later by the band's new label, MCA, with Fist soon to play poor cousin to Tygers of Pan Tang.

April 12, 1980. Mythra issue *The Death & Destiny EP*, on Guardian Records, first as a 7" and then as a 12". Along with Trespass, Mythra—along with perhaps Turbo, Hollow Ground, Weapon and No Quarter—become one of the most well-regarded of the genre's non-LP acts.

April 14, 1980. UK release date for Iron Maiden's self-titled debut, which breaks ground for heavy metal cover art, specifically in that the cover art drives home the point that the music enclosed is very, very likely to be heavy metal, which wasn't generally the case for the harder rocking albums of the '70s. Also, the ghoulish, cartoony image was personified by what would be the first NWOBHM mascot, in the personage of Eddie. Graphics and music work hand in hand, and the album reaches #4 on the UK charts.

Iron Maiden bassist Steve Harris:

It was important the album came out at the time it did, because obviously you need to come out there before a lot of other bands get in there. We just came out before other bands came in. And the fact that we got the deal with EMI was a big thing as well, because it was worldwide distribution and all that so that made a massive difference too. But the fact that we played, again, getting back to the four-and-a-half years before getting signed, that came into play very much so then, because the album came out and it went straight into #4, and it surprised everybody, including me.

But it wasn't a total surprise. It was a surprise we went that high, but we thought that maybe, possibly, we'd chart, because we'd done the groundwork all over the UK, so many gigs all over the place, and built up this following. So we thought, well, even if half of them buy it, we're probably going to be doing all right. And it seemed like everyone bought it, so it went straight into the chart at #4, which was amazing.

And so being the first band to do that and chart that heavily, it made a real statement; it really did. It stood out in a lot of ways. I mean, we didn't even tour with that album in the states or Canada, so basically, you know, fans were going through record shops—and lots of people told me this story—flipping through the album rack and whatever, and "Bloody 'ell, what's that?!" And they turn it over and they see the live thing. Wow, and so they bought the album without really knowing what it was about, just because of the cover. So, you know, definitely made an impact.

Iron Maiden guitarist Adrian Smith on Eddie:

It was kind of unique. It translated great to the stage. It was a great visual tool to use, and to the album. It meant that we could get on with playing and writing music and Eddie could be the outrageous visual side of the band. Although onstage we do our thing. Plus it's just a very eye-catching kind of logo, and people seem to really get into it. They get a tattoo... the first time we'd come to America, we saw people with tattoos on their arms of Eddie and their car spray-painted with the monster all over it. I had one guy who'd built like a 20-foot Eddie on top of his house. I don't know how his parents let him get away with that.

But it just inspired all this sort of almost fanaticism. I think you have to have something to draw attention to music. I mean, that's a time-honoured kind of thing, but if your music doesn't stand up then it's all pointless. But that definitely draws attention to the band. But Eddie, he's got… you can see his brain and he's got green skin and his skin's falling off. I mean who wouldn't love him, really?

Journalist Sandro Buti on early Iron Maiden:
First of all we need to take the line a bit backwards. Because Iron Maiden took a lot from Thin Lizzy, for instance, and less exactly with Deep Purple or other bands which are usually called, let's say, the fathers of hard rock. Because heavy metal was coming from hard rock, but not only. And Iron Maiden had a lot of influence from Thin Lizzy, in my opinion, even if they came ten years before. If Iron Maiden are the fathers of metal, Thin Lizzy can be seen as the forefathers of metal, in my opinion.

What made Iron Maiden so special? First of all they had great songs, they had good quality, they have been able to stand the test of time. The so-called NWOBHM, there were many bands, and most of them were good, but very few of them have lasted. Very few of them kept doing music. So there are some bands like Praying Mantis, for instance, who were, in my opinion, as good as Iron Maiden, but they were not able to leave the same footprint because they did one excellent album and they got lost somewhere.

Iron Maiden had constant quality through the years until now. Maybe the new stuff is not as good as the old, but it's still good. The first two albums from Iron Maiden were raw energy. Then as Bruce Dickinson got into the band, they started developing a more structured sound and I think that sound influenced a lot of metal bands of the '80s, because it was melodic, it was powerful, but it was also structured. But the first two albums, with songs like "Phantom of the Opera" or "Killers" or "Prowler" were fast and quick and easy, definitely good for the time, but not as organized as what was to follow.

April 14, 1980. Judas Priest issue *British Steel*. Although one might argue that musically the record is a slight step away from a still very young NWOBHM sound, the concept of "British steel" alone helps give shape to the reality of the NWOBHM. Plus the album's anthems about rocking out and about metal help make the record a huge success for the band, Priest no doubt leading—as well as being swept along by—Britain's and North America's quickly growing appetite for all things metal.

Judas Priest vocalist Rob Halford:

One of the wonderful memories that I think we all have about Judas Priest is 1980, because here again we have the start of a new decade. You look at what happened in 1980 alone with all the other releases that were happening, it's a remarkable year. It definitely is that New Wave of British Heavy Metal movement.

By then, of course, we've had a few records established, but *British Steel* has become a masterpiece for a lot of people in metal for lots and lots of different reasons. But I think in terms of the band really truly making a defining sound, a statement of this is who we are in 1980, that we at last had found the look and the imagery.

It was kind of filtering around in *Hell Bent for Leather* to some extent, *Killing Machine*, but I think by the time we were into *British Steel* we'd got it. We knew absolutely everything about who we were, what we were trying to do and be. We knew there was still a lot more to do but that was just a great start to an incredibly important decade in metal, 1980. "United" is in there, you know, and it's in the mix of all of those great songs — "Rapid Fire," "Steeler," "Grinder," "Breaking the Law," "Living After Midnight" — every track has something really important to say about the concept of metal, and what we were thinking about metal in terms of the music and the messages in 1980.

Judas Priest guitarist K.K. Downing on the significance of *British Steel*:

The *British Steel* album is what brought a lot of things together, united a lot of things. You think of "The Rage," "Breaking the Law," "Too Old to Be Wise," "Rapid Fire"... a lot of that album was what attracted a lot of the young audience to the band, because it was rebellious, I suppose. And obviously we were all totally leather and studs on that album, and with the *British Steel* theme. That was just something that the youngsters really endeared themselves to. Because everybody, growing up, has some rebelliousness in them. And when you've got seemingly such a complete album, *British Steel*, that was definitely an important turning point in the band's career.

April 25, 1980. Black Sabbath issue *Heaven and Hell*, the band's first album with Ronnie James Dio. By breathing new life into Black Sabbath, Ronnie breathes new life into heavy metal.

DJ Neal Kay on the reason for Black Sabbath's second wind:

It was more about the movement of personnel, and see there was something happening at the senior level, too. If we consider that the NWOBHM bands were like the lowest on the professional ladder, okay? Then you kind of went up and you found UFO and bands like that. Then you climbed above that and you had to look at the family tree of bands like Deep Purple. Very seminal, very important band.

Black Sabbath, probably the first heavy metal band, truly, the world ever knew. But here's the big but! They sounded exactly the same to me on every album, perhaps except *Never Say Die*, until

Ronnie James Dio walked in the door. And Ronnie James Dio came from Rainbow which came from Purple. He changed Sabbath. The old Sabbath fans hated it because it was Americanized, it was melody, it was all the stuff I loved meself, personally. That was the Black Sabbath that I loved. The fans of original Sabbath didn't like it very much. It was still heavy but it was far too commercial in American melodic chord progressions, vocals and all this sort of stuff. But I don't think the new wave did that. I am convinced the NWOBHM did not do that.

It's Ronnie James Dio. If you put Ronnie James Dio against Ozzy, it's a waste of time. I love Ozzy. It's like Lemmy. These people are gods of rock 'n' roll and heavy metal, but it is by virtue of character, not vocal performance. It's outrage. They're this, they're that, they chew the heads off bats, ride Harleys and kill people with their breath. Especially after a drinking session. That's cool, but it ain't

the performance on the stage. Ronnie James Dio is a classic—was a classic; absolute, top of the range vocalist. He had a weapon in his throat and he knew how to use it.

Ronnie probably had to write a lot of that stuff. I mean it's heavy, yes it is. But I mean, my God, how often did you ever hear the members of Black Sabbath play like that? Until *Heaven and Hell*, it wasn't in them.

Martin Popoff

April 26, 1980. Paralex issue "White Lightning"/"Travelling Man"/"Black Widow," on Reddingtons Rare. "White Lightning" was in the running for covering when Metallica was putting together tracks for *The $5.98 E.P.: Garage Days Re-Revisited*, which included a track each from Diamond Head and Holocaust.

April 29, 1980. Venom's first recordings, at Impulse, are "Angel Dust," "Raise the Dead" and "Red Light Fever." Cronos, who works at the place as tape operator, makes cassette copies of these demos and sends them around to various press outlets. The 11:28 demo is entitled *Demon*.

May 1980

May 1980. Angel Witch issue "Sweet Danger"/"Flight Nineteen" as a single ("Hades Paradise" is added to the 12" version).

Angel Witch guitarist Kevin Heybourne on "Sweet Danger:" That was just about a bad dream really, the falling dream, things that happen in nightmares. That song has a Rush influence on it at the beginning, hasn't it? You can't be 100% original, you know what I mean? Everybody's got to get their influence from somewhere. I don't see it as a bad thing. I've never hidden the fact that Black Sabbath is my favourite band. And that is evident in the sound of the music.

Angel Witch bassist Kevin Riddles on "Flight Nineteen:" I very, very well remember sitting in Kevin's flat in South London, when he came up with the riff. He had seen a documentary about Flight 19, the supposed flight that disappeared over the Bermuda triangle, the American Naval aviators who were sadly and hideously lost. So it was about some strange anomaly in the Bermuda triangle and stuff, and it was around the Erich von Daniken time and this idea that we all come from aliens, and were there still aliens here and stuff. And Kevin was able to combine the Flight 19 story with the possibility of alien intrusion, invasion, whatever. He was very good at that. If you listen to the lyric to something like "Baphomet," you would think it's completely about devils and Baphomet himself and Lucifer and all that, but when you read the lyric, it's tied in with something else.

May 1980. The Wolverhampton-based Handsome Beasts issue "All Riot Now"/"The Mark of the Beast." Handsome Beasts actually caused the famed Heavy Metal Records into being, manager of the band Paul Birch forming the label around his biker-rocking act. Neither track hailed from the notorious *Beastiality* album.

Heavy Metal Records' Paul Birch on starting Heavy Metal Records:

Well, back in the 1980s/late 1970s, I was a record company rep and I was going on record jobs. I worked for an independent and we worked on artists like The Tourists, who became The Eurythmics, and we worked on ELO, and I remember there was a particular campaign we were doing which was Steel Pulse. In fact I was working on *Handsworth Revolution*, the album.

And we did retail and radio promotion, and I was at the store, and it was absolutely clear that what was really selling well at the store was heavy metal and there are hardly any titles. In fact EMI had just come out with *Metal for Muthas*, the compilation album. Bands like Iron Maiden were just emerging, as were Praying Mantis. And the only heavy metal labels that we would have known would have been WWA, Phonogram/Vertigo, and however you looked at Atlantic Records. The only independent that I was aware of was Neat Records.

So there was this new wave emerging. Geoff Barton talked about it in *Sounds* magazine, who defined the phrase, NWOBHM, actually. And we could see there was demand, absolutely. I'd come from a northern soul background, but I managed a band and they happened to be heavy metal. We got EMI down to take a look at them; Ashley Goodall from EMI came down to take a look at the band.

They were called The Handsome Beasts. So I couldn't get arrested, as they say. To be fair we tried EMI but there weren't a lot of other options. The other majors weren't really interested in heavy metal, and to be honest with you, for a very long time. By the time the majors were interested, it turned out it was the American majors who were interested. Certainly the British majors were never interested, is the truth of it. And so I decided I'd release a record, as a Handsome Beast myself, and try our own label—and we put "heavy metal" on the label.

May 1980. Derbyshire's Witchfynde issues their debut LP, *Give 'Em Hell*, which gets a three-and-a-half star review from Geoff Barton.

THE DEBUT ALBUM FROM WITCHFYNDE
GIVE 'EM HELL (ABOUT 1) ALSO AVAILABLE ON
CASSETTE (CARB 1) INCLUDES THE INDEPENDENT
CHART HIT
GIVE 'EM HELL c/w GETTIN' HEAVY (ROUND 1)
marketed by ℞ Rondelet Records

Witchfynde guitarist Montalo:
Give 'Em Hell was done in such a short period of time, in a small studio, at hardly any cost, and it still sounds very good. It's that very basic raw sound, which I think is what the band is about, to be honest. We just went into the studio where Def Leppard did their first demos at, and used the same people that produced that as well, and got that basic sound.

May 1980. Jet reissue Quartz' self-titled debut as *Deleted*, given that it had become a "cult album." At this point the band had already been dropped by Jet and were briefly on Reddingtons Rare. So what Quartz had been doing to no effect was now somewhat fashionable again, with the band's strident and authoritative "Mainline Riders" track as elegant "told you so" classic.

May 1980. Vardis issue their second single, "If I Were King."

May 1980. After an MCA reissue of "Don't Touch Me There," Tygers of Pan Tang move forward with "Rock 'n' Roll Man," the single shipped to stores with a quintessential NWOBHM accoutrement, the sew-on patch.

Tygers of Pan Tang vocalist Jess Cox:

The patches came along with the NWOBHM. I don't think there was patches and stuff before that that I was aware of. The punks just had a sort of uniform clothes of chains and bondage stuff and ripped shirts—they didn't have patches. Their patches came later, But when we started off it was badges, which the punks did have.

I remember as the Tygers in 1980, one of our girlfriends making a badge for the band and it was a huge yellow thing with a big safety pin in the back, nearly hand-made, with a hand-drawing was kind of copied 50 times. I know we had a patch in the second single—with "Rock 'n' Roll Man" we had to give away a patch.

If you look at the 1980 *Precious Metal* album, from MCA, there's a kid on there, but they haven't got patches on it. He's got a denim jacket on but it's only got badges. So, I mean we were probably one of the first ones, to tell you the truth. Because "Rock 'n' Roll Man" came out only a few months after *Precious Metal*, and there's nothing on there.

Tank guitarist Mick Tucker:

A lot of kids were just denim jackets, tight jeans, trainers on, badges everywhere. We were in Italy two years ago and everyone dresses like 1980. Incredible. They've all got the striped jeans and the trainers and the cut-off denim jacket and that sort of thing. About 1978, I thought something's happening. There's a void after the punk thing and we'd see bands like Son of a Bitch that later became Saxon; I used to watch bands like that. I'd seen Raven doing Judas Priest covers along with different bands from around the country coming in like Limelight, and you could tell there was something going on there. Something in the air. Mystery to me though where the patches came from, that one. It just suddenly happened—everyone's got patches. Raven bassist and vocalist John Gallagher on the heavy metal uniform:

Well you start with red spandex, I think. No, I mean from the get-go, from the '70s, when I started going to concerts in '73, '74, there was a uniform. You wore denim and you had your denim jacket and everyone had the band's name on there. And since there weren't many patches, you learned to sew. You'd put your band names on the back of your jacket, and these things were like works of art, and that was the uniform. It was already there.

And then obviously more into the '80s, it got more on the leather side of things, and bullet belts, which of course is from our pal Lemmy bringing that out. That was very popular. But there was a denim army waiting, and that kind of music has always been popular in England, specifically, but it's always been an underdog thing.

But yeah, somebody got smart down the line and started making patches so the kids could sew them on their jackets so they didn't have to be quite as artistic. I remember I spent many weeks putting Uriah Heep, pride of place at the top of my jacket. You're not going to get mom to do it—sod it, I'll have to learn. So how much more heavy metal can you get than sitting there with a needle and thread?

Gillan bassist John McCoy:
It was a uniform. It was denim and leather. You would buy a patch of the band that you were the biggest supporter of and buy the T-shirt. But if you couldn't afford that, the kids would just copy the thing in felt tip pen or however, or little paint jobs. You'd see some incredible work. They couldn't afford to go and buy the patch so they painted it on there. It was a uniform, the denim and leather and patches. And you could see it grow over the years where people would have one or two patches sewn onto a jacket. They would turn up a couple of years later and the thing would be completely covered. There were so many new bands coming on and they all had patches.

Journalist John Tucker on buttons and patches:
It was mainstream from punk, almost certainly. What better way for showing your devotion, especially when you get a badge for like 30 pence worth? Not dear, but a good way of showing your allegiances. And to be fair, one of my stories is that another city's football club played my club, and I'm walking down through town, and there's a whole bunch of their fans coming towards me, and they're nasty. And I thought I'm dead.

And one of them took one look at my jacket where there was an Iron Maiden tour patch on the front jacket pocket and said something like, "Cool band, them, great band," and they just parted and let me pass. And it was good because I thought I was in for a pasting. I was about ready to run.

But the badges I don't know about, because I wasn't close enough or aware enough before punk came along. Before punk came along I was quite happy buying my Purple and Sabbath, and then one day someone walked up to me at school and said, "Tucker, you're a fucking dinosaur." I was 14 years old. It left me speechless. So before punk I'm not aware, but certainly as soon as I had my jacket that I could wear them on, then I would buy any badge of any band, and trade if I'd end up with two of the same thing.

May 1980. Neat issue White Spirit's debut single, "Back to the Grind"/"Cheetah."

May 1980. *Metal for Muthas Volume II* is issued. The album winds up in NWOBHM history as more non-LP-destined than the first *Metal for Muthas*, featuring Trespass (two songs), Eazy Money, Xero, White Spirit, Dark Star, Horsepower, Red Alert, Chevy and the Raid.

May 2 – 6, 1980. Fist play their first gigs in London.

May 3, 1980. Whitesnake issue *Ready An' Willing*. Produced by Martin Birch, the album reaches #6 on the UK charts and #90 in the US. The single "Fool for Your Loving" reaches #53 in the US as well. As author John Tucker argues, these old guard bands benefit from the NWOBHM, to be sure, but many of them help fuel the NWOBHM in turn by assembling some of their best work.

May 3, 1980. Motörhead issue *The Golden Years Live EP*.

May 5, 1980. Saxon issue their groundbreaking second album *Wheels of Steel*, which vaults to #5 in the UK and spawns two hit singles; the title track, backed with "Stand Up and Be Counted," is issued as a single concurrent with the release of the album.

Saxon vocalist Biff Byford on "Wheels of Steel:"

We had an American car at the time, and Oldsmobile Towne Car and I just fancied writing a song about it, that's all. I mean, originally my ideas for "Wheels of Steel" was the "Princess of the Night" song, but I switched mid-stream and went with a song about a car. The idea of "Princess of the Night"... I mean, all of my lyrics are pretty much from my childhood or based on experiences or history, which again, is usually from my childhood, Dallas and things.

But "Wheels of Steel" was specifically about the car. It was basically about people's competition between each other with their cars, the hot rod type thing. That's the type of song it is. If you listen to it, it's basically a song about street rods and beating each other. Whereas "Princess of the Night" is about a steam train. When I was a boy, I used to watch the steam trains come over the viaduct near where I lived. At night, they used to light up all the sky with all the fire and everything. And that was going to be "Wheels of Steel" but actually "Princess of the Night" was better. The train was called Princess Elizabeth basically. Millions of people think that song is about a girl but it's actually not. But you know, people can think what they want to. It's up to them.

The "Wheels of Steel" riff is very AC/DC-ish. I was heavily into early AC/DC when I was getting the band together, "Dirty Deeds Done Dirt Cheap" etc. I suppose that riff is influenced by them although it's not really their style because it's just continuous. But it's in sort of the same register. I mean, they're more likely to go up, where we just played it continuous, more like an English riff. But I suppose the original inspiration is from AC/DC.

UK journalist Garry Bushell:
Saxon were lumped into the New Wave of British Heavy Metal, weren't they? By *Sounds*. I wasn't on the road with Saxon; I only really ever saw them play up North so it was slightly different than the bands I'd seen down south in England because the fashions were very different. The kids who turned up at the gigs for Saxon... they had these huge, huge flares. Flares you could park a boy scout in (laughs). Saxon were less hip whereas Maiden was seen as "happening." Saxon was seen as a little bit past, even when they were happening (laughs) in that they weren't quite as up-to-date; they were a bit more mock-able. Biff was drinking tea, for God's sake. He didn't drink like the band. But Saxon had some great songs and maybe those metropolitan attitudes didn't translate across the whole fan base.

Saxon bassist Steve Dawson on winning one for metal:
The turning point for us was a guy came to see us from the *NME*, and he wrote a review. We played in London, and he wrote this review that really slagged us off. Said that we were rubbish, that we were dinosaurs and we sounded like Deep Purple, Black Sabbath and umpteen other bands all rolled up into one. But what he didn't realize was that he alerted a lot of people to our music, and from that day that he wrote that review, our shows were getting more and more people in. And it just went word-of-mouth.

Because we were just a band on the road. We played every day. We didn't have any days off. We just played all the time, and so you would play a small show in England where there was nobody in, to being full. And the next time we would go back there were 200 people outside who can't get in. And then people in the press, like *Sounds* or *Melody Maker* or *NME*, would send somebody to do a review, and it just went from there and snowballed overnight.

And then we made records and Radio One started playing them, because in England, as you know, we have national radio. Not like back in America where every town has a radio station, and you can be big in one town and not in another. In England, if you get airplay, everybody hears you. So after the first single, which was "Big Teaser," got on the Radio One playlist, they were playing it five times a day or eight times a day. And it just started the ball rolling. And from there we released *Wheels of Steel*, and then that just really took off. And that worked for Iron Maiden and a lot of other bands at the same time.

But I can remember that the rock journalists who didn't like our sort of music did everything they possibly could to give us a bad write-up (laughs). But obviously there were great journalists like Geoff Barton who was one of the main factors in helping us become very successful. He liked our music, and he gave *Wheels of Steel* a great review and it just went from there.

When we wrote *Wheels of Steel*, we were angry young men, because we've just been dropped by our management. We were managed by Norman Sheffield and Dave Thomas, who were Queen's managers. They were the managers of Queen and we were signed to Trident for management. And they just spent all our money from the first album, and when it ran out, they just told us to get lost. So we had nothing. And so we were really disillusioned with music from before we got started, really. We just thought right, fuck you, we're going to make you wish you hadn't done that. And we went into this rehearsal studio in Wales, in the middle of nowhere, in the snow, with no heating, and it just made us write those songs — and it worked.

May 13, 1980. Tygers of Pan Tang tour the UK supporting Scorpions, followed by dates with Saxon beginning May 23rd.

Jess Cox on the limited aspirations of the NWOBHM bands:

I mean, I've still got all the 45s. When the Tygers started off, we only did a single for "Don't Touch Me There." And when we signed with MCA, we only signed for a single. We didn't sign for anything else. It was so different then. I mean, people didn't necessarily want to be rock stars—there was no great scheme, no great plan. It was just like, in the NWOBHM, you wanted to impress the girl down the street so you got in a band and you played in the local pub, and that was it. You didn't have these aspirations and five year plans to be the biggest band on the planet. It just wasn't like that.

So it was quite different to what it is these days. Bands form with the idea of how much money they're going to make half the time, and then they just latch onto a sound and try and be like them.

Back then it was so disjointed, all the different bands. There was no set sound of the NWOBHM, and that's because nobody was trying to be the next whatever the hit band was at the time, Whitesnake or whoever. They just wanted to do their own thing, and a lot of them of course just didn't have the musical knowledge to do any of it, like write these great classic songs in a classic style. Some of the early Tygers things, when I look at them now... I mean we'd have four bars and then like six bars in the next verse. It didn't make sense, but to us it sounded good so we just did it. If you'd known about music you probably wouldn't have done that. I think that's what made the NWOBHM so interesting and exciting was the different sounds of the bands.

Tygers Of Pan Tang guitarist Robb Weir:

1980 was a big year for us. We started off on the road with Magnum, opening up for them on a three-week tour. We then did three weeks with Saxon on the *Wheels of Steel* tour. We did a week with the Scorpions, on the *Lovedrive* tour. We then jumped onto the Def Leppard tour, a week with them at the city halls. This was all UK-based. We then did some shows with Iron Maiden, went and recorded *Wild Cat*. Recruited John Sykes.

Wild Cat tour was at the back end of '80, and then '80, '81 we recorded *Spellbound* and then we did a big tour in Europe with Gillan. Came back, John Sykes left and we recruited Fred Purser and we went out and did a big French tour. And then we went out to Japan and did five shows in Japan, I think, three in Tokyo, one in Osaka, one in Nagoya. In fact we played in Osaka the same night as the Scorpions played. They were playing on the other side of town to us, and we actually outsold them by 400 tickets. And the only reason why I know that is because when we went back to the hotel, unbeknownst to us, the Scorpions were staying in the same hotel and we had a party in the nightclub downstairs.

May 1980. MCA joins the hard rock compilation business with *Precious Metal*, assembled by journalist Paul Suter. The US-heavy compilation lets fans know that MCA have got some baby bands as well, in Gillan and Tygers of Pan Tang. Capitol does one to, entitled *America Strikes Back*, the added message being that the UK has been taking over hard rock as of late.

May 23, 1980. Iron Maiden issue "Sanctuary"/"Drifter"/"I've Got the Fire" as a 7".

SAMMY HAGAR, RIOT, APRIL WINE, MINK DE VILLE, MOON MARTIN, PRISM, KRAFTWERK, MOTELS, TEAZE, FACE DANCER, RED RIDER

IN

"AMERICA STRIKES BACK"

AN APOCALYPTIC ALBUM
WHICH IS YOURS FOR
JUST

30p *(plus post and packing)*

PLUS THREE COUPONS CLIPPED
FROM THE NEXT THREE ISSUES
OF SOUNDS.

THIS ALBUM CONTAINS TRACKS
WHICH WILL NOT BE AVAILABLE
IN ANY OTHER FORM AND IS
EXCLUSIVE TO READERS OF
SOUNDS. THE FIRST COUPON
APPEARS NEXT WEEK.

ORDER YOUR COPY NOW!

Journalist Sandro Buti:
Maiden had a unique approach in terms of riffing, the kind of pounding riffs that were typical of the NWOBHM which went on to become a trademark of the band. Difficult to explain in English, but it's the kind of riffing and the kind of melody with double guitars but also galloping guitars. And the guitars were always integrated with the bass sound, another trademark of Iron Maiden. So Steve Harris is writing the music but another identifier is his bass sound, which is unique.

Stratovarius vocalist guitarist Timo Tolki:

The foundation is actually coming from the '80s bands, because when I was 14, I was listening to a lot of Rainbow and Maiden, Black Sabbath with Dio. These bands were really influencing me and my music, and that's where it grew from. That's when I started to really play guitar, actually. When you're 14, you wake up in the morning and you put *Number of the Beast*—incredible feeling. I have never felt like that afterwards, you know? It's a sad thing that when this becomes a profession you lose something in that. I never felt like that again, you know, that freshness of liking something so much. It was very powerful and the vocals were excellent. I really loved them. I saw Iron Maiden in Helsinki in '82 on the *Piece of Mind* tour, and that was the first concert I ever went to.

May 24, 1980. Girlschool issue their second single, and first for Bronze, called "Nothing to Lose"/"Baby Doll," amidst support dates for Krokus on their UK tour. Earlier in the year, Girlschool had played support slot to Uriah Heep.

May 24, 1980. Spider issue their second single, "Children of the Street"/"Down 'n' Out (live)."

Late May – August 1980. Saxon work at Ramport Studios on tracks slated for the band's third album.

June 1980

June 1980. Samson issue their second album, *Head On*. It is the first featuring new vocalist Bruce Dickinson, here known as Bruce Bruce. First single is "Hammerhead"/"Vice Versa," both tracks from the album, followed shortly thereafter by "Hard Times" in remix form backed with non-LPer "Angel with a Machine Gun."

Samson bassist John McCoy:

Let me just go back to that Samson album. I'd just done some sessions with a NWOBHM band called Sledgehammer, with a guitarist called Mike Cook; I did a few tracks with them. And also in that period just after I'd done the Samson album, I was asked to produce a band called White Spirit, the guitarist being Janick Gers who subsequently left White Spirit and replaced Bernie in Gillan. And need I say more? He's gone on to great success with Iron Maiden.

There's also a connection to Iron Maiden as well, because the original drummer in Samson—when I was in Samson and we did the first couple of singles—was Clive Burr, who left Samson to go to Iron Maiden. And then by the second album I did with Samson, we brought in a singer called, at that time, Bruce Bruce, who metamorphasized into Bruce Dickinson, and as everyone knows, joined Iron Maiden.

So I think without that Samson connection, Iron Maiden would not be the band that it is today. It was a small clique of people that were around. You could go out and see Iron Maiden, Angel Witch, Samson—all these bands were just playing anywhere. I don't want to start swearing, but the feeling behind it was punk is shit, this is what we want to do. It was guys learning to play their instruments properly. Coming up with good ideas, good arrangements, good riffs, great singers, with power and heaviness.

I had a great time with the punk thing, don't get me wrong. Great fun. But come on, guys, play it properly. Sing a tune. And that's what the NWOBHM thing was about. It harkened back to the early '70s influences, the Zeppelins and the Purples. That music's going to live forever, and those kids were hit by that, emotionally or however, and the punk thing obviously passed them by. They didn't get it or whatever. And slowly but surely, rock started to take over again. But it was an interesting period. I mean, there are so many guys that came out of that period, you know?

June 1980. Epic reminds music fans that they too have some hard rock in their roster, and issue the *Killer Watts* compilation. Meanwhile, perennial outsiders Dedringer sign to Dindisc.

June 1980. Gillan issue "Sleeping on the Job"/"Higher and Higher" as a single; it's one of the early NWOBHM artifacts to include a free patch. The band quickly follow up with another picture sleeve single the following month, "No Easy Way" backed with "Handles on Her Hips" and "I Might As Well Go Home."

June 1980. Def Leppard issue "Rock Brigade"/"When the Walls Come Tumblin' Down," both album tracks. Subtly, the fact they were both album tracks speaks to a tendency from the major labels to be stingy with fresh material. In other words, it is more likely that a smaller label would treat a single as a piece of stand-alone product, rather than promotion for the album.

June 28, 1980. Girlschool issue their debut album, *Demolition*.

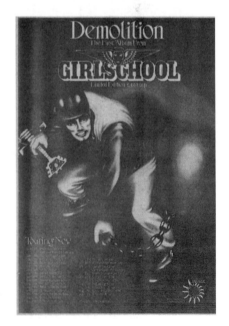

Girlschool bassist and vocalist Enid Williams:
With *Demolition* versus *Hit and Run*, we had been playing the songs a little bit longer. And because it was 1980, it was still very much on the tail end of punk, so it still had a bit of a rawness to it, which I quite like. But I think we were a little bit more polished by the time we came to doing *Hit and Run*, really. I think we found our feet a little bit more.

Late June 1980. Saxon issue "747 (Strangers in the Night)"/"See the Light Shining" as a single.

Saxon vocalist Biff Byford:
"747" is like two songs really, running together. It's a song about a power cut in New York that happened in the '60s or '70s, and there was a plane coming in to land and obviously couldn't land. The lights went off and there was a big panic. It didn't crash; it just went off somewhere else. And there were a lot of people trapped in lifts and there were actually a lot of relationships that happened due to that power outage. I've got two songs really. I've got one about strangers meeting in the dark and one about a plane coming down to land and it's all going on at the same time basically.

Late June 1980. Ethel the Frog issue their self-titled debut album, on EMI. The mysterious black and white cover illustration ably reflected the magic and aura of the NWOBHM.

Late June 1980. Iron Maiden sells out London's Rainbow Theatre.

Future Iron Maiden vocalist Bruce Dickinson:
Well, the first time I saw Maiden was kind of like… when the Marquis de Sade was locked up in jail, he wrote all these terribly ludicrous sex books on odd pieces of toilet paper, representing all his frustrations and fantasies of being locked in a tower with nothing else but hominines for months on end.
Well, for me it was the same thing, but musically. Because I never saw any of the bands that I really got off on, at the start. The Deep Purples or the Jethro Tulls, you know. So in my mind, I had this kind of insane vision of them that they would be leaping around the stage

and doing all these incredible things. I never saw those bands. And I saw those bands—there you go, Freudian slip—I saw Maiden, and I thought, oh my God! This is what I would've really wanted in my dreams; this is sort of the vibe, from what I would've dreamed about some ecstatic Deep Purple concert I never ever saw in my life. And, in a bizarre way, the only thing missing from that dream was me.

Mid-1980. Bitches Sin issue their *Your Place or Mine* 12-track demo cassette followed by the seven-track *Twelve Pounds and No Kinks* cassette.

Mid-1980. Expozer issue "Exposed At Last." The a-side can also be found on the eventful and lively *Heavy Metal Heroes* compilation from 1981. Meanwhile, early hopefuls Money issue "Fast World," (technically *EP.* (sic)), featuring three tracks not on their debut LP from 1979, including an epic nine-minute b-side called "Another Case of Suicide." As with the LP, producer on the project is Chris Tsangarides.

Mid-1980. Red Alert issue "Break the Rules." Red Alert opened 1980's Reading Festival. Not to be confused with the band of the same name who recorded "Open Heart" on the seminal second *Metal for Muthas* comp., or for that matter, the band that had to change their name to Wildfire to be on *Muthas Pride*, the follow-up EP to that compilation.

July 1980

July 1980. Budgie issue their *If Swallowed, Do Not Induce Vomiting* EP, for new label RCA. Although on the scene since 1969, with this EP and the *Power Supply* album (also issued in 1980), the band take a pronounced turn toward a rough 'n' tumble NWOBHM sound—just like Uriah Heep but even more so.

Budgie bassist and vocalist Burke Shelley: Just then, our guitarist Tony Bourge left, so there were domestic upheavals with the band, really. Tony had to leave and sort his life out. And there wasn't any animosity between us; we all got on well and liked each other. But then we moved on and got John Thomas in, and when John Thomas joined, I love the EP that we did, *If Swallowed, Do Not Induce*

Vomiting; I thought it was great (laughs). Some of the tracks on there not a lot of people hear very often. We play them now, because they are more modern now, like "Lies of Jim (The E Type Lover)" and "High School Girl;" I love those.

DJ Neal Kay:
Budgie were a minor band over here. They never did very much to be honest with you. Even less in the new wave. They were nothing to do with the NWOBHM. They're not considered a new wave band. They were around before, and they were a very minor band. They didn't seem to have any part to play whatsoever to me. I played them, but most people weren't interested in them. I think they were a good band, but they didn't have that dynamic, that vital firepower. They were Welshes, you know. They were probably sitting on toadstools half the day. The wave of the fairies, right?

Journalist John Tucker:
Budgie are very much a rock band. There was a documentary from BBC archive footage and they interviewed what looked to be a now very bitter Burke Shelley. Basically it was, "This has nothing to do with us, we didn't talk about Satan, we're not a heavy metal band, we never were." Budgie were sort of more in the Uriah Heep league; they were the next echelon down. And to be fair, my first encounters with Budgie were, like everything else, when they became a heavy metal band with the *Vomiting* EP in 1980, when everything was metal all of a sudden. So I would say theirs was a very limited influence. I'm struggling to think of anybody who's ever actually said, "Yeah, Budgie were an influence for us."

July 1980. Chevy issue "Too Much Loving," on Avatar, home of Dark Star. The a-side is from the well-received self-titled LP, issued in both the UK (also on Avatar) and Germany, on Bellaphon. B-side is "See the Light."

July 1980. Jameson Raid issue "The Hypnotist," amidst the drama of half the band quitting. The four-track *Electric Sun* demo from 1982 would constitute the band's final recordings.

July 1980. Holocaust issue their debut single "Heavy Metal Mania"/"Only as Young as You Feel" as a 7" with an extra track added to the 12".

Holocaust guitarist John Mortimer:
There was this excitement at the time. Every week it seemed,

somebody else was putting out a new self-financed LP or single. And suddenly heavy metal was an accepted term. That was the exciting thing. But until that point, you only had what were known as rock dinosaurs that all the punks slagged off. But suddenly you got this new young wave of heavy metal bands, and yeah, we just bought as much as we could when it came out. It was actually difficult to find the money to buy that stuff, but it was a really exciting time that way. When the likes of Def Leppard, Iron Maiden and Saxon got picked up by the major labels though, it began to be taken over a little bit by the big companies. And it meant that the people who didn't have major league backing kind of fell away into obscurity, and that was a shame.

July 1980. According to John Tucker in *Suzie Smiled... The New Wave of British Heavy Metal*, unemployment in the UK reaches its highest level since 1936, rising from 1.5 million in April 1980 to 1.9 million. By April 1981, it would be at 2.5 million and by February 1983, 3.2 million.

July 3 – 5, 1980. Iron Maiden execute a three date stand at the Marquee. Raven supports on the first night, with the gig being filmed for ITV. Fist supports on the following two nights.

Iron Maiden bassist Steve Harris:
I think when we made the first album, or just before the first album, there was a lot of punk stuff at the time, which we were heavily against. We didn't like that sort of stuff. But I think the difference between us, the newer bands or the older bands at the time, is we were playing faster and also playing stuff with maybe more time changes in it. Probably more harmony guitars, also. A lot of the bands only had one guitar player. A couple of them had two, bands like Thin Lizzy, who influenced us in any way, but a lot of the bands had one guitar, three-piece band, or one guitar with a keyboard player and stuff.
So what we were doing was a bit different with the twin guitar thing, playing heavier twin guitars, and playing faster, more aggressive stuff, with a little bit of prog thrown in. So there were those elements which made us a little different from what was going on before. That's what I like to think anyway.

Raven bassist and vocalist John Gallagher on the dimensions of the NWOBHM sound:
Well, there's the caricature version and then there's the real thing. The real thing is you had bands like Iron Maiden, who were kind of

like a punky, skewed version of Judas Priest. And you had Steve's sensibility, which is totally unique, the way he wrote songs and put stuff together, which was great. That set them apart. Def Leppard, unashamedly, doing the Thin Lizzy template, basically, or at least initially. Another band, just a side-step here, huge influence and everything else, is UFO—they can't be denied either. They were an enormous influence—and Thin Lizzy—right through the '70s.

July 5, 1980. Geoff Barton from *Sounds* gives Venom their first spot of press, by adding the band's demo to his playlist.

Early July 1980. Fist, Raven and White Spirit play Newcastle. These three bands form the North-East New Wave of British Heavy Metal, or the NENWOBHM (as framed in a May '80 article in *Sounds*), along with Mythra and Tygers of Pan Tang.

Raven bassist and vocalist John Gallagher on Newcastle's love of metal:
Just because of the working class existence, you know? I mean, I talk about this with my wife. When we were kids, and you talk about problems kids have with cliques and rich kids, there were no rich kids at my school. There were a couple of kids that were really poor, but everybody else was on an equal footing. All our dads worked in factories—that's it; they worked in factories. You go to school, you get your A levels.

You go to college? What's what? I knew three people that went to college and they came back and ended up working bullshit jobs right afterwards, and it was just really depressing to the point where we did songs about them. "Bring the Hammer Down"... back in like '81, '82, there were riots in the streets because people were just so pissed-off. It was horrible, and that was the climate, and with that kind of thing, people want a release.

So when they went to a concert, they'd go nuts. Headbanging, jumping around, just rush the front. That was the fun thing to do with the city hall. It was a sit-down venue, and soon as the lights went down, everyone got up and pushed the bouncers out of the way and ran to the front. The northeast NWOBHM—NENWOBHM: like let's have the longest acronyms in the world. And then they had the whole thing of us in the studio and talking about Venom and talking about Fist and Whitesnake and all this stuff.

July 19, 1980. Girlschool issue their third single, "Race with the Devil"/"Take it All Away" which hits #49 in the UK charts. The a-side was a Gun song, also covered by Judas Priest.

Girlschool guitarist Kim McAuliffe:

"Race with the Devil" was actually our producer Vic Maile's idea. He thought it would be a great vehicle for us, because girls weren't really playing stuff like that in those days. So for Kelly to play that riff... in fact, that turned out to be quite a great step for us, because Jeff Beck was on a radio show where they actually played it, called *Roundtable*. They were reviewing all the new singles of that week, and Jeff Beck was a guest on there, and he actually said, "There's no way that that's girls playing that." Of course, we really made a big deal out of it and it got into the press that he said this, and that we invited him down to one of our gigs. And then he came down and he took it all back and apologized. So it turned out quite a big deal for us.

July 25, 1980. AC/DC issue *Back in Black*, the first album with their new singer—a "Geordie"—Brian Johnson. The album is huge fuel for the heavy metal fire, and very much so for the Brits, who claim AC/DC as one of their own, for the above reason, for the Scottish roots of the band, for their perennial presence in the UK, as well as, unfortunately, the fact that Bon Scott died on British soil.

Tygers of Pan Tang vocalist Jess Cox:

Well Brian Johnson, obviously, is from my hometown here in Newcastle. You remember, he used to be in a band called Geordie, which is a colloquial term for our language here, or our accent, I should say. When you're from Newcastle they call you Geordies, and this is why Brian Johnson called his band Geordie—it's because you're from the area.

They'd been quite successful anyway; they had a few hits as a pop rock band. And I remember Brian saying to me that he got the job because a fan had written to the band when Bon died, and said, "There's a guy that sounds like Bon Scott; you've got to check him out, from Newcastle, Brian Johnson, a band called Geordie." Of course he was also not that tall and he kind of fit in perfectly. When I saw him he was like, "Oh, I just went along just thinking what the hell, I'll go have an audition." And his first gig was the Houston Astrodome, I think he said. And of course they had a lot of time in England; they spent a lot of time here touring with Bon Scott. Plus the earlier albums with Bon on them were quite popular here anyway.

But they were here all the time. I mean, Bon died here, obviously, in London. So they were here a lot. And they were pretty much thought of as an English band. I know they were Australian. I mean Angus, of course, and his brother, their parents are from Scotland. And Australia, you're not too far away from Britain, really, in the sense of that's where it all started. It was a penal colony from England to start with, so a lot of people are over there still thought of themselves as English. I mean, you've still even got the British flag hooked into the old Australian flag, and the Queen is still the head of state, which is hilarious but true. So there's still quite a lot of connection there.

July 26, 1980. *The Heavy Metal Barn Dance*, at Stafford Bingley Hall, featuring, at the bottom Mythra, Vardis and White Spirit, in the middle, Girlschool and Angel Witch, then second to top, Saxon, headliner being Motörhead. The commemorative shirt for the festival reads, on the back, "Over the Top, H.M.B.D. Mayhem Party, Bingley Hall, July 26th." Girlschool is considered to have won the day, along with Vardis (according to Mick Middles from *Sounds*), with the show standing as the first big gathering of NWOBHM bands.

Angel Witch bassist Kevin Riddles:

> Motörhead were just absolutely brilliant. Bingley Hall, in Stafford, was basically a cattle shed. It's where they used to hold cattle auctions. They used to sell horses out of there and it holds about 12,000 people when it was empty. Sadly, it took about a week to clean it, to get rid of the smell of horse and bullshit.

> And so we were due to play there on the Saturday. On the Friday night, we were playing further north in England, and to get there, we had to drive overnight. We walked into this place about 8 o'clock in the morning, and this huge PA was set up, and there's a huge crowd of people at the other end of the hall.

> And all of a sudden, I saw an arm come out. I don't know if you've ever seen any of the King Arthur or Camelot or Excalibur type films, where the arm comes out of the lake, holding the sword? So that's what this looked like, except he was holding the biggest bottle of Smirnoff blue label vodka I'd ever seen. And this gravelly voice just said, "Morning Kev, fancy some breakfast?"

> And, of course it was Lemmy himself, who obviously hadn't been asleep the night before, and he was just surrounded by sort of acolytes and all that. It was just fantastic. And that's exactly what they were like. Philthy Animal was just like that: he was an animal, just brilliant. And of course Fast Eddie was in the band then and he was the musician out of the band. And we had a great relationship with all of them, I have to say.

Summer 1980. Bleak House issue "Rainbow Warrior." The band is an elder act, with bassist Gez Turner first showing up in Pussy, issuing their classic '69 psych rarity *Pussy Plays*.

Summer 1980. Oxym issue their "Music Power" single, although the band are most remembered for the urgent "Hard Rain" track on the seminal *New Electric Warriors* compilation.

Oxym guitarist Phil Lord of Oxym

The Oxym sound was loud, overdriven, Marshall Master Volume/ DiMarzio classic end of the '70s rock, influenced by UFO, Scorpions, Judas Priest, Montrose, Deep Purple, and Michael and Rudolf Schenker. For me, the NWOBHM was redefining the sound and helping to create a new genre within the already established hard rock circles. In this light, Iron Maiden, Saxon and Praying Mantis, for me, they set the standard. Just like everything in life, things need to move on. There can only be so many top bands within any musical style, so when that number is reached a new style has to evolve, just like thrash and grunge evolved from the NWOBHM.

I loved recording the three songs that made it to vinyl, and still feel very proud of the recordings 30+ years on, especially with the Roxxcalibur cover of "Music Power" having just been released. The whole experience is still one of my dearest memories, as is one particular weekend at Jenks in Blackpool and the 24 hours driving down to London to play at the Kingsbury Soundhouse.

August 1980

August 1980. Demon issue their debut single, "Liar"/"Wild Woman," on Clay.

Demon vocalist Dave Hill:
When we started out, we really started out with Gary, Mal Spooner and myself. Mal actually died in '84. And we'd worked together before Demon, and had written some things. What we liked at the time, in music, was strong commercial songs. I think we got lumped a little bit with the New Wave of British Heavy Metal. I think basically what that was, is that there were a lot of bands who were the same but quite a few that were different that went on to be very successful. But I think we were, first and foremost, strong commercial writers. We were motivated that way so we just continued down that road. There were a lot of bands around and it became this New Wave thing, but our idea was just to write commercial rock songs.

August 1980. Diamond Head issue their second single "Sweet and Innocent"/"Streets of Gold."

Diamond Head guitarist Brian Tatler on the band's lyrical disposition: There were a few kind of horror themes maybe creeping in. I mean, "Am I Evil" could be a little bit bloodthirsty in places; "wounds deep in me" and things like that. And there are a quite a few songs about being on stage, isn't there? About being in a band, that aspirational thing about let's become a rock star, or excite a crowd and get the lights going. I would leave Sean up to whatever he wanted to write about, and I would rarely criticize or comment. I think it's hard enough to get personal feelings out anyway, so I'm certainly not going to say. But Sean would be listening to Zeppelin, Purple, Sabbath, but he also liked Free, things like that, and he did read quite a few books. And I remember him reading Michael Moorcock, and then his lyrics seemed to go down that kind of fantasy route for a while.

August 1980. Post-Strife band Nightwing issue their debut album *Something in the Air*, on Ovation, as well as the band's first single, "Barrel of Pain"/"Nightwing."

August 1980. Witchfynde is busy recording their second album, which would turn out to be a commercial left turn in contrast to the creepy debut.

Witchfynde guitarist Montalo:
We took our time about it. It was a very relaxed album to make. Roy Neave was the person who first did the Def Leppard things, a place called Fairview up in Hull, and it was Roy who did the first Def Leppard demos that came out to be that EP, the *Rocks Off* EP. And at times, there was nobody else doing anything like that. So when we wanted to do something, we said, well, let's go see what Roy Neave could do. And Roy did the first two albums of ours.

August 1980. Silverwing issue "Rock 'n' Roll Are Four Letter Words."

August 2, 1980. Praying Mantis issue their second single, "Praying Mantis"/"High Roller," both tracks non-LP, on RCA, featuring artwork by Rodney Matthews. It comes with a patch that gets stuck to the vinyl, causing much of the shipment to be faulty.

August 4 – September 15, 1980. Motörhead work on what will become their fourth album, *Ace of Spades*.

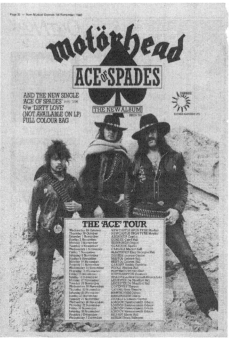

Lemmy on not fitting the NWOBHM narrative:

We were too late for the first one and too late for the second one and too late for Deep Purple and too early for Iron Maiden (laughs)— stuck in the middle there. I don't know; some of them say they were influenced by us. I mean, backstage at a Mötley Crüe show years ago, and they were playing a Motörhead track to warm up. Before they went on stage, they were playing "Overkill," which was most gratifying. And a lot of those bands say they've been influenced by us. You can't normally hear it, but there again, I was influenced by the Everly Brothers, but you can't hear it in Motörhead, although it's there.

We had a punk audience. I mean, it's because they heard us before they saw us, you see? So they liked the music, and then they saw we had long hair, but it was too late, because they liked the music. We sounded more like a punk band than a metal band, didn't we? We were always too fast for heavy metal. I always thought metal was Sabbath's first album and Judas Priest, first couple of albums. Sort of slower, you know? And we were never very slow. You can't be a fan of a whole movement. You have to differentiate. You never mention a movement; you should just ask about individuals. If you asked me about individual punk bands I will tell you what I thought, but the whole thing went from The Damned to Elvis Costello—sorry, I can't like or dislike all that (laughs).

August 8, 1980. Gillan issue their third album, *Glory Road*, which reaches #3 in the UK charts, fueled, again, by the NWOBHM, in other words, all things heavy being in fashion. The album initially comes with a bonus odds 'n' sods album called *For Gillan Fans Only*. Additionally, the band continues its tradition of regularly issuing picture sleeve singles, including "Trouble"/"Your Sister's on My List."

Early August 1980. Jet, who had reissued Quartz' debut as *Deleted*, issues "Street Fighting Lady" as a single. Meanwhile, the band has begun work on their next album, signing with MCA in early August. September dates with Gillan are planned.

> Quartz drummer Malcolm Cope:
> They went through some strange things, MCA did, when we were there. They sort of jumped on the bandwagon and signed a pile of acts all in the same bag—including ourselves—hoping to jump on this New Wave of Heavy Metal. And I just don't think the volume of sales was there across any of us, what they were hoping for. Consequently, they pulled the plug, didn't they, on everybody. And they were in decline. They suddenly, depending on what you heard, they shut the office and they left the handling of the company in the hand of some solicitors for a few years.

Early August 1980. Girl, one of a few baby Def Leppards, issue "Love is a Game"/"Little Miss Ann" as a 7" and a 10". Dedringer issue their "Sunday Drivers" 7", and by the end of the month are slated to open shows for the Michael Schenker Group. Meanwhile, Raven issue "Don't Need Your Money"/"Wiped Out," which constitutes Neat's fourth single.

August 16, 1980. Sounds announces that Witchfynde are slated to headline a metal fest in their hometown of Derbyshire, other bands being Avalanche, Radium, Lammagier, Paralex and Race Against Time.

August 16, 1980. The very first *Monsters of Rock* is held at Castle Donington racetrack. The lineup features Touch, Riot, Saxon, April Wine, Scorpions, Judas Priest and as headliner, Rainbow. A commemorative album is issued.

April Wine guitarist Brian Greenway:
Of course we were the cute little Canadian band there playing our new hit, "Just Between You and Me." And all the headbangers are sitting there going 'What?!' They loved our harder stuff a whole lot better. I remember that it rained and rained and rained. As soon as you got there, they gave you Wellies, you know, rubber boots. And they put hay down everywhere behind the stage area to absorb the water, and of course you would just get huge feet with hay all over them, like you're working on a farm. And the dressing rooms were about a five-minute ride away by a fanatical taxi service of young men in Volkswagen vans.

August 17, 1980. It's the US release date for Iron Maiden's self-titled debut, and America meets a bona fide heavy metal cartoon character called Eddie.

Iron Maiden bassist Steve Harris on Eddie:
Adding the Eddie thing meant that we didn't have to be on the front covers, which has always been a good thing. And I think it takes you to another element. A lot of people actually said to me—especially in the States where we didn't even tour with the first album—they look through the album racks as people used to do in those days, and they'd see that front cover and go, wow, what is that? And then they'd turn it over and they'd see the live picture of the band on the back. And then they say, well, I've got to have this—before they've even heard what it is.

So you know, you've already captured people. Although that's not really why we did it initially, the Eddie thing as such, because it started off as a bit of a joke, really, in the sense that we had... well it wasn't original, but the second singer we had, he used to do a bit of a Kiss thing where he used to put a sword through his mouth and the blood and guts and all this stuff. And when he left we didn't want to incorporate that within the band itself, but we thought we'd try to incorporate it in some other way.

So we came up with this Kabuki-type mask, which eventually became Eddie, because we don't pronounce the H in London, so you just say Eddie the 'ead. And then it became this thing. And then we just had this real simple thing like a fish pump pumping blood through the mouth. So you get it all over the drummer's head, because in the pubs it'd be sitting right above him. He used to love it, actually; he was in his element. He was like part of the show.

And then we used to put lights around it and the eyes lit up with smoke coming out, and sort of embellish it like that. We always wanted to put on a show, even in pubs. We would go into the change room and get changed, because we always felt you don't want to look like every other band that gets up there. You need to look around in a pub and think, who's in the band, then? Because everyone's wearing jeans and T-shirts or whatever. And then four guys or five guys will get up and, okay, it's them, then.

We would go off and get changed and just think, well we're going to put on a show, even in a pub. Even though it's a room probably not much bigger than this, we'd put on a show visually ourselves, and add elements of theatrics within what we're doing.

But Eddie meant that we didn't have to be that persona. We could have the Eddie thing and it would be like outside of us as such. And we wanted to entertain people and not freak people out, because it wasn't that kind of thing. But it was just something different as well and made people take notice. Because we always felt that once you got people in, then you can prove what you can do, and they either like it or they don't, but you gotta get people in in the first place.

And trying to fill up pubs in them days wasn't easy. But right from the start we got a real good following happening, and word of mouth thing—you gotta go and check this band out. Because it's the music and the theatrics also. It was visually something to see as well as go and enjoy the music. You know, it was important. And those elements are still there now, obviously. You make it an event so people go away thinking, wow, I've just seen something a little bit different, a little bit special.

I think people saw that it worked. I think people saw the Eddie thing was doing exactly what it was meant to do, and entertain people. But also get people excited and talking and basically go see you. Once you've got people there, you can prove what you can do, but the hardest thing is getting them there in the first place. You just had to do everything you could.

And you couldn't really afford big advertising campaigns. Yeah, you could go get a few posters together, maybe, and go slap them about. But if there wasn't the buzz about the name that was on those posters or some sort of striking image on there like Eddie or whatever, then it makes it that much more difficult. And I think anything that's going to make it easier to get people in to see you, you've just gotta get them there in the first place. Once they're there, I think you can hook them in. If you're good enough, you can hook them in, but it's very tough getting them there.

August 22 – 24, 1980.
England's venerable Reading Rock festival goes full-on heavy metal. The complete lineup (in order of performance) is as follows: Friday: Red Alert, 01 Band, Hellions, Praying Mantis, Fischer Z, Nine Below Zero, Krokus, Gillan and Rory Gallagher. Saturday: Trimmer And Jenkins, Headboys, Writz, Broken Home, Samson, Q Tips, Pat Travers Band, Angel City (did not play), Iron Maiden, UFO. Sunday: Pencils (did not play), Sledgehammer, Tygers of Pan Tang, Girl, Budgie, Magnum, Gary Moore's G-Force (did not play), Ozzy Osbourne (replaced by Slade), Def Leppard and Whitesnake.

Iron Maiden bassist Steve Harris on Reading 1980:
Well, that was great for us, because obviously it was a big fantastic festival. I'd been there in '73 to see Genesis and loads of other bands and so to actually play there was amazing, and UFO were playing, and so that was a really big thing for me as well, and just the whole vibe of it. And the reaction we got was incredible. I think everybody was just willing us to do well. You know, wherever we were playing, the crowd was growing with the band, effectively. Because they just wanted to see us go to the next stage and the next level. And whenever we went and did something that, it was a big thing, a turning point for us, a festival like that for example, and then they were really behind it and wanted us to do well. It was like they were all willing us along. It was quite a fantastic time to be involved with the band, really.

August 23, 1980. Tygers of Pan Tang's debut album, *Wild Cat*, emerges on MCA. The album reaches #18 in the UK. August 8th marks the release of the album's first single, "Suzie Smiled"/"Tush." Also John Sykes, not there for the album's recording, joins the band at this time. History has come to view *Wild Cat* as one of the albums most representative of the NWOBHM in a positive sense, i.e. youthful and yet aspiring, raw and yet brimming with fresh heavy metal ideas.

Tygers of Pan Tang vocalist Jess Cox:

I think that *Wild Cat* album is just a classic album. It's like AC/DC *Back in Black* or the first Iron Maiden, or the second and third Iron Maiden album. It's just something that will stand out. It was eclectic, different, you had themes in there that weren't the norm, let's say, in a sexist kind of rock lyric way. We were singing about euthanasia, although it was a tongue-in-cheek thing. It wasn't supposed to be supporting euthanasia. I'd just been given a survey about euthanasia and I just thought it was a bizarre thing to be asked about.

So we tried to write about things that were a bit outside of the box because we'd all been to college; we were all fairly clever. I mean Rocky was very much into sci-fi, so some of his things, like "Fireclown," was more Rocky than me, which was a guy trapped in a spaceship heading towards the sun. But you know, "Insanity" was trying to look at mental health. There's quite a few different themes in there.

Musically as well, it wasn't necessarily just what I would call metal-by-numbers. It wasn't standard riff, middle eight, chorus, riff, verse, whatever. There was a bit more to it. I mean, I know every metal band in the world said that about themselves, but I just think it was different. It stood the test of time.

I mean, my whole life has been on from *Wild Cat*. Everything I've achieved in life has been from *Wild Cat* because when I went home, I was able to get the opportunity to then go on and do some music journalism and then onto working for Neat. I sold Neat Records to Sanctuary for quite a substantial amount of money and I've been able to have a whole career out of *Wild Cat*, you know?

Tygers Of Pan Tang guitarist Robb Weir:

Well, with the album *Wild Cat*, I'd written what I wanted to write and what I thought was hard rock. I listened to heavy metal and the dividing line is quite thin. Part of me says we were slightly more melodic heavy metal, but a bit more intense, not quite as cheerful, shall we say. I'm not saying heavy metal isn't cheerful, but it's little more grandiose.

And I had my influences at the time, which were early Zeppelin, early Sabbath, Jimi Hendrix, early Uriah Heep, even early Judas

Priest. I mean that *Sad Wings of Destiny* album is fantastic. And the guy who actually did some engineering on that, a guy called Chris Tsangarides, he'd just produced a live album called *Marauder* for Magnum, and I really liked the guitar sound on that album, and I said to our manager at the time, if the record company is looking for anybody, why don't we give this guy a go because the sounds that he's got on this live Magnum album are fantastic. So that was conveyed to MCA, MCA got in touch with Chris, and off we went into the studio and recorded *Wild Cat*. And I think—and I have a slightly biased opinion obviously because it's one of my babies, which has grown up to be quite a formidable monster—I think *Wild Cat* personifies the NWOBHM movement. I think that is what the NWOBHM is all about.

As for the album cover, for me, it's quite groundbreaking, really, in as much as it says what's in the tin. The band's called Tygers Of Pan Tang, very colourful, snarling tiger's head, and the album is called *Wild Cat*, and that's what this creature is on the front—it's a wild cat. It's going to jump out and rip your head off, hopefully while you're busy listening to the music.

Tygers of Pan Tang producer Chris Tsangarides:

They were actually lucky, insomuch as they were signed by MCA. They start with a small record company in Newcastle, Neat Records, where they made a single, MCA had heard it, picked them up, signed them to a worldwide deal. And they were on tour with Magnum, and I'd worked with Magnum, on some live stuff, and that's how we… yes, Tony Clarkin had told the guys, if they were making a record, they should ask me to do it. And that's exactly what happened. And we went in, did it properly, MCA marketed it in such a way that the very first album went straight into the charts at #18. Proper charts. That kind of thing would not happen now, but it did then. And, oh crikey, it set them up.

But it was quite fun, really. We got to do the first record, which was done very, very quickly and organically; the whole thing took three weeks from start to finish, and it was hugely successful. Like I say it went straight into the mainstream charts which is ridiculous for a New Wave of British Heavy Metal band, as they tended to be called in those days.

End of August 1980. Quartz issue "Stoking Up the Fires of Hell," as an advance single from the forthcoming *Stand Up and Fight*. The b-side, "Circles," features Brian May production and Ozzy on background vocals.

Quartz drummer Malcolm Cope:
"Circles" was recorded as a demo way before the first album. In fact, "Circles" was done in about three different versions, way before we did it with Tony Iommi. And Ozzy is singing in the background as well, on one of the original versions. Ozzy used to, every now and again, come down to the studio. And then on one occasion, Brian May came down. I don't know if you're aware of it, but the way Queen used to put a load of their songs together, especially in the early days, is that they'd do two or three songs, and then just put them together, splicing things together, and then just build the song up with edits. Well, they were looking for different things to do, so Brian May came around, and Tony said to Brian, he said, "Well, why don't you see what you can do with your skills, with your editing on this?" which was "Circles." And at that point he said to us, "Why don't you go have a meal? Come back…" which happened. Anyway, we come back, there was just a pile of tape on the floor. It's all in bits and pieces—just a mess (laughs).

End of August 1980. Trespass issue their second single, "Jealousy"/"Live it Up." The band now has a new lead vocalist.

DJ Neal Kay on Trespass:
Not so much an album, more tracks and songs. They never made it, unfortunately. "One of These Days" was the name of their classic song that made the Soundhouse charts. A very, very good band. Had some small measure of success in Japan.

August 29 1980. Iron Maiden take a break from their first headlining tour to support Kiss who were promoting *Unmasked*. One suspects that the band must have felt quite confident, given that this was Kiss at their nadir commercially, creatively, and in terms of heaviness. The *Unmasked* tour finds Maiden traipsing around Europe for the first time.

Iron Maiden guitarist Adrian Smith on the band's signature twin lead sound:
Yeah, it thickens out the sound, yeah. I've played in three-piece bands, it's great fun, but you tend to play differently. Filling in all the gaps. Like I say, you've got more discipline between the two of you;

otherwise it'll sound just like a big mess. Funny enough, a lot of the songs I wrote didn't have—certainly in the '80s—didn't have guitar harmonies. Ironically Steve wrote a lot of the guitar harmonies in "The Trooper" and "Hallowed" and a lot of the classic Maiden stuff. Steve was really specific; he was really into the idea of two guitars. And he wrote a lot of that stuff, the two guitar parts. In the latest incarnation of the band, I started writing more for three guitars, you know? But yeah, a lot of the classic harmony lines you hear is the guitar stuff that Steve wrote.

September 1980

September 1980. MCA issues their *Brute Force* compilation, a classic of the early comps, chock full of new bands, quality and not so pro, without singles.

September 1980. Tygers of Pan Tang issue "Euthanasia" as the second single from the ass-kicking *Wild Cat* album, backed with the non-LP "Straight as a Die."

Tygers of Pan Tang producer Chris Tsangarides on the value of Tygers working first with indie Neat Records:

The roots of pretty much any music today is the small guy who actually bothers, not because he has a load of money, but because he loves and is passionate about the music, first and foremost. So he'll sign, or do what he can to help that particular band or artist to get up and away. And that becomes, for the majors, a really good sort of sorting ground for what's on the streets. Because it all starts at street level. If you're in there with the fans at base, that's where you begin. They discover you. As a fan you feel proud of discovering Metallica or whatever, without the big business behind it. It's more, "Hey, have you heard such and such?" And that's how it always used to work—word-of-mouth.

It was a fascinating time and it was a kick; we were getting a little bit up ourselves in the music industry at that point, really. Just briefly, when Sex Pistols were signed to A&M, all their acts were threatening to leave because they signed this nonsense. They had Supertramp, God knows what, and so, you know, they got rid of them!

But they had just given them £75,000 or whatever it was, and they did the same thing with EMI and so on. And it did sort of point the finger at the idea that music had become bigger than itself, if you like, too pompous. And the punks basically said you don't need that. We can just run around and do what we like and have a great time. And that kind of attitude spilled over into the New Wave of British Heavy Metal. But by this time we were getting a few sort of players, and so we have a few big New Wave of British Heavy Metal Bands that are still playing now.

Tygers Of Pan Tang guitarist Robb Weir:
We were out playing with all sorts of guys, before we got our record deal. And getting written about in the national press at the time, the *Sounds* newspaper, *New Music Express*, *Melody Maker*, and then *Kerrang!* came out in the early '80s, which was an offshoot from *Sounds*, using Geoff Barton from *Sounds* and some other guy. And it was really Geoff's fault because when Geoff actually put a name to this kind of music, that's when people sort of all jumped into the boat and said, "Yes we're NWOBHM, that's us, hello." So it also gave the live venues an angle to put on their appetizer, "Tygers Of Pan Tang, NWOBHM band." Kids could tell themselves, "Okay, well I've read about that in the paper, this is NWOBHM, so I've got to be there." It's kind of be there or be square.

It appeared to me back then every record company wanted British heavy metal; all the record companies were scrambling for their own signing. EMI signed Iron Maiden, Phonogram signed Def Leppard, Carrere, the French label signed Saxon, Arista signed Krokus, and MCA got us. And oddly enough, because Iron Maiden and Def Leppard and the Tygers were all kind of signed within a few months of each other, from what I remember, I don't know whether it was management at the time's fault or whatever, but they actually got us the lowest advance, cash advance, than the other bands, which was a bit of a hindrance, really, to be honest with you. Iron Maiden got £100,000 pounds to push the boat out into water, as it were. Def Leppard at the time got an industry record £250,000, and we got a lowly £25,000, which we were always up against it, unfortunately. The £25,000 had to pay for the studio, it had to pay our wages, it had to pay for our stage clothes, it had to pay for running our office, it had to pay for everything.

Tygers of Pan Tang vocalist Jess Cox:
We had no enemies as such. We felt a rivalry of course, only because we were all being written about in the media at the same time. As we toured the UK, Maiden, Saxon, Girlschool, Leppard etc. all did the same 'toilet' circuit. We'd leave messages on dressing room walls like

"Maiden shag sheep." The next time we came back to that venue, Maiden and other acts would have added a line to it, getting more and more obscene. It was a nice way of keeping in touch, and it saved on the phone bill (laughs).

September 1980. Rage, previously known as Nutz, issue "Money"/"Thank That Woman," on Carrere.

September 1980. Diamond Head issue their debut album, *Lightning to the Nations*.

Diamond Head guitarist Brian Tatler:
  I started the band with Duncan straight from school and all we literally had was, I had my brother's old guitar, which cost £14, and Duncan had a set of biscuit tins. So we just started as absolute beginners, and we auditioned some school chums until we found Sean—he was the only one who could sing. And we started writing our own material from then, and by the time we did that first album, *Lighting to the Nations*, we had been going probably four years and we had written probably a hundred songs. And I think we had played about 50 or 60 gigs, so we had honed our stuff down to the best seven that appeared on that album.
  We were striving to be as progressive as we could, as much as we could play, really. We were almost playing out of our skin. Songs like "Streets of Gold" and "The Prince" were really hard to play, when you'd only been playing a couple of years. We would listen to bands like Judas Priest and Sabbath and Deep Purple, and we would almost be trying to find the fastest and heaviest sections of those bands, and saying, well, we like that little bit there, and we would try and come up with something a bit like that, the way they've done it. But we wanted to be fast and exciting, because we were playing live, and we realized that playing slow songs didn't really go over well, especially when nobody had heard them before. We were aiming all the time for faster and more exciting material. "It's Electric" was the oldest song, although we actually wrote "Wild in the Streets" before that, which didn't appear until *Death and Progress*. "It's Electric" was a little bit AC/DC at the time, because we liked AC/DC.
  So with Diamond Head, we probably brought some speed to the table, and the arrangements. We seemed to be doing fairly complicated songs—you think of "The Prince" and "Helpless"—with quite a lot in them, that not too many rock bands were doing. They

seemed to be able to come up with riffs, but then they would stick to the idea, and then verse, chorus, verse, chorus. And we would think, how could we take it in this direction, add that little bit there? So we threw loads into the pot, really.

I think "Am I Evil?" is a good song; it's well-written; I think the arrangement is good, and it's got a lot of dynamics. Dynamics are hard to get into songs, and that's got a lot of dynamics. It goes from the moody intro and then goes into the widdly widdly bit, and it's a great riff, for the main chunk of the song. Then it goes into a fast section, and then there's a big guitar solo, tapping, and so it kind of takes you on a roller coaster ride of emotions, really, that song. 7:40 long—people must've thought, how can this young band, 19, 20-year-old, write this epic song? And if they can write this epic song, there must be more that they could do in the future. There's a lot of potential in a song like that, and a song like "The Prince."

September 1980. White Spirit issue their self-titled debut. The band tour as support for Gillan. The first single is "Midnight Chaser"/"Suffragettes" and the second single is "High Upon High"/"No Reprieve"/"Arthur Guitar."

White Spirit producer John McCoy:

Great band, with MCA. I was asked to go see them and I went up to Hartleypool, in the Northeast, a wonderful place. Saw this band, and I was really, really impressed. They were a Deep Purple-esque kind of band; did a couple of Purple numbers, the lineup with Simon. The musical instruments was the same as Deep Purple, and there was definitely a big influence there.

But it was much more a kind of progressive rock, with quite complex arrangements and lots of overdubs and things on that album.

They impressed me, and in particular Janick Gers stood out as a really hot player. And we went and did the album very, very quickly. I would have liked more time to work on it, to be honest. The last time I listened to it, some of the tracks are great, but some of the mixes aren't. I have to be honest (laughs). But it was in a rush, yeah. As for signing with MCA, I can't remember the guys' names at the company at the time, but they were right on the button. They were going out and just looking at bands because record companies, if there's a buzz on the street they want to know about it. They want to get in there first. They don't want to be the label that didn't get to sign whoever it might be, the flavour of the month. But yeah, MCA were pretty hot at that time.

September 1980. Saxon issue "Suzie Hold On"/"Judgement Day (live)." The Suzie in question is an acquaintance of the band's who unfortunately got cancer and later died.

September 1, 1980. Saxon issues their third album, *Strong Arm of the Law*, which debuts at #11 on the UK charts. *Sounds* gives it a five star review.

Saxon guitarist Graham Oliver: *Strong Arm* was done in The Who's studio—same as *Wheels of Steel*—and I remember doing "Dallas 1 PM," and the moment that Pete Gill laid that beat down and Steve started thumping on the E string, it inspired me to write a great riff, and that's what happened with "Dallas 1 PM." And so when we were recording it, we were very fresh with it, and I can remember doing it with the screens around, and Pete Gill was just laughing, with his headphones on, because we were having so much fun and it was sounding great—it was just a great time.

NOT FOR THE INNOCENT.

SAXON, England's deadliest rock and roll strike force, hits hard with their newest collection of unmenaced metal muscle— "Strong Arm Of The Law." With the power to totally protect you from the criminally mundane.

Awesome Saxon. "Strong Arm Of The Law." Rock and roll with authority.

On Carrere® Records and Tapes.

CARRERE

Produced by Saxon and Pete Hinton. Distributed by CBS Records.   © 1982 CBS Inc.

In fact, Pete Gill said that on a couple of the sessions on *Strong Arm*, that he felt the presence of Keith Moon. And I don't know how... and Pete is not one to say things, he doesn't suffer fools and he's not a liar and is very straight. In fact, talking straight maybe got him into trouble sometimes. And he felt the presence of, what he thought was Keith Moon, when the lights were down and we were recording backing tracks, which is quite awesome.

It was an old church, for a start, the Who studio, so it's quite eerie. And it even had the pulpit still in there, and so it was an excellent place to record metal music (laughs). We were recording right where the pulpit was and everything. They left certain architectural features in there, and I can remember doing things like "To Hell and Back Again," with Quinn-y and everybody just jamming out and having a great time. It's a long time ago, but I can remember having breaks and going upstairs and listening to tracks and playing on the pinball machine upstairs in the recreation room, which was the original one from the film. They had that it in there.

Strong Arm was remixed for America. Because what happened is, because *Wheels of Steel* had done so well, and Pete Hinton had been involved, the record company deemed that Pete Hinton should be involved. And I think Pete Hinton got delusions of grandeur, and started sitting behind desks. And we were still a bit naïve and thought, well, he was right on *Wheels of Steel*, he must be right on this.

We didn't really understand that—and people don't do that now—if you release a big album like *Wheels of Steel*, like Metallica did on their big album in 1991, they tour for like two or three years on that one album. Def Leppard toured for two or three years on *Pyromania*. What we should've done is tour on *Wheels of Steel* for a couple of years, and not rush back into another album. I think that's why it was a bit scrappy. We had the songs, but it was put together six months after the release of *Wheels of Steel*. And hindsight is a wonderful thing, but I think that was a mistake. And we weren't strong enough then as individual band members to say that's a bit wrong; we should take our time a bit. We were guided by people who were doing things, and you don't really think they could be wrong at that stage.

Saxon bassist Steve Dawson:
For *Wheels of Steel*, we wrote some great tunes, and then, more or less, our management wanted us to do another album straightaway. Which was unheard of. We made two records in one year. And looking back on it, it was probably a mistake (laughs). We should have kept touring on *Wheels of Steel* a bit longer. So *Strong Arm of the Law* was written quick. But we were on a songwriting roll, so we wrote all those songs together, and so obviously then there's more money coming in, and then you've got more time to write your next record.

Diamond Head guitarist Brian Tatler on the immediacy of Saxon:
As for other bands, maybe some of them were a bit more commercial. I mean, Saxon probably, I don't know if it was their idea, but they might've been encouraged to write singles and get on *Top of the Pops*, and I mean, bands like Zeppelin never really did that, did they? Purple had a few singles. Sabbath had a couple singles. I never saw them as single bands—they were album bands. So maybe they were more, "You've got to get a hit single, you've got to get on the radio, you've got to get on MTV." So maybe that came into it.

I mean, Zeppelin *III* got terribly slated when it came out, and I remember some of the Sabbath albums, you'd get little acoustic guitar bits in-between songs, and I never liked that. I always wanted it to go from "Children of the Grave" to "After Forever" or vice versa, rather than have a little filler bit. But when you get to Saxon, they didn't do any of that. They just go from this to this to this, and not mess about. Just slabs of hard rock. And not have any airy fairy bits.

September 6, 1980. *Sounds* announces that Saxon's *Wheels of Steel* had gone silver. Meanwhile, the band is in North America supporting Rush.

Saxon vocalist Biff Byford on *Wheels of Steel*:

I think musically and lyrically—because obviously you have to split them in two—I think musically it was a great coming together of our influences, altogether, the five of us. I think more predominantly, the four of us really. The two guitarists, Dawson on bass, and me, fiddling around on the guitar and things. Although Pete Gill was there sometimes, I think the majority of the ideas came from the four of us. It was just a great combination of styles.

Myself and Paul were more into the musical-oriented stuff and I think Oliver and Dawson were more into Free. In fact SOB, Son of a Bitch, *Tons of Sobs* was the name of a Free album, so they were heavily into that, which was quite old-fashioned. And I think myself and Paul jazzed that up a little bit.

And lyrically, I think I just got my shit together at that particular point in time. I think up to that point on the first album, two or three songs were mine and Paul's, like "Judgement Day," "Militia Guard," "Frozen Rainbow," and the co-written songs were like "Stallions of the Highway" and "Backs to the Wall" and the SOB-influenced song was probably "Freeway Mad." So it was a mixed album and I really wasn't getting my talents as a lyricist together yet. It was all a bit weird. "Stand Up and Fight," "Frozen Rainbow," you know?

So on *Wheels of Steel*, I actually got it together and started writing quite memorable lyrics and really good titles for songs as well. Because the two things really go together. The riff has to fit the title with me. I'll keep a title for years if I don't hear a riff. Really I will.

I was a biker, so I mean, "Motorcycle Man" was my theme song. I was in a club as well, actually originally. I did used to ride bikes up to my daughter being born about seven years ago. And then I decided to pack it in because I seriously risked being killed every day, as you do on a motorcycle. My wife used to do show-jumping on horses and I used to ride bikes, and we made a pact to stop doing it basically, so we did. But I was heavily into bikes and I still am heavily into bikes. And we do actually play a lot of biker festivals.

September 6, 1980. Spider issue their third single, "College Luv"/"Born to Be Wild." By this point they have their well-known logo. Spider also claim to be the only bar band with a laser light show.

September 12, 1980. Vardis issue their "Let's Go" single, in advance of the *100 M.P.H.* debut (live) LP.

Mid-September 1980. Fist issue their "Forever Amber"/"Brain Damage" single, in advance of their debut album.

September 19, 1980. Quartz issue the immense *Stand Up And Fight* on MCA, their fourth label, after Reddingtons Rare, Jet and licensee Logo. The album is produced by Derek Lawrence of Deep Purple and Wishbone Ash fame. Headlining pub dates span September 6 to the 21st after which the plan is to go out with Gillan. MCA also features on its roster Fist and Tygers of Pan Tang.

Quartz drummer Malcolm Cope:

It's amazing how people see things. When we did *Stand Up and Fight*, we weren't happy with it at all. But the reviews that it's got, especially recently, it stands up for itself. So it's quite a shock, really. I mean, Derek Lawrence, our producer, did a great job, and he was a nice guy; we got on quite well with him. The only thing, we'd been used to guys help constructing the songs. When we got in the studio, we were used to people making suggestions, even from the point of engineers saying, "Why don't you try that?" or "Have you thought about this?" There wasn't anything like that. And that was one of the things that was strange. As we played, he just wanted to get it on tape and he was quite happy with that. And any effects on that album are all down to us, not anybody else, an engineer or Derek or anybody else. It's us saying, we'd like to try this here, we'd like to try that.

Actually, we were thrown in the deep end quite quickly, because if my memory serves me correct, the deal with MCA sort of came out of the blue. And as soon as we'd done the deal, they wanted us in the studio. And so all those songs we wrote very, very quickly, within about two weeks. And that was one of the reasons we had to put one of the old songs, "Can't Say No To You" on there, which we didn't want to do. But "Revenge" they liked. "Stoking Up the Fires of Hell," they put out as a single. Without even asking us, if I remember rightly, with "Stand Up and Fight" on the other side of the single.

Quartz guitarist Mick Hopkins:

I came up with most of the stuff on *Stand Up and Fight*. I was sitting in the front room with two cassette recorders, bouncing ideas from one to the other, and I was working at Reddingtons Records at the time, and we had three weeks to get the album complete. As a mad rush. Some people, particularly, like Brian May, will spend days on a guitar solo. We took days to do the actual full thing. So it was a bit of a rush, really. We always had bad luck that way.

But we missed out on touring with Sabbath again. Ronnie, he didn't want us on the shows. I can't understand it, because it's like, if you're top of the bill, you want somebody to warm the fans up for you. That's the way I look at it. But Ronnie had a different way of looking at it. He didn't want us to go on, so we just put the gear back in the van and came back home.

September 20, 1980. Logo Records issues their seminal *New Electric Warriors* compilation, while simultaneously, the BBC issues their *Metal Explosion: From the Friday Rock Show* compilation, another classic documenter of the genre. Amusingly, both are panned by Geoff Barton, who declares the NWOBHM over with.

Diamond Head guitarist Brian Tatler on metal as a movement strong enough that so many compilations could be commercially viable:
Well, maybe it just didn't exist before that. Now there were suddenly enough bands giving precedent to this kind of music. There weren't that many really heavy bands, were there, before the New Wave of British Heavy Metal? Obviously, Sabbath and Judas Priest, but if I wanted to go and buy another heavy metal album, there weren't many about. And so maybe the fact that the floodgates are opened, and everybody started to think ah, there's something giant here we can belong to. It's a whole scene; it's suddenly a scene. It's not just, "We like this band." It's a whole style of music.
And it's very loyal; it's fantastically loyal. When you get into rock or metal, it never seems to leave you. I've never moved away from it. I do listen to other things, but I've never gone off it. I still like rock and heavy metal, and so maybe, once you've got it in you, in your system, it will never go away. It will never leave you, and you'll always like it. And you might not like all the latest harder and heavier and faster darker bands, but you still appreciate what they're trying to do, and appreciate the classics from yesteryear.

September 25, 1980. John Bonham dies after a night of drinking. With Deep Purple gone and now Led Zeppelin, we have come to the end of the old guard. Adding to the pronounced feeling of transition is the questionable status of Uriah Heep and Black Sabbath. A similar situation is confronting the biggest American acts, namely Ted Nugent, Kiss and Aerosmith, all of whom are in the process of losing band members, resulting in marked declines in both critical and commercial success.

October 1980

October 1980. Dark Star issue, on Avatar, quintessential anthem "Lady of Mars." B-side is the non-LP "Rock 'n' Romancin'." The band bill themselves as "the kings of mysterious metal."

October 1980. Angel Witch issue their second single "Angel Witch"/"Gorgon." Both singles thus far are in exciting advance of the groundbreaking self-titled debut.

Angel Witch bassist Kevin Riddles:

"Angel Witch" was our anthem, if you like. What you have to remember is, in large part, the band was going before I joined, in slightly different guises. When I came on board, probably 70% of the set we did had already been written. My contribution at the time was to try and do some rearrangements. Bear in mind, Kevin was so young and actually we were all really young at that time, but I'd had some classical training at school, so I was able to—how can I put it?—rein in the more naïve parts, and sort of jumble them around to make them a bit more coherent and make sense.

But for all intents and purposes, they're still Kevin Heybourne songs, and they were there, so "Angel Witch" was already there; we just swapped a few bits around. And the fact that it was called "Angel Witch," I think came before the name of the band came about. As far as I understand it, Kevin came up with that when the band was called Lucifer, sort of six months before I joined.

And "Gorgon," that again was one that was already written, but needed a fair bit of rearranging, and there's a couple of riffs in there of mine. It was based on Greek mythology. A lot of people think that we were all into devil worship and all that, which wasn't true. A lot of the stuff, if you listen, it was more Greek and Roman mythology. Gorgon was based on Medusa and the head of snakes and how her look could turn you to stone.

Kevin had a very wide interest in ancient myths and legends. But he was also able to bring it up-to-date with things like "Flight Nineteen;" anything that piqued his interest that was a bit epic, shall we say. He'd find it quite easy to come up with an idea for a song. And whereas the way I write, I always write the music first. Once I've got a title in my head and I know what the song is going to be called, then I can start writing the songs. I could pull a riff out and say, oh, that riff goes with that title, and along will come the lyrics, usually the last thing. Kevin would pretty much do the whole thing as he's going along. As he was writing the riff, the words would be forming in his head, and what he was writing this song about, that would be the title. It's a horrible word that people use nowadays, but it was all very organic. It just sort of arrived—completed songs used to come out. And that went for most of the tracks on the album and the ones that came after.

October 1980. Manchester's AIIZ issue a debut live album called *The Witch of Berkeley*, which features a strangely Satanic front cover. The album, recorded at Hazel Grove High School, emerges on Polydor and the band garners a back-up slot with Girlschool and Black Sabbath.

October 1980. Guitarist Dennis Stratton leaves Iron Maiden, after butting heads with Steve Harris and manager Rod Smallwood. He would be replaced by Adrian Smith.

Early October 1980. Fist issue their debut album, *Turn the Hell On*, on MCA. It is announced that they will be support for upcoming UFO dates. Hobbled by a thin mix, the album would fail, with the band being dropped by the label early into 1981.

Tygers of Pan Tang guitarist Robb Weir:
Quartz just did one album on MCA, and that didn't do very well, so they were dropped—which was the same as Fist. Fist were another local Newcastle band. Great band to see live, but when they recorded their album and I listened to their album, it was nothing like they are live—it was just flat. It didn't capture the excitement of what Fist were live.

October 10, 1980. Budgie issue *Power Supply*, on RCA. The album is a flagrant cash-in, with the band wholesale adopting a gritty NWOBHM sound.

Budgie bassist and vocalist Burke Shelley:

Power Supply is one of my favourite albums, but the only thing I'm not too pleased about is the production. The producer on that one messed up on something rather critical. He had my bass out of phase, which meant, the more you turn up the album, the less bass you get, actually. And once again, you just pull your hair out trying to get people to understand. They had no idea what ambience is about, I realized. They have an idea in their head about what they think ambience is, but when you play live in a huge hall, you know what ambience is. And these people didn't. And I still could've done with that album being bigger, more spread-out, instead of so tight. That's one of the things I would've done with it. But having said all that, that is still a really good album.

John Thomas is a great guitarist, with great style and technique and he had a big sound at the time, and it was great. Plus he was a good laugh, John is. *Power Supply* was the first one we did with John, and I think that's a good album. Like I say, I can do with a bit more thump in it though, production-wise, but I do like that album. It's pretty 4/4 rock, most of it, tight as the nuts. I think you probably know this, but maybe you don't, but he got ill and had a stroke, and that's why he had to leave. It became impossible for him to play the way he used to.

Raven bassist and vocalist John Gallagher on Budgie's heavy turn: Yeah, but they had to because they already lost it when they did… it got a little weird when they did *Brittania*, and it was liked not so much. That was back '76. All these bands… Zeppelin did *Presence*, Aerosmith did *Night in the Ruts*, which has got that funky type of thing going on, and Pat Travers did *Crash and Burn*. Too much on the funk side of things. That really kicked in. It's probably, I think, because all those guys were all out of their mind on cocaine at the time. And one year after that, they all started dying.

October 10, 1980. Venom record a second demo, known as The £50 Demo Session. Mantas suggests Cronos sing "Live Like an Angel" in place of Clive; shortly thereafter, Clive is let go from the band and the classic Venom lineup is birthed.

Mid-October 1980. Wakefield, West Yorkshire boogie kings Vardis issue their debut LP, *100 M.P.H.*, which generates a single release for non-LPer "Too Many People" paired with album track "The Lion's Share." Odd for a debut but not unprecedented, the album is live—both Stampede and AIIZ would also issue a live debut album. *100 M.P.H.* would rise to #52 in the British charts.

Late October 1980. Grand Prix issue, on RCA, a self-titled debut. The band is most famous for eventually coughing up Phil Lanzon and western Canadian Bernie Shaw to Uriah Heep (Shaw first to Praying Mantis), along with second vocalist Robin McAuley to the McAuley Schenker Group. Concurrent single release is "Thinking of You"/"Feels Good."

October 27, 1980. Motörhead release as an advance single, "Ace of Spades"/"Dirty Love," which peaks at #15. On the same day, Lemmy's ex-band Hawkwind issue their tenth record, *Leviathan*, which is somewhat reflective of what was going on in the NWOBHM.

Motörhead guitarist Fast Eddie Clarke on "Ace of Spades:"

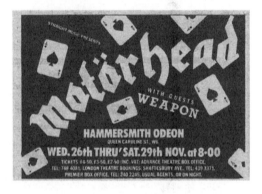

This track was not as straight forward as it might have been. We had gone down to a live in rehearsal room in Wales called Rockfield and had decided to write the album there; it was as yet untitled. Motörhead didn't really do the country thing, so we spent a lot of time drinking and falling over and at first, did very little work.

After about a week, we did start to do a bit of playing, surprisingly, and the songs started to take shape. We decided it would be good to record the rehearsals, so we hired in a 16-track mobile recording unit. We recorded the songs as they were so far and split back to London.

Eventually, we decided to go to a studio and put some vocals on the tracks and this was the first time the title "Ace of Spades" appeared. Lemmy threw down a few lyrics and we moved on to another track. Not much more was said at this time as they were, after all, only demos for the album.

Discussions were taking place regarding producers and that is when we were steered towards Vic Maile, who was favoured by the record company and management. We didn't really care too much; we just wanted to record the album and get back on the road.

We started laying down the backing tracks but when we got to "Ace of Spades" we decided that the riff needed a makeover. This was unusual for us, as we were always in a hurry. The result was that the main riff was completely changed and wedded to the old part of the song. We all got very excited about the new arrangement and we knew we had a killer track on our hands. This new approach was then applied to some of the other songs and the results were equally impressive. It was only a matter of hours before we agreed the album title would be *Ace of Spades*.

October 27, 1980. Iron Maiden issue "Women in Uniform," a Skyhooks cover, backed with "Invasion." 12" version adds a live performance of "Phantom of the Opera."

Nouember 1980

November 1980. Budgie issue "Crime Against the World"/"Hellbender," the only single from the heavy and gritty *Power Supply* album.

November 1980. Leicester's Blitzkrieg issue a three-track demo cassette consisting of "Blitzkrieg," "Inferno" and "Armageddon."

November 1980. Saxon issue "Strong Arm of the Law"/"Taking Your Chances."

November 1980. Guardian Records assembles (and quickly issues) their legendary *Roksnax* compilation, one of the top NWOBHM collectibles in the full-length record department. The album features three North East bands, Samurai, Saracen and Hollow Ground, performing four tracks each.

November 1980. Vertigo issue a heavy metal compilation called *Living Legends*, featuring the established hard rock bands on their label, but also newcomers Def Leppard.

November 1980. Manchester's Tora Tora issue their debut single, "Red Sun Setting." The band are featured in the very first issue of *Kerrang!* in June 1981.

November 1, 1980. Whitesnake issue *Live... in the Heart of the City*. The UK version was a double, trimmed to a single in North America. The album reached #146 on the Billboard charts and #5 on the UK charts.

November 1, 1980. Witchfynde issue their second album, *Stagefright*, which yields a single release for "In the Stars" backed with the heaviest track on the album, "Wake Up Screaming." Vocalist Steve Bridges had already left the band, serving notice the previous month.

Witchfynde guitarist Montalo:

"Wake Up Screaming" was one of the songs we'd had left over from *Give 'Em Hell*. That was a song that we'd been playing live before we actually recorded the *Give 'Em Hell* album, really. In fact, that was one of the songs that Tony Iommi had put ideas through on that. We sent him the original demo ideas for "Wake Up Screaming" and he just gave us a few pointers on various things, and we were very appreciative.

Yeah, so why's that album so diverse? I guess it was just a matter of exploring the theme of songwriting, and trying to get different sounds in the studio. We had a lot more time in the studio for that album. In hindsight, that might've been a dangerous thing (laughs).

But to be fair, we do have that sort of light-hearted background to the band. We're not terribly... I don't know want to say we're not serious, because ultimately we are. I mean, we're not a comedy band (laughs), but we don't like to take ourselves too seriously. I don't really see the point in that. We do like to enjoy ourselves as well.

So there's a song called "Big Deal" that is just totally the story of the whole setup of the band, really, and I listen to it now and I still laugh about that. It does make me smile, some of the things that did go on. "Doing the Right Thing"... Steve had quite an involvement in that song; that was a chord progression that I came up with and we thought it matched Steve's style well. He could just handle that type of music a lot easier.

"Would Not Be Seen Dead in Heaven" was Gra's involvement on the lyric side, which, he loved playing around with words and titles—that is his forté. That was Gra doing what he was best at, turning the lyrics around. And it still is a good title, quite a funny title, not terribly serious.

Also on *Stagefright*, "Moon Magic" is still quite a favourite of mine, because of the guitar, the different guitar notes and progressions on it. Which is quite a clever sort of guitar chord, quite nicely put together. And it still is quite a valid type of song for us. Although conversely, "In the Stars" was a bit of a disaster, really. It's quite a well put-together song production-wise, but it did really lose the point. It was us experimenting, really. "Trick or Treat," I remember Gra loved all the various guitar ideas on that, and all the things that sort of go in and out. That again was Gra's lyric. And "Madeline," yeah, I forgot all about that one. I think it's best that I have (laughs)."

On the guitar side, I expect *Stagefright* is fairly Thin Lizzy-ish, if I dare say that. I'm sure that's where I was coming from at the time. Lizzy was the first band that we actually ever played with, as Witchfynde. I'm sure it was; yes it was. That was when they'd just got Brian Robertson and Scott Gorham. Fact is, I think it was their first gig with the Scott Gorham and Brian Robertson's lineup, in Darby. The thing was, it was our home crowd (laughs), so we had quite a good crowd reaction. And that was the first time they had done that lineup, so they were a bit nervous, I guess. And the other bizarre thing about it, the last gig that we played, as the lineup after the third album, with Luther, was Phil Lynott's last gig before he died. That was with the Mama's Boys in Nottingham, a guest appearance of John Sykes and Phil Lynott together.

November 8, 1980. Motörhead issue their classic *Ace of Spades* album, which peaks at #4 on the UK charts. The success of the album allows for Motörhead to be one of the rare NWOBHM-era acts to tour North America, and eventually, to become one of the four most successful bands across the pond, along with Iron Maiden, Saxon and Def Leppard.

Motörhead drummer Phil Taylor on his creative role in the band:

Not in the actual music. Because I don't play guitar or anything like that. I mean my contribution was, I would help with coming up with suggestions for the arrangement, or maybe we should do a stop here or there. Just little things. I don't know an E flat from an elbow, so I'm saying I don't play guitar, but occasionally I would have a tune going through my head or whatever, and I would kind of like hum it, but it's not quite the same.

But Eddie and I wrote a couple of songs like "Chase is Better than the Catch" from *Ace of Spades*; we wrote that in Eddie's flat, with me playing on a cardboard box. When me and Eddie worked together, Eddie was a lot more understanding than Lemmy, and I would make guitar noises, just make a change or this and that, and Eddie interpreted it very well. So that was from my point of view, how my input was. And in lots of other ways, but not necessarily musically.

We started out as a family, and to be honest, that was the way of keeping the band together, by including everybody, because famously, throughout history or whatever, drummers have never been included in the publishing, just because they don't necessarily play music, but they always have a certain input, and Lemmy and Eddie both insisted that they split the publishing three ways, so that we could stay together as a band. And as I say, I did have input in my own way. I wasn't just a freeloader, put it that way (laughs)."

November 10 – December 12, 1980. Gillan conduct an intensive US and Canadian tour. It is a significant event, in that, as alluded to above, very few NWOBHM bands got over to North America, one of the reasons cited for the genre's lack of successful bands and subsequent quick displacement by a metal movement born in California.

November 21, 1980. Iron Maiden finish their first headlining tour, after taking a break to support Kiss. All shows, besides one in Belgium, were up and down the UK, Maiden solidifying their home country support, underscored by their overt and proud British-ness.

November 22, 1980. Motörhead issue their *Beer Drinkers* EP.

Late 1980. The Midlands' Grim Reaper whip up an eight-song, four-track cassette demo called *Bleed 'Em Dry*.

Late 1980. A NWOBHM supergroup called Lionheart forms, featuring Jess Cox and Dennis Stratton, plus two members from The Next Band, Rocky Newton and Frank Noon, the latter also serving as early drummer for Def Leppard. Jess Cox is soon to be replaced by Reuben Archer. Frank Noon would be succeeded by two famed drummers himself, namely Les Binks and Clive Edwards. The band's song "Lionheart" would surface on the 1982 compilation *Heavy Metal Heroes Vol. 2*.

Late 1980. Black Axe issue "Highway Rider." Black Axe, along with Xero pulled up the rear on the otherwise mid-tier *The Friday Rock Show* compilation. Meanwhile excellent songwriters Trespass issue "Jealousy" and Triarchy gives us "Metal Messiah."

Late 1980. EMI issue their *Muthas Pride* EP compilation, featuring Quartz, Wildfire, White Spirit and Baby Jane. *Metal for Muthas* was intended to comprise a trio of full-length albums, and the fact that EMI could only bring themselves to issue an EP for the third installment indicates some level of metal fatigue, even if the sleeve suggested that EMI stood for 'Eavy Metal In'nit?.

December 1980

December 1980. Angel Witch issue their classic self-titled debut, on Bronze. It's as good as Iron Maiden's first record, but this doom band is doomed.

Angel Witch guitarist Kevin Heybourne on the John Martin painting used for the cover of *Angel Witch*:
    We had to get the rights from the gallery, Tate Gallery, to use the transparency. I originally saw it in a book by Dennis Wheatley. I've always been interested in that stuff but I've never taken it seriously. I see religion as religion is, you know what I mean? I think it can be just as bad as Satanism. So yes, I tracked it down to the Tate Gallery, same as the Baphomet as well, the goat thing, same gallery. I mean we were just into the old Hammer horror films. It's just imagination and fantasy. I thought, you know, a lot of bands sing about love and stuff like that, real issues, and I just wanted to get away from that, do pure

fantasy. A lot of people out there want to hear that, you know?

As for our producer, Martin Smith, he hadn't produced anything before us. When I knew him then, he was in Electric Light Orchestra, but that was it as far as I know. He's still around and he's still doing it. He's got his own little set-up and he does a few little bits and pieces. He was a member of ELO, but I don't know for how long. All told, the album took about three weeks of playing and a week of other stuff to get done. Bronze didn't give us much of a recording advance, and come to think of it, it wasn't much of a publishing advance either (laughs).

Song-wise, "Atlantis" was a real trick to get down, the drums, and I think in the end, they had to play them the other way around, sort of "snare bass bass" instead of "bass snare snare." That was a very, very trying time, a real pain in the ass. Basically Martin didn't want big drum rolls and stuff like that. He wanted to try and cut this out and cut that out which I thought sucked a bit. But I kind of knew what he wanted to achieve. He wanted to make it more basic so people could hear what's going on instead of it been cluttered. Lyrically, that was just straight out of me own box (laughs).

"White Witch," that's when I was working in a mental institution as a porter as my day job at the time. There was this weird girl there that just made my imagination run wild. She told me a few things. She told me she was a witch and she had died and I kind of wrote the thing around her. Obviously the things in this song didn't happen to her (laughs). And "Confused," I didn't write the lyrics for that. My ex-wife actually wrote them. Obviously I wrote the music. And actually I thought the lyrics were pretty good. I thought, yeah, this is actually what people feel like, the kind of people that go to those things, go to gigs. They have a bit more of an open mind. You can say what you like to them and nobody really holds against you what you say.

The press do, on the other hand (laughs). I'd say reviews were about 50/50; we had some bad ones and some good ones. Some people raved about it and some people absolutely hated it. You're talking about one person's opinion of your album, and that sort of annoys me. It goes out to the public and you say, "They believe this?! You've got a mind of your own." It's dangerous. I really like that whole album. I'm very proud of it because it's the first one and because of the fact that I wouldn't be where I am now without it. I feel I have a bit of respect because of that album.

Angel Witch bassist Kevin Riddles on how Angel Witch's first record was as good as Iron Maiden's:

I think so, yes. I mean, with hindsight, it was certainly as influential. Because everywhere I go, every gig I play now with Tytan, I'm still getting people coming up to me. We just did a gig in Italy two weeks ago and we've never been to Italy and I'm still getting people coming up with albums for me to sign, posters for me to sign, and it's 30 odd years later. So it obviously means something to people. Even people who weren't even born then, it still means something. And it's amazing how many times that I get asked, and Kevin Heybourne gets asked, to put the original Angel Witch back together.

December 1980. Sledgehammer issues "Living in Dreams"/"Fantasia," the latter of which can also be found on the *Brute Force* compilation from MCA.

December 1980. Holocaust issue "Smokin' Valves"/"Out My Book." 12" version adds "Friend or Foe."

Holocaust guitarist John Mortimer on the band's record label, Phoenix:

They were initially just an independent record store in Edinburgh. Because at that time, after the punk thing, there were a lot of self-financed labels coming on the scene. The guy there, John Mayer, he had quite a lot of money and he just decided, "Hey, I'm going to have a label as well." He did various different things but he knew heavy metal was an up-and-coming thing, and Garry, our singer, worked for him in that store. He just said, "We've got a band; come on down and see us." So he came and saw us play in a church hall (laughs) and we just went from there. I mean, they were a new label at the time and didn't really have a track record. Good guy though, everything went great the whole time. I still know him now. He's a high-flying lawyer now, an advocate, which is the Scottish equivalent of the English QC, top-notch.

December 1980. Chevy issue their debut album, *The Taker*, on Avatar, promoting the album on an English tour supporting Hawkwind, December 12 - 21.

December 6, 1980. Girlschool issue "Yeah Right" as a single, backed with "The Hunter," quickly followed by "Hit & Run"/"Tonight," which rises to #32 in the UK charts.

Girlschool bassist and vocalist Enid Williams on "Yeah Right:"

"Yeah Right" I remember quite well because I wrote a lot of the lyrics for it. And it's quite funny, because the other three members of the band are big drinkers, and I'm not. But I guess I drank more in those days and I started to pull back quite early. Because I'm one of those people, I have two glasses of wine or two beers or something and I'm on my back. So I'm a cheap date.

So with "Yeah Right," it was very much about... we were still quite young then, and it was kind of like we're going to go out and have adventures and we're going to drink and be really crazy and wild. And on one level our parents were sort of accepting of it, and on another level they didn't know what we were up to (laughs). So it's quite a good time, fun song, about yeah, just going out and being crazy.

And then of course we got Philthy in to do the bit in the middle, which I suppose was loosely based on an amalgam of our parents (laughs). And he dressed up for the video as well. So it's him going, "And don't come home late, and don't drink too much!" You know, our parents were very supportive of us doing the whole band, and they came to a lot of gigs and they knew that we drank and that we were a little crazy, but I don't think they knew quite how crazy. Parents have to sort of say don't come home too late and don't drink too much. It's their job really, and we go yes, yeah right. I'm going to do what I want anyway. It's a teenage song, in a way. But there was still an element of that spirit about us, a bit of don't tell us how to live our lives. Yeah, right. We're just going to do what we do anyway.

December 20, 1980. Motörhead cancel their remaining tour dates after Phil Taylor breaks his neck horsing around with his road crew at their hotel, the Europa, in Belfast, Northern Ireland. Fast Eddie receives a call in his room the following morning about the incident and wonders, "Could this be the end?"

Recap

I think we would all have to agree that 1980 became the penultimate year of the NWOBHM, a 12-month period in which everything came together in a clanging kerrang of power chords—and that goes for new bands, old bands, baby bands and big bands.

However, dispensing with the horrible, and the negative, both AC/DC's Bon Scott and Led Zeppelin's John Bonham would die in 1980, and under similar circumstances, both felled by alcohol. As history would have it, the career arcs for these two bands couldn't be more different, Led Zeppelin promptly closing up shop and AC/DC returning with one of the most beloved albums—and biggest sellers—of all time, *Back in Black*.

Other old guard bands would do brisk business as well. In 1980. Judas Priest would finally shake their cult status and swan into the mainstream with *British Steel*, ingratiating themselves into the New Wave of British Heavy Metal, and temporally, somewhat being allowed to sneak in there anyway, given both their grinding metal dedication through six previous albums and the fact that they were not viewed as original first wave metal, but rather somewhat from the second wave, a placement also bestowed upon the likes of Thin Lizzy, AC/DC, Rainbow and UFO.

With somewhat similar spring in the step came a newly tanned and toned Black Sabbath, offering *Heaven and Hell*, whipped into shape through the arrival of American metal legend Ronnie James Dio. Also of note (although commercially it meant zip), was the fact that Budgie went full-on the metal this year, with some level of acceptance awarded, given the band's thankless toiling in the forge since their first album back in 1971.

I was going to liken the sturdy seat that was the New Wave of British Heavy Metal in 1980 as a three-legged stool, but I've come to realize that this chair has four legs. One leg is represented by the aforementioned vim and vigour of the old bands, and I suppose the other three would have to stand and support as follows: 1) the massive amount of mostly independent singles generated by a toiling base of baby bands; 2) the extent and quality of the heavy metal compilations coming out this year; and 3) the impressive productivity in full-length albums from most of the bands we associate and celebrate with and through the genre, even though, incredibly, we've still got 1981, 1982, 1983 and 1984 to come in our tale (please proceed to volume 2 of this undertaking, *This Means War: The Sunset Years of the NWOBHM*).

So yes, first consider the mortar between the bricks (signifying that we definitely had a movement on our hands), the fact that a high quantity and high quality of singles were being issued out of every corner of the UK, by bands that would never make albums, by bands that were about to make an album, and by bands that were already making albums, some of them on major labels.

And consider as well (making it plain that there was a huge appetite for heavy metal in the UK), the fact that every manner and magnitude of label, from indies like Guardian up to EMI, were issuing compilation albums. *Axe Attack*, a couple of *Metal for Muthas*, *Metallurgy*, *Killer Watts*, *Brute Force*, *Precious Metal*, *New Electric Warriors*, *Roksnax*... some of these were utterly pointless to the deep metal fan, because we were already buying the full-lengths from whence the songs originated. But then again, on the other hand, buying something like *Roksnax* was like snatching up four or five singles all in one place, and with some sort of knowledge-imbuing context to boot.

Finally, what makes 1980 virtually and ridiculously something like one half of the NWOBHM, is the fact that many of the classic full-length cornerstones of the genre emerged in this first year of the new decade.

Martin Popoff

Motörhead was all guns blazing on *Ace of Spades*, along with various single and EP output, and even more productive was Witchfynde, who suggested for our collections *Give 'Em Hell* and *Stagefright* in the same year, and more historically important Saxon, who cranked out *Wheels of Steel* and *Strong Arm of the Law*, again, two records in one year, the second admitted by the band to be not a patch on the first.

But the real story is that of the debut albums, 1980 giving us no less than Girlschool's *Demolition*, Ethel the Frog's self-titled, Diamond Head's *Lightning to the Nations*, Girl's *Sheer Greed*, and highest up the totem pole, Tygers of Pan Tang's *Wild Cat*, the malevolent self-titled from Angel Witch, *On Through the Night* from Def Leppard, and at the tip of the spear (to mix metaphors), Iron Maiden's *Iron Maiden*, the record so good they hadda name it twice.

And there you have it—a round of applause for 1980, please. But before we leave you to ponder what comes next (again, all covered in follow-up volume *This Means War*), I just wanted to mention that such a boatload of great music precipitated as well, an overflowing of opportunities for these bands in the live environment. It was inevitable that there would be great packages, such as the *Metal for Muthas* tour, as well as landmark three and four band bills about the country. But I suppose of tantamount importance concerning the live subplot 1980 would be the heartening heaviness of the annual Reading festival this year, filling out the supposition that, along with all the press and the compilations and all of these records modest and majestic in the shops, that heavy metal had executed a loud 'n' proud coming out party in 1980.

Now, what will be demonstrated in *This Means War: The Sunset Years of the NWOBHM* is two-fold. First, the productivity of the UK bands would continue quite unabated for at least another year or 18 months, with the NWOBHM generating a ton of great music for the discerning headbanger at hand. Second, we will come to realize that the marked and inexorable decline in 1983 and 1984—through saturation and other factors—would possess within it a silver lining, namely the happenstance that there would exist a boomerang effect, with heavy metal quite simply and surgically shifting headquarters to California, where it would crunch and crash long into the night for the entirety of the rest of the 1980s, essentially granting a modicum of victory to the metalheads of yore.

Text Credits

The majority of the quotations in this book are from the author's 20-year archive of interviews with NWOBHM acts, with additional material by kind permission of Sam Dunn and Jeb Wright.

Design and Photography Credits

This book was skillfully and artfully designed by Eduardo Rodriguez, who can be reached at eduardobwbk@gmail.com. Cover photography and inside pages scans are from the author's archive.

About The Author

At approximately 7900 (with over 7000 appearing in his books), Martin has unofficially written more record reviews than anybody in the history of music writing across all genres. Additionally, Martin has penned 51 books on hard rock, heavy metal, classic rock and record collecting. He was Editor In Chief of the now retired *Brave Words & Bloody Knuckles*, Canada's foremost metal publication for 14 years, and has also contributed to *Revolver, Guitar World, Goldmine, Record Collector*, bravewords.com, lollipop.com and *hardradio.com*, with many record label band bios and liner notes to his credit as well. Additionally, Martin has been a regular contractor to Banger Films, having worked for two years as researcher on the award-wining documentary *Rush: Beyond The Lighted Stage*, on the writing and research team for the 11-episode *Metal Evolution* and on the 10-episode *Rock Icons*, both for VH1 Classic. Additionally, Martin is the writer of the original metal genre chart used in *Metal: A Headbanger's Journey* and throughout the *Metal Evolution* episodes. Martin currently resides in Toronto and can be reached through martinp@inforamp.net or www.martinpopoff.com.

Martin Popoff — A Complete Bibliography

Wheels of Steel: The Explosive Early Years of the NWOBHM (2015)

Swords And Tequila: Riot's Classic First Decade (2015)

Who Invented Heavy Metal? (2015)

Sail Away: Whitesnake's Fantastic Voyage (2015)

Live Magnetic Air: The Unlikely Saga Of The Superlative Max Webster (2014)

Steal Away The Night: An Ozzy Osbourne Day-By-Day (2014)

The Big Book Of Hair Metal (2014)

Sweating Bullets: The Deth And Rebirth Of Megadeth (2014)

Smokin' Valves: A Headbanger's Guide to 900 NWOBHM Records (2014)

The Art Of Metal (co-edit with Malcolm Dome; 2013)

2 Minutes To Midnight: An Iron Maiden Day-By-Day (2013)

Metallica: The Complete Illustrated History (2013)

Rush: The Illustrated History (2013)

Ye Olde Metal: 1979 (2013)

Scorpions: Top Of The Bill (2013)

Epic Ted Nugent (2012)

Fade To Black: Hard Rock Cover Art Of The Vinyl Age (2012)

It's Getting Dangerous: Thin Lizzy 81-12 (2012)

We Will Be Strong: Thin Lizzy 76-81 (2012)

Fighting My Way Back: Thin Lizzy 69-76 (2011)

The Deep Purple Royal Family: Chain Of Events '80 – '11 (2011)

The Deep Purple Royal Family: Chain Of Events Through '79 (2011)
Black Sabbath FAQ (2011)
The Collector's Guide To Heavy Metal: Volume 4: The '00s (2011; co-authored with David Perri)
Goldmine Standard Catalog Of American Records 1948 – 1991, 7th Edition (2010)
Goldmine Record Album Price Guide, 6th Edition (2009)
Goldmine 45 RPM Price Guide, 7th Edition (2009)
A Castle Full Of Rascals: Deep Purple '83 – '09 (2009)
Worlds Away: Voivod And The Art Of Michel Langevin (2009)
Ye Olde Metal: 1978 (2009)
Gettin' Tighter: Deep Purple '68 – '76 (2008)
All Access: The Art Of The Backstage Pass (2008)
Ye Olde Metal: 1977 (2008)
Ye Olde Metal: 1976 (2008)
Judas Priest: Heavy Metal Painkillers (2007)
Ye Olde Metal: 1973 To 1975 (2007)
The Collector's Guide To Heavy Metal: Volume 3: The Nineties (2007)
Ye Olde Metal: 1968 To 1972 (2007)
Run For Cover: The Art Of Derek Riggs (2006)
Black Sabbath: Doom Let Loose (2006)
Dio: Light Beyond The Black (2006)
The Collector's Guide To Heavy Metal: Volume 2: The Eighties (2005)
Rainbow: English Castle Magic (2005)
UFO: Shoot Out The Lights (2005)
The New Wave Of British Heavy Metal Singles (2005)
Blue Öyster Cult: Secrets Revealed! (2004)
Contents Under Pressure: 30 Years Of Rush At Home & Away (2004)
The Top 500 Heavy Metal Albums Of All Time (2004)
The Collector's Guide To Heavy Metal: Volume 1: The Seventies (2003)
The Top 500 Heavy Metal Songs Of All Time (2003)
Southern Rock Review (2001)
Heavy Metal: 20th Century Rock And Roll (2000)
The Goldmine Price Guide To Heavy Metal Records (2000)
The Collector's Guide To Heavy Metal (1997)
Riff Kills Man! 25 Years Of Recorded Hard Rock & Heavy Metal (1993)

See martinpopoff.com for complete details and ordering information.

Smokin' Values: A Headbanger's Guide To 900 NWOBHM Records

If you like *Wheels of Steel: The Explosive Early Years of the NWOBHM*, you might also dig this one.

Taking cue from the do-it-yourself attitude of their country's punk movement, Britain's up-and-coming heavy metal bands that comprised the New Wave of British Heavy Metal (NWOBHM) were not content to wait for record labels to come knocking. Instead, they took to issuing their own music, typically in the form of 7 inch singles but also 12s and full-length album, many indie, some on small labels, and some on the major labels smart enough to get on board (essentially EMI and MCA).

Martin Popoff, author of 51 books on heavy metal (and at 7900, writer of more record reviews than anybody in history across all genres), has undertaken the task of documenting virtually every record large and wee from heavy metal's most fabled period (beginning essentially in '79 with a hard stop at 1983) providing catalogue information, mini reviews as only he can do, plus a gob of thumbnails of those wonderful 7" picture sleeves and LP covers.

Note: the lion's share of the material in *Smokin' Valves: A Headbanger's Guide To 900 NWOBHM Records* combines rewritten and expanded text from Martin's long out-of-print *The New Wave Of British Heavy Metal Singles* plus the relevant reviews of full-length albums from his *Collector's Guide* series, specifically the '70s and '80s book. These reviews have also experienced judicious editing and rewrites.

Additional features:
- includes a few hundred rare 45 picture sleeve and album cover images
- every record rated out of 10
- layout designed so that albums are distinguished from 7", 10" and 12" singles/EPs by larger, bolder typestyle
- label, year of release and catalogue number for almost every entry
- two appendices, displaying all 9's and 10's for singles as opposed to LPs

Final note, one thing I like about an experience like this book in the internet age, hopefully the idea is that you will read some of these glowing 8 to 10 rated reviews of hopelessly obscure singles you ain't never going to get alerted to otherwise, and then check out if they can be heard and enjoyed on youtube (many of them can!), so you can decide for yourself, or begin some sort of whacky digital collection of this stuff to park in yer metal library. In that respect, I'm just being a DJ that instead of talking, types.

Available directly from the publisher at www.wymeruk.co.uk